CYBER-PHYSICAL ATTACKS

CYBER-PHYSICAL ATTACKS

A Growing Invisible Threat

GEORGE LOUKAS

AMSTERDAM • BOSTON • HEIDELBERG • LONDON • NEW YORK • OXFORD
PARIS • SAN DIEGO • SAN FRANCISCO • SINGAPORE • SYDNEY • TOKYO
Butterworth-Heinemann is an imprint of Elsevier

Acquiring Editor: Tom Stover
Editorial Project Manager: Hilary Carr
Project Manager: Punithavathy Govindaradjane
Designer: Matthew Limbert

Butterworth-Heinemann is an imprint of Elsevier
The Boulevard, Langford Lane, Kidlington, Oxford OX5 1GB, UK
225 Wyman Street, Waltham, MA 02451, USA

ISBN: 978-0-12-801290-1

British Library Cataloguing-in-Publication Data
A catalogue record for this book is available from the British Library

Library of Congress Cataloging-in-Publication Data
A catalog record for this book is available from the Library of Congress

For Information on all Butterworth-Heinemann publications
visit our website at http://store.elsevier.com/

Working together
to grow libraries in
developing countries

www.elsevier.com • www.bookaid.org

Dedication

For Georgia

CONTENTS

1

A CYBER-PHYSICAL WORLD

Chapter Summary

Conventional cyber attacks affect primarily the confidentiality, integrity, and availability of data and services in cyberspace. Cyber-physical attacks are the particular category of cyber attacks that, whether intentionally or not, also adversely affect physical space by targeting the computational and communication infrastructure that allows people and systems to monitor and control sensors and actuators. This chapter provides a brief introduction to the concepts and components that bridge cyberspace with physical space, and defines what is and what is not a cyber-physical attack in relation to its impact on sensing and actuation.

Key Terms: Actuator; sensor; wireless sensor network; controller; embedded system; cyber-physical system; Internet of Things; cyber-physical attack

In the past, it was safe to assume that the primary aim of a cyber attack would be to cause damage in cyberspace, and of a physical attack to cause damage in physical space. This is no longer the case.

Our increasing dependence on computerized and highly networked environments is generating considerable new threats where the two spaces overlap. For clarity, by physical space, we refer to the space governed by the laws of physics. Cyberspace cannot be defined as succinctly. For our purposes, it is a metaphor referring to the electronic transmission, manipulation, storage, and retrieval of information in computer systems and networks.

Modern automobiles, smart buildings, wireless implants, intelligent traffic lights, full-body scanners, and industrial control systems are realistic targets for an attacker who wants to cause damage in physical space. An autonomous vehicle that has been compromised electronically can be used to intercept communications, transmit false data, launch a cyber attack from a convenient location, or even drive or fly itself into a crowd. Because documentation and code for exploiting weaknesses of widely used industrial control systems are available online, a cyber attack against a gas pipeline or water management facility may require considerably less planning and resources than a physical attack with the same aim.

Note that an attack in cyberspace can affect one or more of the three basic information security attributes collectively known as the CIA triad: **confidentiality**, **integrity**, and **availability**. In broad terms, confidentiality ensures that information can be accessed only by those authorized to access it; integrity ensures that information or a system's configuration can be modified only by those authorized to modify it; and availability ensures that those authorized to access particular information or a service can indeed access it when necessary. To these, it is common to add authenticity, accountability, nonrepudiation, and other increasingly overlapping attributes.[1] For the sake of simplicity, throughout this book we will refer mainly to the CIA triad and occasionally to authenticity. We will also frequently use five information security terms: adversary, threat, vulnerability, attack, and

---

[1]Maconachy, W. V., Schou, C. D., Ragsdale, D., and Welch, D. (2001). A model for information assurance: An integrated approach. In *Proceedings of the 2001 IEEE Workshop on Information Assurance and Security*, Volume 310, New York, USA.

Box 1.1 Basic Information Security Terminology

Vulnerability: A flaw or weakness in a system's design, implementation, operation, or management that could be exploited to violate the system's confidentiality, integrity, or availability.

Threat: Any circumstance or event with the potential to exploit a vulnerability and adversely affect a system through unauthorized access, destruction, disclosure, or modification of data, or denial of service.

Attack: An intentional assault on system security that derives from an intelligent threat. An **active attack** is one that attempts to alter system resources or affect their operation, while a **passive attack** is one that attempts to learn or make use of information from a system but does not affect that system.

Adversary: An entity that attacks a system or is a threat to a system. The terms "intruder," "attacker," "cyber attacker," "cracker," and "hacker" can also be used.

Countermeasure: An action, device, procedure, or technique that meets or opposes (i.e., counters) a threat, a vulnerability, or an attack by eliminating or preventing it, by minimizing the harm it can cause, or by discovering and reporting it so that corrective action can be taken.

countermeasure, for which the explanations (following the Internet Engineering Task Force's *Internet Security glossary*[2]) can be seen in Box 1.1, Basic Information Security Terminology.

Basic Concepts and Definitions of a Cyber-Physical World

Few like definitions. They can be too specific and limiting, or so general and vague as to be of little use in practice. Different schools of thought lead to distinctly different definitions, which are almost always incomplete. More than anything, definitions show what the industrial or research team behind each one considers a challenge and where it has focused its attention. But that is precisely why they are useful for areas of science and technology that are new and rapidly changing, currently expanding their real-world applications and impact to society. To appreciate and understand how an attack in cyberspace can have an impact in physical space, it is useful to have a basic understanding of the devices and systems involved, including sensors, actuators, controllers, embedded systems, cyber-physical systems, and recent computing paradigms such as the Internet of Things. We will use some of the most popular

[2]Shirey, R. W. (2007). RFC 4949, Internet security glossary, Version 2, IETF.

definitions proposed to describe these, although it is possible that some of these terms will be out of fashion in the near future. Nevertheless, they all point toward a world where cyber and physical spaces meet and new security threats appear where the two overlap.

Transducers

Computers are designed to generate, manipulate, transmit, and receive information in the form of pulses of electrical energy. (For example, a 0 may be represented as a low-voltage pulse and a 1 as a high-voltage pulse.) To be able to cross the cyber-physical boundary from information to physical effect and vice versa, they need transducers, which are devices that can convert between different forms of energy.[3] Within the scope of this book, we are interested in transducers that can be classified as sensors or actuators.

Sensors are devices "that transform real-world data into electrical form"[4] for the purpose of measurement or observation of the physical environment. The quantity, property, or condition measured is called stimulus or measurand, and can be acoustic, biological, chemical, electric, magnetic, mechanical, optical, radiation, or thermal. They may involve a number of transducers converting energy from one form into another until one produces an electrical signal that can be interpreted by an information processing system, such as a computer.

Strictly speaking, a sensor does not need to be a man-made object. Natural sensors on living organisms can also be included. For example, at the back of the human eye's retina there is a layer of photoreceptors (light-sensitive nerve cells), whose job is to convert light rays into an electrical signal.[5] This signal is then transmitted through the optic nerve to the brain, where it is processed and converted into an image. From our point of view, natural sensors should not be outright excluded from a discussion on cyber-physical attacks, as it is possible for an information security breach to lead to a stimulus that can be intentionally damaging to a human being (see the section, *Health*, in Chapter 2).

[3]Song, E. Y. and Lee, K. (2008). Understanding IEEE 1451-Networked smart transducer interface standard—What is a smart transducer? *Instrumentation and Measurement Magazine, IEEE*, Volume 11, No. 2, pp. 11–17.
[4]Richard, W. M. (1987). A sensor classification scheme. *IEEE Transactions on Ultrasonic, Ferroelectrics, and Frequency Control*, Volume 34, No. 2, pp. 124–126.
[5]Atchison, D. A. and Smith, G. (2000). *Optics of the human eye*, Butterworth-Heinemann.

Thanks to advances in low-cost electronics and a variety of energy-efficient communication technologies, it is possible to deploy large numbers of inexpensive sensors that can communicate and report their measurements through a wireless network. Wireless sensor networks were originally conceived for military applications, where the sensors would be airdropped on an otherwise inaccessible terrain and would remotely report information about the battlefield. Today, they are commonly used in disaster response, detecting pollutants in the environment, monitoring a smart home, and so on.[6]

Electric **actuators** are in a sense the reverse of sensors, as their job is to initiate a physical action when instructed to do so by an electrical signal.[7] For example, in wheeled vehicles, a rotary encoder is a sensor that measures position or speed by converting the angular motion of a wheel into an electrical signal. On the other hand, the electric motor that moves the vehicle is an actuator because it converts electrical energy into torque (the rotary force) that rotates the wheel. For simplicity in discussing cyber-physical attacks, we will consider as sensor any device that can gather information about its physical environment (hear a sound, see an image, measure temperature, detect motion, etc.) and as actuator any device that can initiate a physical action in its environment (move a lever, close a valve, switch on a light, turn off a heater, etc.).

Sensors are of interest to cyber attackers because by gaining access to a computer that controls them, one is able to observe a remote physical environment. Actuators possibly are of even greater interest because they allow that physical environment to be altered.

Controllers

Think of a simple heater with a thermostat. The user sets a target temperature (the setpoint) and then the thermostat compares it to the actual temperature sensed and switches the heating on or off as appropriate. In engineering and mathematics, such devices that monitor and adjust the operating conditions of dynamical systems are called controllers. They are the devices that ensure that an aircraft stays on the predefined flight path set on its autopilot, a refrigerator maintains a specific temperature, a DVD player's spinning motor rotates at a precise speed, and an industrial robot

---

[6]Akyildiz, I. F., Su, W., Sankarasubramaniam, Y., and Cayirci, E. (2002). Wireless sensor networks: a survey. *Computer Networks*, Volume 38, pp. 393–422.
[7]Janocha, H. (2004). *Actuators: Basics and Applications*, Springer Berlin Heidelberg.

faithfully carries out the same action without losing accuracy and, above all, safely. Depending on the requirements of the system that they are tasked to balance, controllers can be on/off (aptly also called bang-bang[8]), as in the simple thermostat example above, or continuous, where actuation is not abrupt but depends on how different the measured value is to the setpoint. An example of continuous control is a car's cruise control system, which may be based on a proportional control scheme, adjusting the throttle proportionally to the error (the slower the car the more throttle is needed to reach the desired speed), or more commonly based on a scheme called proportional-integral-derivative control,[9] taking into account also distance and acceleration.

In practice, controllers create a direct link between sensing and actuation, which can be exploited by an adversary. An error in the sensing process, whether natural or the result of an intentional attack, can lead to undesirable actuation. While many controllers are mechanical, hydraulic, or pneumatic, our focus here is on electronic ones based on computers and embedded systems, where it is software that constantly processes the measurements coming from the sensors and determines the parameters of the actuation.

Embedded Systems

Steve Heath has described an embedded system as "a microprocessor-based system that is built to control a function or range of functions and is not designed to be programmed by the end user in the same way that a PC is."[10] However, technically every modern PC is based on a microprocessor (a single chip) as its central processing unit (CPU), and more and more devices that are not PCs can now be programmed extensively. (Especially, smart phones and tablets have blurred the lines of what is and what is not a computer.) Instead, Berkeley's Edward A. Lee has focused on the software that they run: "Embedded software is software that is integrated with physical processes,"[11] where the technical problem is to cope with

[8]LaSalle, J. P. (1960). The "Bang-bang" principle. In Proceedings of the First International Congress of the International Federation of Automatic Control, Moscow, Volume 1, pp. 493–497.
[9]Ioannou, P., Xu, Z., Eckert, S., Clemons, D., and Sieja, T. (1993). Intelligent cruise control: theory and experiment. In *Proceedings of the 32nd IEEE Conference on Decision and Control*, pp. 1885–1890, IEEE.
[10]Heath, S. (2002). *Embedded systems design*. Newnes.
[11]Lee, E. A. (2006). The future of embedded software. In *ARTEMIS Conference*, Graz, Austria, May 2006.

challenges of the physical world, such as time limitations and the fact that multiple processes run concurrently. On the other hand, the Technical University of Dortmund's Peter Marwedel refers to embedded systems as "information processing systems embedded into a larger product."[12] These information processing systems are small computers that need to cope with limited resources.

In practice, there is no universally accepted definition or comprehensive list of characteristics of an embedded system.[13] From the perspective of cyber-physical security, they are "computers masquerading as non-computers."[14] They are hidden inside microwave ovens, satellite navigation devices, coffee makers, parking meters, thermostats, and hundreds of other devices and appliances that we encounter and often rely on every day in our lives. Unlike general-purpose computers, they do not run a full-blown operating system such as Windows 10 or Mac OS. Instead, they are programmed to perform only a specific set of limited functions required by the system in which they are embedded. For example, a washing machine's embedded system needs to be able to set washing programs, not to work out calculations on spreadsheets. Nevertheless, from the point of view of a cyber attacker, embedded systems are computers that run some form of software and often feature network communication capabilities. Consequently, they are conceivable targets.

Cyber-Physical Systems

New disciplines that emerge from the intersection of well-established ones are not easy to describe with precision. They have too much in common with the disciplines to which they are related. Sztipanovits has described cyber-physical system research as "a new discipline at the intersection of physical, biological, engineering and information sciences,"[15] which is not particularly enlightening but illustrates the breadth of its

---

[12]Marwedel, P. (2006). *Embedded system design* (Vol. 1). Secaucus, NJ: Springer.

[13]Graaf, B., Lormans, M., and Toetenel, H. (2002). Software technologies for embedded systems: An industry inventory. In *Product Focused Software Process Improvement*, Springer Berlin Heidelberg, pp. 453–465.

[14]Boutekkouk, F., Benmohammed, M., Bilavarn, S., and Auguin, M. (2009). UML2. 0 Profiles for Embedded Systems and Systems On a Chip (SOCs). *Journal of Object Technology*, Volume 8, No. 1, pp. 135–157.

[15]Sztipanovits, J. (2007). Composition of Cyber-Physical Systems. In Proceedings of the 14th Annual IEEE International Conference and Workshop on the Engineering of Computer Based Systems, pp. 3–6, March 2007.

applications. According to Edward A. Lee, cyber-physical systems are "integrations of computation and physical processes,"[16] but this does not differ that much from his own definition of embedded software. When it was first introduced, the term would have sounded like a fancy new name for embedded systems, or possibly the next stage in their evolution. The term does indeed encompass most embedded systems, but it is used to emphasize their physical characteristics, especially in applications that involve multiple networked systems, which receive information from the physical world through sensors and affect it through actuators. A more complete definition has been provided by Helen Gill of the National Science Foundation: "Cyber-physical systems are physical, biological, and engineered systems whose operations are integrated, monitored, and/or controlled by a computational core. Components are networked at every scale. Computing is deeply embedded into every physical component, possibly even into materials. The computational core is an embedded system, usually demands real-time response, and is most often distributed."[17]

A cyber-physical system is usually a closed-loop system of networked sensors and actuators, where data collected by sensors are communicated to embedded systems (controllers) that adjust the system's operation through the actuators. Kim and Kumar have tracked its origins back in 1973 and the introduction of real-time computation paradigms, which demanded that a computer should not only perform a task correctly but should also complete it in time.[18] Today, examples of cyber-physical systems include computerized and networked medical equipment, manned and unmanned vehicles, home automation systems, intelligent traffic management systems, industrial control systems, among others.[19] Whereas a standalone airbag system is an embedded system, an automobile is a cyber-physical system containing a large number of different interconnected embedded systems controlling sensors and actuators and

[16]Lee, E. A. (2007). Computing foundations and practice for cyber-physical systems: A preliminary report. *University of California, Berkeley, Tech. Rep. UCB/EECS-2007-72.*
[17]Gill, H. (2008). From vision to reality: cyber-physical systems. HCSS National Workshop on New Research Directions for High Confidence Transportation CPS: Automotive, Aviation and Rail, November 2008.
[18]Kim, K. D. and Kumar, P. R. (2012). Cyber−physical systems: A perspective at the centennial. Proceedings of the IEEE, 100, Special Centennial Issue, pp. 1287−1308.
[19]Rajkumar, R. R., Lee, I., Sha, L., and Stankovic, J. (2010). Cyber-physical systems: the next computing revolution. In Proceedings of the 47th Design Automation Conference, pp. 731−736, ACM, June 2010.

exchanging information with each other. A security breach that affects the operation of these embedded systems or the network infrastructure that supports their communication can have a direct effect in physical space.

The Internet of Things

Historically, the Internet has been used almost exclusively for the connection of conventional computers, sharing ideas or information generated by human beings (someone's typed text, recorded video, digital picture, etc.).[20] The Internet of Things is "the vision of a global infrastructure of networked physical objects,"[21] where information is not generated by human beings but by physical objects, such as appliances, buildings, vehicles, and clothes. Initial publications on the Internet of Things focused on radio frequency identification (RFID)[22] as a prerequisite technology, with the vision of a world where every object can become a "smart object" by embedding to it a RFID tag. This allows identifying it uniquely and wirelessly communicating information about the object and its immediate environment. Technological advances in high-speed mobile communications, wireless sensor networks, and data storage, analysis, and visualization are also contributing in this direction.[23] It has been estimated that there will be as many as 26 billion devices on the Internet of Things by 2020.[24]

Both the Internet of Things and cyber-physical systems are paradigms that are based on networked embedded systems as the core technology. To many the two concepts are identical. To others, the former focuses on machine-to-machine communication, while the latter on the interaction with the physical environment. In the Internet of Things, everything is intelligent and networked (see Figure 1.1). An Internet-connected smart fridge keeps track of its contents through RFID or some other technology, and when running low on eggs, it sends a reminder

---

[20]Ashton, K. (2009). That "Internet of Things" thing. RFID Journal, June 22, 2009.
[21]Kortuem, G., Kawsar, F., Fitton, D., and Sundramoorthy, V. (2010). Smart objects as building blocks for the Internet of Things. *Internet Computing, IEEE*, Volume 14, No. 1, pp. 44–51.
[22]Welbourne, E., Battle, L., Cole, G., Gould, K., Rector, K., Raymer, S., Balazinska, B., and Borriello, G. (2009). Building the Internet of Things using RFID: the RFID ecosystem experience. *Internet Computing, IEEE*, Volume 13, No. 3, pp. 48–55.
[23]Gubbi, J., Buyya, R., Marusic, S., and Palaniswami, M. (2013). Internet of Things (IoT): A vision, architectural elements, and future directions. *Future Generation Computer Systems*, Volume 29, No. 7, pp. 1645–1660.
[24]Middleton, P., Kjeldsen, P., and Tully, J. (2013). Forecast: The Internet of Things, Worldwide. Gartner, November 18, 2013.

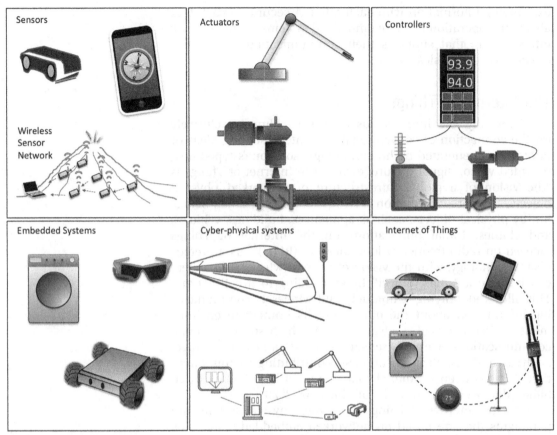

Figure 1.1 (Top left) Sensors are devices that gather information from their physical environment (examples shown: ultrasound sensor used by robots to measure distance from obstacles; magnetometer used by smartphones to orientate; and a network of wireless acoustic and seismic sensors used to monitor volcanic eruptions). (Top middle) Actuators are devices that initiate a physical action, such as the servo motors of a robotic arm, or the valve actuators used to control gas and oil pipelines. (Top right) Controllers are devices that monitor and adjust the operating conditions of dynamical systems. (Bottom left) Embedded systems are small computers with dedicated functions that are hidden inside microwave ovens, satellite navigation devices, coffee makers, parking meters, thermostats, and other devices and appliances. (Bottom middle) Cyber-physical systems are systems where computation (often in embedded systems), communications, and physical processes are closely related and depend on each other (examples shown: a modern train control infrastructure, as well as the train itself; and an industrial control system for remotely monitoring and controlling sensors and actuators in the field). (Bottom right) The Internet of Things is a computing paradigm where every physical object is intelligent and networked.

to the owner to purchase more, or better yet connects to the supermarket's web site and purchases them itself. Such automation can be very convenient, but news items on smart light bulbs leaking their owners' Wi-Fi passwords[25] and (probably

[25]Wakefield, J. (2014). Smart LED light bulbs leak wi-fi passwords, BBC News, July 8, 2014.

incorrect) claims of smart fridges sending spam e-mails[26] paint a picture of an Internet of Things that, still in its infancy, is poorly understood, poorly implemented, and vulnerable to cyber attacks.[27]

Defining Cyber-Physical Attacks

Cyber-physical attacks are usually seen in relation to cyber-physical systems and the vulnerability of their computation and communication elements.[28] This is understandable as these are the kinds of systems that are defined by their cyber-physical interactions. For example, a malicious user taking control of the computing or communication components of water pumps, medical implants, cars, and gas pipeline valves can use these to affect physical space by damaging property or the environment and putting lives at risk. As a result, security is universally considered as one of the grand challenges in designing trustworthy cyber-physical systems.[29] Valasek and Miller have referred to cyber-physical attacks as the cyber attacks "that result in physical control of various aspects" of a cyber-physical system, such as an automobile,[30] while Yamploskiy et al. have defined them more generally as the cyber attacks that have "physical effect propagations."[31]

In fact, every action in cyberspace has some form of impact in physical space, whether it involves a system that can be classified as cyber-physical or not, and it may or may not have the potential or the intent to cause damage. For example, in every computer, information is transmitted in physical space in the form of energy through wires or over the air, images are displayed on screens, sounds are produced through speakers, LED lights blink, hard disks spin,

---

[26]Thomas, P. (2014). Despite the news, your refrigerator is not yet sending spam. Symantec, January 23, 2014.

[27]Babcock, C. (2014). HP warns of IoT security risks. Information Week, July 29, 2014.

[28]Ma, C. Y., Rao, N. S., and Yau, D. K. (2011). A game theoretic study of attack and defense in cyber-physical systems. In *2011 IEEE Conference on Computer Communications (INFOCOM) Workshops*, pp. 708–713, IEEE, April 2011.

[29]Lee, E. A. (2008). Cyber physical systems: Design challenges. In 11th IEEE International Symposium on Object Oriented Real-Time Distributed Computing (ISORC), pp. 363–369, IEEE, May 2008.

[30]Miller, C. and Valasek, C. (2014). A Survey of Remote Automotive Attack Surfaces, Black Hat 2014, Las Vegas, Nevada, USA.

[31]Yampolskiy, M., Horvath, P., Koutsoukos, X. D., Xue, Y., and Sztipanovits, J. (2012). Systematic analysis of cyber-attacks on CPS-evaluating applicability of DFD-based approach. In Proceedings of the 5th International Symposium on Resilient Control Systems (ISRCS), pp. 55–62, IEEE, August 2012.

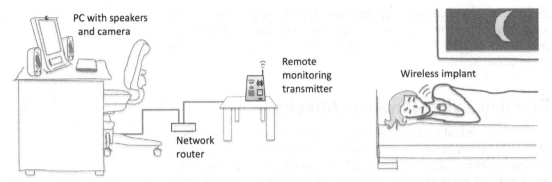

Figure 1.2 The politician is sleeping at night, with her computer left on and a remote monitoring device collecting real-time data on the operation of her heart from the sensor of her implantable cardioverter defibrillator.

printers produce ink on paper, and so on. All these are physical effect propagations. Instead, we propose the following general definition:

A cyber-physical attack is a security breach in cyberspace that adversely affects physical space.

By way of example, consider the hypothetical scenario of a senior politician who, due to heart problems, is wearing an implantable cardioverter defibrillator (an implant that can deliver an electric shock if its sensors detect an episode of arrhythmia or an external clinical device instructs it to do so). The implant features short-range wireless capability for communicating data about the operation of her heart to a transmitter device, which then reports this information in real time to her doctors at the hospital. It is late at night and she is sleeping in the room where she has her personal computer, which she has left on (see Figure 1.2).

Two foreign intelligence agents have been tasked to target the politician's weak heart. Agent A is focusing on the remote monitoring transmitter and is looking for known vulnerabilities that would let him hijack it and then use it to wirelessly disable the implant or instruct it to deliver dangerously powerful electric shocks. However, he does not go very far on this line of thought. As he quickly finds out online, the particular transmitter does not feature any functionality for sending commands to the implant, only for receiving data from it and forwarding it to the doctors. Agent B focuses on a different system. His goal is to remotely install malware on the personal computer to take control of it; then try to violently wake up the victim by playing a sound abruptly and at maximum volume through the computer's speakers. His attempt fails, either because his assumptions about the physical dependencies in this scenario are incorrect if not plain silly (a loud sound would not lead to a heart episode) or because he did not really manage to produce a loud sound in physical space (if the knob on the actual speaker device is set to just above 0, no matter what the volume setting in the operating system is, the sound produced cannot be loud). He knows that he has failed because agent A has managed to intercept the real-time reports of the politician's heart rhythm from the wireless transmitter and it appears normal, or because he sees her the next day on television. Nevertheless, the two agents are still confident in the usefulness of their offensive cyber-physical skills, especially because the hijacked personal computer features a camera, through which they can see in the room and collect intelligence that would otherwise be inaccessible.

There are three cyber attacks in this scenario that can affect actuation or sensing. One attempts unauthorized actuation (to produce a loud sound through the PC speakers) and two attempt unauthorized collection of information from sensors (live image from the camera and the real-time reports of the heart rhythm). Unauthorized actuation related to the implant (disabling it or delivering powerful shocks) would not be realistic in the specific case. Even if the attacker could gain full control of the network router and from there of the transmitter, there would still be no logical attack path from the transmitter to the implant.

Following our definition, the eventual impact of a cyber-physical attack in physical space is a consequence of its impact in cyberspace (Figure 1.3). Jointly, the three types of cyber impact (breach of confidentiality, breach of integrity, and breach of availability) can lead to five types of physical impact:

- **Breach of physical privacy.** Traditionally, this occurs when "a person is looked at, listened to, or recorded against his or her wishes."[32] For instance, an adversary remotely taking control of a computer's on-board camera or intercepting a Skype call initiated at that computer would also breach its user's physical privacy. We can extend this type's scope to include attacks that breach the confidentiality of a person's real-time blood sugar level, the number of occupants in a house, and other private information collected from sensors.

---

[32]Moreham, N. A. (2014). Beyond information: physical privacy in English Law. *The Cambridge Law Journal*, Volume 73, No. 2, pp. 350–377.

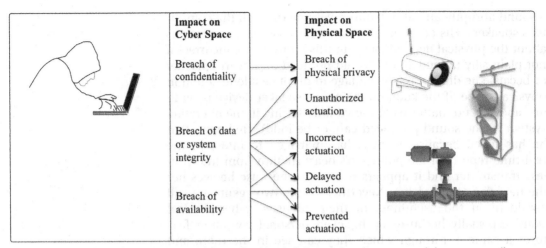

Figure 1.3 Cyber-physical attacks can be characterized by their impact in cyberspace and the corresponding impact in physical space.

- **Unauthorized actuation**. An unauthorized user initiates actuation by breaching the integrity of a computer system that controls an actuator. An example would be an adversary unlocking a door in a smart building or changing the facing of a surveillance camera.

- **Incorrect actuation**. The adversary does not initiate actuation but aims to affect an actuator's operation by breaching the integrity or availability of the instructions sent to it, the sensor data on which it relies, or its controller's operation. An example would be an attack that would consistently lower the speed values reported by a car's sensors, so as to cause its cruise control system to keep accelerating.

- **Delayed actuation**. The adversary aims to delay actuation by breaching the integrity or availability of the data and systems involved. Suppression of warnings can also be included in this category. An example would be a denial of service attack that would delay measurements on dangerous pressures to be reported to a gas pipeline's safety valve controllers.

- **Prevented actuation**. The adversary aims to block actuation altogether by breaching the integrity or availability of the data and systems involved. Examples would be a sleep deprivation attack that exhausts the battery of a surveillance robot or a medical implant until it can no longer function, or a malware infection that suppresses the operation of a car window by injecting a "close" command every time an "open" command is received.

Note that the five types of physical impact are not mutually exclusive. For instance, an attack can effectively prevent actuation by delaying it until it is not useful any more. In fact, most cyber-physical attacks involve multiple types of breach in cyberspace, followed by multiple and often cascading effects in physical space.

It is important to emphasize that technical methodologies used for a cyber-physical attack are not somehow magically different than the ones used in conventional cyber attacks. A SQL injection attack is a SQL injection attack whether it targets someone's bank account details or the controls of an actuator. A worm is a worm whether it causes the disruption of a company's corporate network or of medical equipment. There are certain examples of attacks that are possible only by exploiting the unique physical characteristics of their target in the attack process, but they are rather rare. It would be naïve to limit a discussion on cyber-physical attacks to these only. It is the physical impact that defines them and not any particular technical methodology in cyberspace. Note, also, that the physical impact does not need to be intentional. For example, it is rather common for a computer worm epidemic to have considerable and widespread physical impact even if that was not the intention of its creator.

Cyber-physical attacks can be seen in contrast to physical-cyber attacks,[33] which are attacks initiated in physical space but which affect cyberspace (discussed in detail in Chapter 7), physical attacks that do not affect cyberspace and are primarily the realm of physical security professionals, and cyber attacks that do not affect physical space and are primarily the realm of information/cyber security[34] professionals.

It may be useful to emphasize that for an event to be characterized as a cyber-physical attack, it needs to involve an unauthorized action in cyberspace (a breach of confidentiality, integrity, or availability). If an authorized person uses a cyber-physical system to cause physical damage, this does not constitute a cyber-physical attack. It is merely a misuse of the trust placed on that person by whomever authorized him or her.

---

[33]Yampolskiy, M., Horvath, P., Koutsoukos, X. D., Xue, Y., and Sztipanovits, J. (2013). Taxonomy for description of cross-domain attacks on CPS. In Proceedings of the 2nd ACM international conference on high confidence networked systems, pp. 135−142, ACM, April 2013.

[34]Note that we use the terms cyber security and information security interchangeably, as they both boil down to ensuring confidentiality, integrity, and availability. Due to this book's close relationship with cyber-physical systems, we have generally opted to use the term cyber security despite it being less mature and sometimes derided for being too vague.

Who Should Read This Book

This book is intended to serve as an accessible introduction to the variety of cyber-physical attack approaches and applicable countermeasures that have already been employed in the real world or in a research setting. It has not been written for experienced computer security professionals or postdoctoral researchers, but for undergraduate students and nonexperts, including physical security professionals with limited exposure to computer science. Note that we purposefully refrain from providing detailed instructions or sample code for cyber-physical attacks. The aim is to help understand their characteristics, not encourage them.

Outline

This book can be read from cover to cover, but this is not necessary. After Chapter 1, where we have already defined the scope of cyber-physical attacks and of the book, the reader can continue reading the chapters in any order. At the end of every chapter, there is a summary and a few follow-up questions and exercises to help review its content. Individually, the topics covered by each chapter are as follows.

Chapter 1: A Cyber-Physical World

A brief introduction to the devices, systems, and computing paradigms that allow interaction between cyberspace and physical space. It includes sensors, actuators, controllers, embedded systems, cyber-physical systems, and recent computing paradigms, such as the Internet of Things, followed by a discussion on what is and what is not a cyber-physical attack.

Chapter 2: A History of Cyber-Physical Security Incidents

A timeline of cyber-physical security incidents publicly reported to have occurred either in the real world or in an experimental laboratory setting. Its aim is to illustrate the breadth, chronological evolution, and potential impact of such incidents. The focus is on the sectors of energy, water, health, transport, and defense.

Chapter 3: Cyber-Physical Attacks on Implants and Vehicles

A detailed analysis of cyber-physical threats related to small-scale cyber-physical systems, such as implantable medical devices, and medium-scale ones, such as unmanned aerial vehicles and automobiles.

Chapter 4: Cyber-Physical Attacks on Industrial Control Systems

A detailed analysis of cyber-physical threats related to industrial control systems, with an emphasis on supervisory control and data acquisition in the energy sector. The chapter includes a section on Stuxnet as the primary example of an advanced cyber-physical attack. It continues with a discussion on new threats appearing with the advent of the smart grid.

Chapter 5: Cyber-Physical Attack Steps

A general view of the steps employed by adversaries that aim to affect physical space, including the preliminary research and reconnaissance steps, discovery, intrusion, attack delivery, and antiforensics. Where appropriate, we match each attack component with the corresponding countermeasures that are discussed in more detail in Chapter 6.

Chapter 6: Protection Mechanisms and Secure Design Principles

This chapter presents new protection mechanisms developed specifically for cyber-physical attacks, as well as traditional protection mechanisms and age-old secure design principles that have been developed for conventional cyber attacks and are largely applicable in this context too. The focus is on the protection of cyber-physical systems.

Chapter 7: Physical-Cyber Attacks

It is possible for attacks in physical space to affect availability, integrity, or confidentiality in cyberspace. We refer to these as physical-cyber attacks. The focus here is on physical and electromagnetic attacks affecting availability, intentional manipulation of physical input to sensors affecting integrity, and exploitation of compromising emanations affecting confidentiality. There is also a brief discussion on cyber-physical-cyber and physical-cyber-physical attacks.

Summary

Sensors, actuators, controllers, embedded systems, cyber-physical systems, and the Internet of Things are the main components and concepts that bridge cyberspaces and physical spaces, and allow an action in the former to affect the latter. Sensors allow the flow of information from physical space to cyberspace, while actuators allow information in cyberspace to become an action in physical space. Controllers, embedded systems, cyber-physical systems, and the Internet of Things allow the intelligent monitoring and control of our physical environment through sensors and actuators.

We have chosen to define cyber-physical attacks as the cyber attacks that affect physical space adversely. By this, we mean any breach of the confidentiality of information received from sensors, as well as, rather more interestingly, any incident of unauthorized, incorrect, delayed, or prevented actuation that is the result of a breach of integrity or availability in cyberspace.

Follow-Up Questions and Exercises

1. Which of the following activities can best be described as occurring in physical space only, and which as occurring in cyberspace too?
   a. A full-body scanner emitting X-rays
   b. An MP3 music file being accessed from a car's media player software
   c. A user visiting a web site
   d. A user receiving spam e-mail
   e. An electric vehicle receiving electricity at a charging station
   f. A robot's wheels turning
2. Fill in the blanks with the following terms: adversary, vulnerability, threat, attack, countermeasure.
   In August, Thomas purchased a video surveillance camera from the high street electronics retailer inSecure Inc. to install at home. The particular model was priced very competitively and would let him connect it to his home wireless router and turn it on/off, rotate it, and change other settings from any Internet browser or a smartphone app while away from home. That was exactly what he needed. However, a

few days later, when watching television in his living room late at night, he briefly noticed from the corner of his eye the camera slowly rotating toward him. Astonished, he rushed to pull the plug and switch it off. When he had a minute to calm down, he searched for the particular problem online. One of the results was on a(n) _____ first reported in January, which would cause the camera's authentication process to malfunction and allow logging in as an administrator if an extremely long name were typed in the login field. As a result, there was the realistic _____ that a(n) _____ could exploit it to launch a(n) _____ against the camera and hijack its controls. Interestingly, a(n) _____ had already been produced in the form of a software update, but Thomas had not been made aware of it by the retailer or the manufacturer.

3. Which of the following are best characterized as sensors and which as actuators?
   a. A smart fridge's thermometer
   b. A surveillance camera's swivel mechanism
   c. An occupancy detector
   d. A police radar gun
   e. A car's sunroof mechanism
   f. An altimeter
   g. A valve on a water pipe
   h. A computer's speakers

4. The boundaries between what is and what is not an example of an embedded system, a cyber-physical system, or an Internet of Things device can be blurred and are not within the scope of this book. From the perspective of cyber-physical attacks, what matters is the existence of cyber-physical interactions that can be exploited. Which of the following can be considered realistic targets of a cyber-physical attack? Provide your reasoning.
   a. An electric toothbrush
   b. A pacemaker implanted in a patient's body
   c. An e-banking account
   d. A modern car's door locking system

5. Choose the types of impact in physical space that were exhibited by the attack described in exercise 2.
   a. Breach of physical privacy
   b. Unauthorized actuation
   c. Incorrect actuation
   d. Delayed or prevented actuation

2

A HISTORY OF CYBER-PHYSICAL SECURITY INCIDENTS

Chapter Summary

Although the concept of a cyber-physical attack is not new, in recent years we have become so dependent on computerized and networked systems that such attacks are now considered a key threat to critical national infrastructures and a realistic threat to private cars, home automation devices, and even pacemakers. Cyber-physical security incidents can be accidents caused by misconfiguration and sheer bad luck or they can be state-sponsored attacks several months in preparation. They can be targeted, they can be opportunistic, and they can even be the result of indiscriminate malware infections. This chapter is not about what they can be but about what they have been. A brief history of incident reports demonstrates a remarkable variety of targets, motives, attack mechanisms, and impacts. We focus in particular on the sectors of energy, water, health, transport, and defense, and briefly discuss landmark real-world incidents that have been publicly reported, as well as some of the most noteworthy staged attacks that have been carried out by researchers.

Key Terms: History; cyber-physical incident; industrial control system; SCADA; malware; normal accident; kinetic cyber

Dependable and accurate reports on cyber-physical attacks are rare. As with all types of information security breaches, organizations are reluctant to publicly report them, fearing that they will be seen as easy targets and therefore attract further attacks. Being relatively novel, a cyber attack with a physical impact may also be more newsworthy, even further damaging the reputation of the organization that would report it. As a result, a history of cyber-physical security incidents can only be incomplete. It cannot help us deduce their actual frequency or severity and it cannot show how to best defend against them. What it can do is help illustrate their breadth, chronological evolution, and potential impact.

The incidents discussed in this chapter were publicly reported to have occurred either in the real world or in an experimental laboratory setting. There have been many others but it is not this book's aim to disclose classified information or to provide an exhaustive list of many similar incident reports. Our focus is on incidents that are notable for their impact or for the new approach that they demonstrated. We have chosen to present this history by sector affected, starting with the one that has seen most of the high-profile incidents: the energy sector. It is primarily the cyber-physical attacks in this sector that have sparked a series of public research programs around the world on the security of critical national infrastructures.[1]

For convenience in referring back to these incidents throughout the rest of the book, each one is assigned an identifier, starting with E1 as the first one mentioned in the energy sector, W1 in the water sector, and so forth. A graphical timeline is provided at the end of this chapter.

---

[1]Note that what constitutes Critical National Infrastructure differs from nation to nation. For example, in Australia, it comprises the sectors of Energy, Water, Communications, Banking and Finance, Health, Transport, and Food. In the United Kingdom, it additionally includes Government and Emergency Services, and in the United States, it has been extended to the Defense Industrial Base, the Chemical Industry and Hazardous Materials, the Post, the National Monuments and Icons, and Critical Manufacturing. In some countries, the emphasis is not on sectors but on threats and risks. In Russia, the term most commonly used is "critically important object," which is defined by the human, material, and spatial impact of a catastrophe that would involve it.

Reported Incidents by Sector Affected

Energy

An oft-repeated story from the Cold War recounts that in June 1982, somewhere in the Siberian wilderness, a natural gas pipeline exploded so spectacularly that it could be seen from space[2] (E1). The story contends that, through a Soviet defector a year earlier, the CIA had become aware that the Soviets were trying to steal pipeline control software from a Canadian company. Allegedly, the CIA made the company insert flaws in the code that would cause the pipeline's valves to misbehave and lead to pressures beyond its limits. The only account of the operation and the explosion comes from a US official's memoirs of the Cold War and has never been confirmed from other sources. It may or may not be true. What we can confidently consider as true, though, is that the possibility of such cyber-physical sabotage was already known to the US intelligence services. The defector had provided a list of the most important technologies that the Soviets were trying to steal from the West and the CIA would run a large deception operation around them. According to the CIA's "Farewell Dossier" that was declassified in 1996, "contrived computer chips found their way into Soviet military equipment, flawed turbines were installed on a gas pipeline, and defective plans disrupted the output of chemical plants and a tractor factory."

Since the wide adoption of supervisory control and data acquisition (SCADA) systems started in the 1980s, production and delivery of energy is controlled remotely and in a largely automated manner. As a result, a flaw in software code can indeed affect power stations and pipelines. (See Box 2.1 for more information on SCADA systems.)

Most of the industrial control systems installed worldwide were designed decades ago, with little consideration for security. Yet, in order to improve efficiency of day-to-day operations, they are often retrofitted with modern networking capabilities, such as connection to IP-based corporate networks of organizations (and even to the Internet, albeit rarely). As a result, they can be as vulnerable to common security threats as any of the networks to which they are connected.

Even though there is little evidence that the Cold War spy story of the Siberian pipeline is accurate, a more recent, widely reported pipeline incident (though not a cyber attack) proves

---

[2]Reed, T. (2005). At the abyss: An insider's history of the cold war. Presidio Press.

Box 2.1 Industrial Control Systems

This is a general term for systems used to monitor and control physical processes in manufacturing, power generation, water treatment, mass transit, and other critical infrastructures. The primary types used today are the programmable logic controller (PLC), the distributed control system (DCS), and the supervisory control and data acquisition (SCADA) system.

A PLC[3] is a microprocessor-based controller that allows an engineer to configure the logic of a system involving sensors and actuators. For instance, using a relatively simple graphical programming language called ladder logic, the engineer may specify that "if the temperature is over 200 °C and the rotational speed is over 1,000 rpm, then open valves A and D." For our purposes, they are computers used to automate the control of machinery. Unlike personal computers, they are designed to resist vibrations, electrical noise, humidity, heat, and other adverse environmental conditions, to ensure the safe operation of the machinery they control. They typically have multiple input and output points for connecting to sensors and actuators, and as their name implies, their logic can be programmed. This is usually done on an accompanying programming terminal or a separate personal computer running specialized software and then loaded on the PLC via cabling. Most modern PLCs also have some form of network connectivity for communicating with other systems, especially when they are themselves components of DCS or SCADA systems.

While a PLC controls machinery, a DCS is a distributed system that may control a whole plant's industrial processes, such as an entire production line in a manufacturing plant. A DCS may oversee multiple subsystems and particularly PLCs. Also, it is typically expected to stay online for very long periods of time and to be reconfigured while it is online. DCS systems are usually found in manufacturing plants, chemical plants, refineries, and so on.

SCADA systems are used where there is a need to centrally monitor and control geographically dispersed assets. While the emphasis of DCS is on processes, the emphasis of SCADA is usually on real-time data gathering. They monitor remote terminals units (RTUs; also known as remote telemetry units) that are responsible for sensing, process the data centrally, and allow a human supervisor or an automated process to remotely issue commands to field devices such as motors, valves, and pumps. RTUs and PLCs share a lot of functionality, but RTUs have traditionally placed more emphasis on data gathering and wireless communication, whereas PLCs have placed more emphasis on the control of machinery. We refer to either as field controllers, as they control field devices, such as sensors, pumps, and valves. An important component of a SCADA system is the human machine interface (HMI) that displays the remotely gathered real-time information in a manner that is easy for the human operator to understand and act upon. So, a typical SCADA system's architecture would be composed of RTUs for gathering sensor data from the field, a control center for processing the data, and a HMI for displaying them and for issuing commands remotely to the field devices of a plant (see Figure 2.1). Communication between the various components may be wired or wireless and is increasingly based on the Internet protocol (IP). SCADA systems are typically used for the management of wastewater collection systems, ships, rail systems, and oil and gas pipelines. In the case of the electrical grid, it is a DCS that controls the

(Continued)

---

[3]Bolton, W. (2009). *Programmable logic controllers*. Newnes.

Box 2.1 (Continued)

operation of the power generation facility, but it is a SCADA system monitoring supply and demand across the grid that determines how much energy the facility should produce.[4]

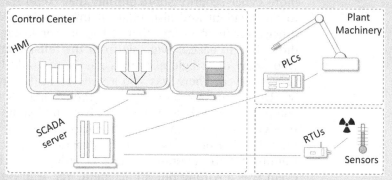

Figure 2.1 A simplified representation of a SCADA architecture with field controllers (PLCs, RTUs, etc.) controlling field devices and gathering sensor data.

that the story is in fact plausible. In 1999, a pipeline in Bellingham, Washington ruptured because of a slow-down of the SCADA system controlling it[5] (E2). Prior to this, a contractor had caused external damage to the pipeline while installing water lines across it. Due to that damage and misconfiguration of some newly installed valves, pressure started to build up. This normally would be detected and mitigated through the SCADA system but the latter had become unresponsive. Although it was configured to collect the latest data from RTUs every few seconds, the operator's HMI would not display an update for several minutes. Later investigation showed that at that time a system administrator had been programming new reports on the live database of the SCADA system without having first tested them offline. Another mistake was that there was a single login account for all users, and this was an administrator account with a priority setting that allowed all available computational resources to be assigned to it. As a result, a programming error could not only directly affect the operation of the live SCADA system but it could also consume all its

[4]Stouffer, K., Falco, J., and Scarfone, K. (2011). Guide to industrial control systems (ICS) security. *NIST Special Publication*, pp. 800–882.
[5]Abrams, M. and Weiss, J. (2007). *Bellingham, Washington, Control System Cyber Security Case Study.* NIST.

resources. With it being unresponsive, the controllers were unable to operate pumps remotely to alleviate the impact of the pressure buildup in time. The gasoline ignition that followed caused three deaths and substantial environmental damage.

Investigation after the Bellingham event showed several more cyber security shortcomings that could have contributed to the incident and also made it impossible to determine the precise chain of events that led to it. For instance, there was direct dial-in access available from the outside and any person who knew the single account's password could have been the user involved. There was also a network bridge[6] connecting the SCADA control room's network to the company's administrative computer network, and the latter even had some Internet connectivity. Although there was no virus protection and generally no indication of a cyber security program in place or any such training for the operators, there is little doubt that the whole event was anything but an accident. Yet, it illustrated just how easy it would have been for an intruder gaining access to the network of a pipeline control company to willfully cause catastrophic damage. A similar accident occurred in San Bruno, California, in 2010 (E9). A natural gas pipeline explosion that killed eight and injured 60 others was also partly attributed to erroneous and unavailable SCADA pressure readings.[7] A power failure led to the erroneous reporting of low pressure values, which in turn led to the regulating control valves opening fully and increasing the pressure in the pipeline.

Control systems may also be affected by malware, and there are plenty of such examples in the energy sector. In 2003, the Slammer worm that had already infected thousands of personal computers worldwide entered the network of the Davis-Besse nuclear power plant in Ohio and disabled its safety display[8] (E3). The IT infrastructure of the plant had been correctly designed with a firewall that isolated the plant's control network of SCADA systems from the corporate network used by the plant's employees for their daily business. The aim of this was to ensure that any malware infection picked up by the

---

[6]Computers can normally communicate with other computers only if they belong to the same network. A network bridge is a hardware device or software that connects different networks and allows computers in one network to communicate with computers in another.

[7]Parformak, P. W. (2012). *Pipeline Cybersecurity: Federal Policy.* Congressional Research Service Report for Congress, August 16, 2012.

[8]United States Nuclear Regulatory Commission (2003). NRC Information Notice 2003-14: Potential Vulnerability of Plant Computer Network to Worm Infection. Washington DC, USA, August 29, 2003.

employees' computers on the corporate network would not affect the plant. However, external contractors could connect to the control network directly, effectively bypassing the firewall and its access control policies. Consequently, when a contractor's infected computer connected to it, the worm launched a denial of service attack against the control network. This type of attack typically involves a number of computers (referred to as bots) that have been compromised by a hacker, which are instructed to send large amounts of meaningless data to a target computer. By doing so, they overwhelm its computational or network resources and effectively disable it.[9]

In the case of Davis-Besse's Slammer infection, the resulting overload of the network resources rendered the system for monitoring radiation and core temperatures inaccessible for 5 hours. Fortunately, at the time the plant was shut down for repairs and there was no real safety incident. Still, it was alarming, because this was not a targeted attack. Slammer was a tiny 376-byte code that was replicating at a spectacular rate, looking for computers that had not been patched against a particular vulnerability in a Microsoft database product. By indiscriminately spreading through the Internet, malware had indirectly disabled a critical process of a nuclear power plant even though the plant did not have direct Internet access itself, and even though Microsoft had released a patch for the specific vulnerability a long time ago. It was by then becoming evident that the increasing interconnectivity of modern industrial control systems was putting critical national infrastructure at risk of cyber attacks. As a US senator put it in his letter to the power plant's chairman, "future computer worms will not be polite enough to attack only defueled plants."[10]

The potential of cyber attacks causing major disruption in the energy sector had already started being discussed within the scientific community. In 2004, a US government accountability report[11] emphasized the potential of a state-sponsored organized attack against the electric grid "with a high degree of anonymity, and without having to set foot in the target nation." In 2007, CNN broadcast footage of a diesel generator being

---

[9]Loukas, G. and Öke, G. (2010). Protection against denial of service attacks: a survey. The Computer Journal, Oxford University Press, Volume 53, No. 7, pp. 1020–1037.
[10]Senator Markey, E. J. to United States Nuclear Regulator Commission Chairman Nils Diaz (2003). Infection of the Davis Besse Nuclear Plant by the "Slammer" Worm Computer Virus – Follow-up Questions. EDO Principal Correspondence Control G20030637, October 20, 2003.
[11]Government Accountability Office (2004). *Critical Infrastructure Protection — Challenges and Efforts to Secure Control Systems* (GAO-04-354). Washington, DC, USA.

attacked remotely and bursting into thick black smoke. Since this was a $1 million generator and one of the most widely used in the United States, the footage created considerable interest worldwide (E4). The footage was from a staged attack, the so-called Aurora Generator Test, which had been carried out a few months earlier by scientists from Idaho National Laboratory. The scientists were trying to illustrate the vulnerability of the electric grid to cyber attacks. The approach was relatively simple and has since been shown to be applicable to many other systems.[12]

In 2008, an incident at another nuclear power plant showed that lessons from Davis-Besse (E3) had not been learned. After an engineer installed a software update on a computer sitting on Hatch Nuclear Plant's corporate network, the safety systems on the control network started to erroneously report a drop in the water reservoir levels[13] (E5). The engineer knew that the two networks were connected but did not know that the software update was designed to synchronize data between them. As a result, after the computer was rebooted and its data were reset, the control systems' data were also reset. The safety systems interpreted the difference in reported measurements before and after the reset as a sudden drop in the level of the water reservoirs, and this in turn triggered an automated shut down of the plant.

After the airing of the Aurora Generator Test's footage, there was an increase not only of public interest but also of public announcements regarding cyber security concerns in the energy sector. In 2009, senior officials in the United States reported that cyberspies from foreign states had been attempting to map the infrastructure of the country's electric grid and had deposited software that could be used as part of a future attack.[14] At the same time, several research grants for the cyber security of critical national infrastructures were announced by funding agencies in the United States, the European Union, the United Kingdom, Australia, and many other countries. The security of SCADA systems in general, and especially those involved in power stations, had by then become an area of intense scientific and political interest.

[12]Swearingen, M., Brunasso, S., Weiss, J., and Huber, D. (2013). *What You Need to Know (and Don't) About the AURORA Vulnerability.* Electric Power, September 1, 2013.
[13]Krebs, B. (2008). *Cyber Incident Blamed for Nuclear Power Plant Shutdown.* Washington Post, June 5, 2008.
[14]Gorman, S. (2009). *Electricity Grid in U.S. penetrated by spies.* Wall Street Journal, April 4, 2009.

The same year, two former employees in the energy sector were arrested for having attacked the industrial control systems they had been previously working on. The one had attacked the system used to detect leaks in a marine oil platform of California-based Pacific Energy Resources (E6),[15] and the other had attacked an energy forecast system at a nuclear reactor owned by Texas-based Energy Future Holdings (E7).[16] The industry was beginning to accept that the primary security threat to their systems was the threat of insiders, including former employees. They have the capability, the knowledge, and often the opportunity to cause harm. The attack on Energy Future Holdings was simply the result of forgetting to disable access to the virtual private network (VPN)[17] for the particular employee after firing him. High-impact attacks from other classes of adversaries were considered less likely. What came next was a surprise.

In 2010, a number of cyber-security companies started reporting the existence of Stuxnet, a new worm with an unusual payload that would affect only a specific type of Siemens SCADA systems and would not have any impact on any other type of machine (E8). Stuxnet was exceptionally complex. It exploited a long list of vulnerabilities, four of which were previously undiscovered. These vulnerabilities allowed it to self-replicate through USB flash media, update itself over a network, connect to a command and control server to download and execute malicious code, evade common antivirus packages, and eventually modify code on the actual SCADA system. Most interestingly, more than half of the computers infected by the worm globally were located in Iran.[18] In November of the same year, Iran's president confirmed that malware had affected the operation of some centrifuges at the Natanz nuclear facilities.[19] The controllers of these centrifuges were not directly connected to the Internet. To infect them, Stuxnet first would have to infect a mobile device or USB stick of a contractor who would

---

[15]Goodin, D. (2009). (Former) IT consultant confesses to SCADA tampering. The Register, September 24, 2009.

[16]Leyden, J. (2009). Feds quiz former worker over Texas power plant hack. The Register, June 1, 2009.

[17]VPN technologies allow an authorized user (e.g., a current employee) to connect to an organization's private network securely across the Internet.

[18]Fallier, N., O'Murchu, L., and Chien, E. (2011). *W32.Stuxnet Dossier.* Symantec.

[19]Erdbrink, T. (2010). Ahmadinejad: Iran's nuclear program hit by sabotage. Washington Post Foreign Service, November 29, 2010.

connect to the control network at a later point in time and unknowingly allow the worm to reach its target. This is what had happened at Hatch Nuclear Plant (E3) (albeit unintentionally) at around the same time that Stuxnet was in development. Most significantly, the main functions of Stuxnet are relatively generic and are able to be modified to deliver different payloads. For instance, DuQu, a worm discovered a year later, is very similar to Stuxnet and may have been based on it or may have been developed by the same group. However, instead of targeting industrial control systems, its aim was to steal digital certificates and gather intelligence, such as keystrokes and system information, presumably in preparation for future attacks.[20] A few months after its discovery, there were already 15 DuQu variants identified by the computer security company Symantec.

Reports of attacks in the energy sector have since continued to multiply. According to the cyber emergency response team that the US Department of Homeland Security has set up, around half of the security incidents reported to involve industrial control systems occur in the energy sector.[21] Despite the increased public interest and involvement of the public and private sector in securing such systems, many are still completely insecure. As researchers demonstrated at the 2013 Black Hat USA convention, hacking into an oil well, turning its pumps on and off, and overflowing containers requires only basic computer skills.[22]

At this point, it is important to note that an attack does not have to target physical components of an energy firm to affect its processes. In August 2012, Aramco, Saudi Arabia's state-owned oil and gas firm, and RasGas, Qatar's second largest producer of liquefied natural gas, were both attacked by self-replicating malware (E10). The attacks did not propagate to their control networks but did cause severe disruption to their business processes and may have indirectly affected their generation or delivery of energy.[23]

---

[20]Bencsáth, B., and Pék. P. (2012). Duqu: Analysis, Detection, and Lessons Learned. In *ACM European Workshop on System Security (EuroSec)*. Bern, Switzerland, ACM, April 2012.

[21]ICS-CERT (2013). *ICS-CERT Monitor Report Between April-June 2013*. Department of Homeland Security, June 17, 2013.

[22]Meixell, B., and Forner, E. (2013). *Out of Control: Demonstrating SCADA Exploitation*. Black Hat.

[23]Bronk, C., and Tikk-Ringas, E. (2013). The Cyber Attack on Saudi Aramco. *Survival: Global Politics and Strategy*, International Institute for Strategic Studies, Volume 55, Issue 2, pp. 81–96, April 2013.

Water

The first notable incident in the water sector took place in 1994, when a hacker using a dial-up modem gained access to the computer network of the Salt River Project in Arizona (W1). The intrusion involved at least one 5-hour session where the hacker had access to water and power monitoring data.[24] This incident is often misreported and linked with an alleged hacking incident of Arizona's Roosevelt Dam,[25] but investigation concluded that there was no threat to any dams and there was generally no indication of any intention beyond bragging rights or the satisfaction that a successful hack gives. According to an Idaho National Laboratory report, the perpetrator was a prolific hacker who "believed that he had the right to pursue his intellectual freedom through his hacking activities."[26]

It was another 6 years before a confirmed incident clearly involving malicious intent occurred. It is known today as the Maroochy attack, named after the area in Queensland, Australia where it occurred[27] (W2). This is an area of natural beauty with several water canals, parks, and approximately 120,000 residents. In 2000, its Council had only recently installed a complex SCADA-based infrastructure for managing its 880 kilometers of sewers and 142 pumping stations when its engineers started noticing unusual behavior. Failures of equipment would not always be reported on time, pumps would not respond to remote commands, and communication with central control would often be lost. At the beginning, these were thought to be teething problems of the new infrastructure but it gradually became obvious that there must have been some human involvement. Even after all software had been reinstalled, the configuration of the pumps was changing unexpectedly in a manner that could only be attributed to a human user. The suspicions were confirmed when an engineer who had been called to investigate detected unknown wireless equipment connecting to the system. At one point, he even got into a "duel" trying to revert the changes that were being introduced by an unknown user. The engineer concluded that the user was connecting to

[24]Turk, R. J. (2005). *Cyber Incidents Involving Control Systems.* INL/EXT-05-00671. US-CERT Control Systems Security Center, Idaho Falls, Idaho 83415, October 2005.
[25]Gleick, P. H. (2006). Water and Terrorism. *Water Policy,* Volume 8, No. 6, pp. 481–503, IWA.
[26]Turk, R. J. (2005). *Cyber Incidents Involving Control Systems.* INL/EXT-05-00671. US-CERT Control Systems Security Center, Idaho Falls, Idaho 83415, October 2005.
[27]Abrams, M., and Weiss, J. (2007). *Bellingham, Washington, Control System Cyber Security Case Study.* NIST.

pumps with a laptop, rapidly moving from station to station.[28] The attacks lasted two and a half months until a man was pulled over by the police for a traffic violation near one of the pumping stations and was arrested after suspicious computer and radio communication equipment was found in his car. The man arrested was Vitek Boden, previously an external contractor's employee working as a site supervisor for the installation of the communication infrastructure of the Maroochy SCADA project. After resigning from that position, Boden had sought employment by the Maroochy Shire Council but was twice refused. That is when the unusual behavior of the SCADA systems started being observed. Based primarily on the evidence found on his laptop, he was sentenced to 2 years in jail for having caused the release of 800,000 liters of raw sewage into parks, public waterways, and the grounds of a hotel.

The damage caused by the Maroochy attack was a wake-up call for the industry. Although this was a brand new project with SCADA systems that controlled a critical function of a large residential area, there were no technical cyber-security defenses or policies in place. Possibly more importantly, the contract with the external contractor had not specified adequate personnel security measures for protecting from disgruntled employees. The Council had never employed Boden. Yet, with the specialist knowledge and experience from his employment with the external contractor, he was an insider. He had access to the specialist software used to control the pumps, knew how to connect to the pumping stations and understood well the procedures involved in SCADA-based sewage management. As a result, the attack highlighted not only the potential of cyber-physical attacks in the sector but also the significance of the insider threat.

Two years later, in 2002, the FBI issued a bulletin indicating that Al-Qaeda members had been seeking information on SCADA systems used in water supplies, as well as information on wastewater management practices in the United States and abroad. The bulletin had come after the discovery of instructions on poisoning water sources by a suspected terrorist and analysis of visits to relevant web sites.[29] There is no evidence yet of a successful terrorist attack in the water sector, but incidents involving the failures of SCADA systems have since become increasingly common. More often than not there is no malicious intent behind them. For

---

[28]Slay, J., and Miller, M. (2007). Lessons learned from the Maroochy Water breach. *Critical Infrastructure Protection*, Chapter 6, pp. 73–82, Springer US.
[29]Gleick, P. H. (2006). Water and Terrorism. *Water Policy*, Volume 8, No. 6, pp. 481–503, IWA.

example, the catastrophic failure of the remote monitoring system at the Sauk Water Storage Dam that led to the release of a billion gallons of water in 2005 was an accident (W3). This was followed by two high-profile incidents that did involve unauthorized access. In 2006, a hacker connecting from outside the United States was reported to have intruded into the network of a water filtering plant in Harrisburg, Pennsylvania (W4). The attack involved the installation of malware that could but did not affect the plant's physical operations.[30] The next year, a former electrical supervisor of a small canal system in California was sentenced to 10 years in prison for having installed unauthorized software on a SCADA system, causing water to be diverted from the Sacramento River (W5). He was reported to have carried out the attack on the day he was dismissed after 17 years of employment.[31]

As a result of these security incidents and a growing political interest, an increasing number of scientists started working on the security of water infrastructures, developing defense as well as new attack mechanisms. In 2010, scientists from Mississippi State University demonstrated a variety of attacks against a mock water tank control system in their laboratory, affecting the availability of its SCADA network and forcing it to report false water levels[32] (W6).

The 2011 failure of a water plant in Springfield, Illinois was widely reported as the first foreign cyber attack on a public utility in the United States, but it was later shown to be a normal failure of a pump that had malfunctioned several times in the past (W7). Suspicions had been raised because of a user who had connected to the network from a Russian IP address. After investigation, the user proved to be a contractor who had legitimately accessed the network remotely while in Russia on personal business.[33] Unaware at the time that it was only an accident, a 22-year-old hacker called pr0f was furious that US officials were playing down the incident. Determined to show that such an attack was not only easy but also potentially

[30]Government Accountability Office (2007). *Critical Infrastructure Protection: Multiple Efforts to Secure Control Systems Under Way, but Challenges Remain (GAO-07-1036).* Washington, DC, USA.

[31]Nicholson, A., Webber, S., Dyer, S., Patel, T., and Janicke, H. (2012). SCADA security in the light of Cyber-Warfare. *Computers & Security*, Elsevier, Volume 31, No. 4, pp. 418–436, June 2012.

[32]Gao, W., Morris, T., Reaves, B., and Richey, D. (2010). On SCADA control system command and response injection and intrusion detection. In *eCrime Researchers Summit (eCrime)*, IEEE, pp. 1–9, October 2010.

[33]Hartman, S. M. (2012). Protecting Accelerator Control Systems in the Face of Sophisticated Cyber Attacks. In the *International Particle Accelerator Conference (IPAC'12)*, New Orleans, Louisiana, USA, pp. 2101–2105, May 23, 2012.

catastrophic, he began by looking for Siemens Simatic S7 controllers[34] on the Internet and found one used by a water treatment facility in South Houston, Texas (W8). In less than 10 minutes he had connected to it using the default 3-digit password that was publicly available in the device's manual and had gained access to the water plant's HMI. From there he could control all aspects of the system. He did not cause any damage but took some screenshots and posted one online to prove the intrusion.[35]

Beyond exposing the poor security of the specific facility, the South Houston incident highlighted the potential of opportunistic cyber-physical attacks on critical infrastructure. As was demonstrated at the 2011 Black Hat conference, the IP addresses of several units controlling pumping stations are easily discoverable via common search engines, including Google.[36] More significantly, attackers can use Shodan, a search engine designed specifically to expose "webcams, routers, power plants, iPhones, wind turbines, refrigerators, VoIP phones" [37] and any other device connected to the Internet. Shodan does not operate in the same manner as conventional search engines that crawl the Internet for web sites. Instead, it scans the network ports[38] of devices connected to the Internet, indexing them and making the results available to its users. Port scanning has always been a powerful tool in the hands of cyber attackers. The difference with Shodan is that it conducts port scanning at a global scale, stores the results in a database, and makes them searchable with simple keywords and accessible by anyone. A Shodan search at the time of this writing revealed 629 results for "Siemens Simatic S7."

Health

Until recently, life-threatening system failures in the health sector were a matter of safety engineering. For example, the failures of the Therac-25 computerized radiation therapy machines that led to four deaths in the 1980s were the result of poor

---

[34]These are the same PLCs that were targeted by Stuxnet.

[35]O'Harrow, R. (2013) *Zero Day: The Threat In Cyberspace*. Diversion Books.

[36]Mills, E. (2011). *Researchers warn of SCADA equipment discoverable via Google.* CNET, August 2, 2011.

[37]http://www.shodanhq.com

[38]Network ports are software constructs that allow different applications on the same computer to share the same network resources without interfering with each other. For example, web sites typically use port 80 and e-mail uses port 25. Network devices, such as printers and cameras, use less well-known ports.

software design (H1). Its developers had not duplicated in software all the safety mechanisms that previous less computerized versions of the machine had provided in hardware. As a result, on a few occasions the machine malfunctioned and delivered lethal overdoses of radiation to patients.[39] Over the next two decades, cyber-physical incidents in the health sector continued to be the result of software flaws or misconfiguration of medical equipment rather than intentional attacks. An exception was the unusual case of the defacement of the not-for-profit Epilepsy Foundation's web site in 2008. Hackers replaced part of the web site's content with flashing animations chosen to cause migraines or seizures to visitors that suffer from epilepsy[40] (H2). At least some of the visitors in fact were affected. The incident is significant for demonstrating the possibility of a web site being hijacked in manner that can physically affect a human being.

Cyber attacks started becoming an area of genuine concern when implantable medical devices introduced wireless communication features. Implantable cardiac defibrillators, pacemakers, neurostimulators, and drug pumps that contain embedded computers and can be programmed wirelessly have helped enormously in treating a large variety of physiological conditions within the body. At the same time, however, they have effectively introduced cyber vulnerabilities to it. In 2008, a team of researchers showed that some of the most widely used pacemakers and implantable cardiac defibrillators could be reprogrammed remotely and without authorization[41] (H3). A malicious attacker could program such a device to deliver a life-threatening electrical shock. In 2011, Jerome Radcliffe, a security specialist suffering from diabetes and a user of insulin pumps himself, showed that it is possible to alter insulin injection levels remotely from a range of 30 meters. He intercepted the signals sent wirelessly and caused the glucose monitors to display the wrong values[42] (H4). However, the specific attack required knowledge of the serial number of the device. A year later, another security expert, Barnaby Jack, demonstrated how

[39]Leveson, N. G., and Turner, C. S. (1993). An investigation of the Therac-25 accidents. *Computer, IEEE*, Volume 26, No. 7, pp. 18–41, July 1993.
[40]Poulsen, K. Hackers Assault Epilepsy Patients via Computer, Wired, 28 March 2008.
[41]Halperin, D., Heydt-Benjamin, T. S., Fu, K., Kohno, T., and Maisel, W. H. (2008). Security and Privacy of Implantable Medical Devices. *Pervasive Computing, IEEE*, Volume 7, No. 1, pp. 30–39, January 2008.
[42]Radcliffe, J. (2011). Hacking medical devices for fun and insulin: Breaking the human SCADA system. In *Black Hat Conference*. Las Vegas, Nevada, USA, August 2011.

to deliver a lethal insulin dose wirelessly from a range of 90 meters using a high-gain antenna, and more significantly, without knowledge of the serial number[43] (H5).

As the security of implantable devices started capturing the imagination of the general public, HBO's series *Homeland* featured a fictional assassination based solely on hacking the victim's pacemaker. In an interview in 2013, Jack stated that not only was this feasible but he had even developed software that could deliver a lethal shock to anyone wearing a pacemaker within a 50-foot radius. He was due to demonstrate this attack at the 2013 Black Hat USA convention but a few days earlier he was found dead in his apartment due to unrelated causes.[44]

Beyond implantable devices, other medical equipment used in hospitals may also be vulnerable to cyber attacks. For example, the *Conficker* worm was first reported to have infected magnetic resonance imaging (MRI) machines in 2009, and was again the cause of equipment malfunctioning at James A. Halley Veterans' Hospital in Tampa, Florida 3 years later (H6). This time it had infected an X-ray machine, a mammography device, and a gamma camera. According to records from the Department of Veteran Affairs, malware infected at least 327 devices in their hospitals between 2009 and 2013.[45] Considering that many critical medical devices are still based on old and often unpatched versions of Microsoft Windows, their susceptibility to infections by common Internet-borne malware is anything but surprising. As Fu and Blum have pointed out, "operating system software with production lifecycles measured in months does not match well with a medical device having production lifecycles measured in years or decades." It is highly unlikely that a very expensive MRI machine that was bought a few years ago and is based on Windows XP or earlier operating systems would be withdrawn by a hospital any time soon. Yet, Microsoft has not supported Windows XP since April 2014, which renders these machines extremely vulnerable to newer security threats.[46]

At the same time, the operation of hospitals heavily depends on building automation control. In 2009, a security guard that was in the night shift of the Carrell Clinic in Arlington, Texas,

[43]Hei, X. and Du, X. (2013). *Security for wireless implantable medical devices.* Springer.
[44]Finkle, J. (2013). *Famed hacker Barnaby Jack dies a week before hacking convention.* Reuters, July 26, 2013.
[45]Weaver, C. (2013). *Patients put at risk by computer virus.* The Wall Street Journal, June 13, 2013.
[46]Fu, K. and Blum, J. (2013). Controlling for cyber security risks of medical device software. *Communications of the ACM*, Volume 56, No. 10, pp. 21–23, October 2013.

broke into the clinic's computers to install malware that allowed the remote control of heating, ventilation, and air conditioning (HVAC) systems (H7). The security guard, who was also the leader of a hacker group, was caught after he posted pictures on the Internet of the compromised HVAC system.[47] He was sentenced to 9 years in prison and although the attack did not cause any damage, it publicized one more cyber threat to hospitals. By accessing the systems that control heating, ventilation, and air conditioning, one could remotely damage pharmaceuticals and affect patients' health. Attacks that target the automation of smart buildings and smart homes are becoming a favorite subject for researchers presenting their exploits at cyber security and hacking conferences. In 2011, researchers demonstrated a device that can be plugged into a power outlet outside a building to jam the signals that control lights, doors, air conditioning, and physical security systems.[48]

Transportation

In 1998, a teenager from Massachusetts became the first juvenile in the United States to be charged in federal court with hacking (T1). A year earlier he had broken into a telephone company's network and had caused a crash that disabled digital loop carrier (DLC) systems at Worcester Regional Airport. These systems are used to integrate voice and data communications from several telephone lines for digital transmission over a single high-capacity cable. This is much more efficient than having hundreds of lines from every part of an airport's infrastructure separately connected to the control tower, but if a DLC is disabled, then all associated communications are disabled too. The specific DLCs were accessible to external modems, so that the company's technicians could maintain service remotely.[49] The teenager identified their telephone numbers and connected to them with his personal computer's modem. He then disabled the transmitter responsible for activating runway lights, as well as communication with the control tower, fire department, airport security, and weather service for 6 hours. Although the outage did not cause any serious problem, the US Secret Service considered the incident a matter of national security.

[47]Bradbury, D. (2011). The World's Dumbest Hackers. *Infosecurity*, Elsevier, Volume 8, No. 2, pp. 16–19, March–April 2011.
[48]Kennedy, D. and Simon, R. (2011). Pentesting over power lines. In *DEFCON conference*, Las Vegas, Nevada, USA, August 5, 2011.
[49]Rindskopf, A. (1998). *Juvenile computer hacker cuts off FAA tower at regional airport*. US Department of Justice Press Release, March 18, 1998.

Since then, mass transit operations have gradually become more dependent on IT infrastructures that include general-purpose personal computers and operating systems and are often connected to the Internet. In 2001, the Port of Houston, Texas had taken the security precautions that were reasonable at the time, but its web-based systems used to assist ships in mooring were disabled by a Denial of Service attack (T2). Interestingly, the port's computers might not have been the targets of the attack, but the compromised bots. By sending large amounts of data against an unrelated target on the Internet, they were themselves slowed down in the process. In addition to its impact on one of the busiest ports in the world, this case has also been significant for its legal angle. The defendant's attorney did not contest the fact that the attack was launched from his computer. The evidence for this was convincing. He claimed instead that foreign hackers had remotely gained control of the computer at the time of the attack and they were the ones who launched it. Although no traces of such an intrusion were found on the computer, the prosecutors did not manage to rebut this claim beyond reasonable doubt and the accused was acquitted.[50]

As with all other sectors, cyber-physical attacks in the transportation sector have also often been the result of untargeted worm infections on unpatched Microsoft Windows machines. For example, in 2003, the Sobig.F worm infected computers that controlled the dispatching and signaling systems of the US railway CSX, causing commuter traffic in Washington, DC to stop for several hours[51] (T3). Similar disruption was caused to 300,000 Sydney commuters in Australia in 2004 when the Sasser worm entered the network of RailCorp railway[52] (T4), and in 2006 a computer virus forced the US Federal Aviation Administration to shut down some of its air traffic control systems in Alaska[53] (T5).

Another area where the transportation sector has been affected by cyber attacks is road traffic, and in particular traffic

---

[50]Brenner, S. (2010). *Cybercrime: Criminal Threats from Cyberspace.* Praeger Publishers, pp. 104–108.

[51]Turk, R. J. (2005). *Cyber Incidents Involving Control Systems (INL/EXT-05-00671).* US-CERT Control Systems Security Center, Idaho Falls, Idaho 83415, USA, October 2005.

[52]BBC (2005). *Sasser creator avoids jail term.* July 8, 2005. http://news.bbc.co.uk/1/hi/technology/4659329.stm

[53]De Cerchio, R., and Riley, C. (2011). Aircraft systems cyber security. In the *30th IEEE/AIAA Digital Avionics Systems Conference (DASC)*, pp. 1C3-1–1C3-7, Seattle, Washington, USA, 16–20 October 2011.

lights. The concept is not new. In fact, key in the plot of the 1969 movie *The Italian Job* was an attack on Turin's computerized traffic control system that would paralyze the city and allow the perpetrators to escape in their agile Mini Cooper cars while the Italian police would be stuck in traffic. Although not quite as flamboyant, a real such attack took place in Los Angeles, California in 2006. When traffic engineers went on strike, the city temporarily blocked their access to the computer that controlled 3,200 of its traffic signals (T6). Two of the striking engineers hacked into the computer by stealing the credentials of one of the top managers and increased the duration of the red lights. This further aggravated congestion at four critical intersections, causing a gridlock that lasted several days before managers realized what had happened. The engineers were sentenced to probation 3 years later.[54]

A large number of traffic lights in the United States have been fitted with traffic signal preemption, a system that allows incoming emergency service vehicles to override their operation. Usually activated together with the vehicle's emergency warning lights, a mobile infrared transmitter communicates with a receiver on the traffic lights to give right-of-way to the vehicle. An infrared flash at the frequency specified for emergency vehicles turns the traffic lights to green. During the first years of operation of this system, impatient drivers could purchase such devices online for about $500 and could use them in the same manner. There even existed a web site that described the process of building such a device with parts that would cost less than $20. Since 2005, the practice has been outlawed and legal transmitters used by the emergency services now feature some form of authentication, which has reduced the particular problem considerably.[55]

Current concerns for the potential misuse of traffic lights are related to what researchers from the University of Michigan have characterized as "a systemic lack of security consciousness"[56] in the design and implementation of intelligent wireless traffic management systems. In a large-scale experiment that they conducted with the permission of a local road agency in 2014, they demonstrated practical cyber attacks against nearly

---

[54]Applegate, S. D. (2013). The Dawn of Kinetic Cyber. In the 5th *International Conference on Cyber Conflict (CyCon)*, IEEE, pp. 1–15, Tallinn, Estonia, June 4–7, 2013.

[55]Poulsen, K. (2005). *Traffic Hackers Hit Red Light*. Wired, August 12, 2005.

[56]Ghena, B., Beyer, W., Hillaker, A., Pevarnek, J., and Halderman, J. A. (2014). Green Lights Forever: Analyzing the Security of Traffic Infrastructure. In Proceedings of *the 8th USENIX Workshop on Offensive Technologies*, August 2014.

100 traffic lights of a type that is used throughout the United States (T7). They were able to remotely take control of the operation of all traffic lights, reducing the duration of green lights, turning them green or red on command, and so on. The three security flaws that they exploited are common in wirelessly networked cyber-physical systems found in most critical national infrastructures: communication to its controllers is neither encrypted nor authenticated; usernames and passwords are left to the default ones (which manufacturers publish online); and services for testing the system during its development are often left enabled and can be easily accessed by attackers.[57] The same year, another researcher conducted field tests in three large US cities to show that the sensors embedded in roadways to feed data about traffic flow to traffic signal controllers exhibit similar vulnerabilities.[58] By intercepting and altering the data these sensors transmit, one can indirectly affect the operation of the traffic lights.

Cyber-physical attacks are often described as close calls; examples of what may happen but has not yet happened. An exception was the 2008 incident in Lodz, Poland, where a 14-year-old schoolboy took control of the city's tram system and started operating track switches as if playing with a toy train set[59] (T8). According to the police statement, he had been studying the trams and tracks for a long time before the attack and had built a device akin to a TV remote control to move tracks and redirect trams. In one case, a tram was taken to the left while its driver was trying to steer it to the right, forcing the rear wagon to derail and crash into another tram. In total, four trams were derailed and 14 passengers were injured. The incident is considered to be the first case of an intentional cyber attack directly causing injury to people.

In the meantime, researchers had started expressing their concerns regarding privacy and security in the automotive sector. Today's automobiles contain a variety of in-vehicle networks, generate several types of data, and depend on a multitude of Electronic Control Units (ECUs), which are independent computers controlling critical elements of the vehicle's

---

[57]ICS-CERT (2010). Vulnerability note VU#362332: Wind River Systems VxWorks debug service enabled by default.

[58]Zetter, K. (2014). Hackers can mess with traffic lights to jam roads and reroute cars, Wired, July 30, 2014.

[59]Templeton, S. J. (2011). Security Aspects of Cyber-Physical Device Safety in Assistive Environments. In the 4th *International Conference on Pervasive Technologies Related to Assistive Environments (PETRA), ACM*, pp. 53:1–53:8, Crete, Greece, May 25–27, 2011.

operation. ECUs have limitations in computational power, memory, and bandwidth, which render them vulnerable to denial of service attacks. They operate in an intensely real-time environment where delay caused by any software or network malfunction cannot be tolerated. Yet, network security technologies designed based on traditional IP networks may not be applicable, as network traffic patterns in vehicular communications are different.[60] Privacy considerations have also been raised, especially in relation to number plate recognition, Global Positioning Systems (GPS), Event Data Recording (EDR), and Crash Data Retrieval (CDR) technologies. Nevertheless, most of these threats were theoretical until a large team of researchers from the University of Washington and the University of California San Diego demonstrated experimentally a wide range of cyber attacks on an actual automobile[61] (T9).

In a paper published in 2010, they described the approach they used to take control of an ECU and neutralize the brakes and door locks. Most impressively, they managed to selectively cause one wheel to brake, so as to make the vehicle veer toward one side while at speed and even roll. It took the team around 2 years to discover and exploit the relevant vulnerabilities.[62] For example, a Bluetooth vulnerability allowed them to execute malicious code by using an app on a smartphone connected to the car via Bluetooth, and an infected music file was used to compromise it through the audio system. Two years later, Miller and Valasek demonstrated custom software that allowed taking control of two different makes of cars by physically connecting a computer to their diagnostics ports (T10). This allowed disabling brakes, stopping the engine, manipulating speed and fuel gauges, and affecting the steering and the seat belts. The researchers provided a detailed description of the whole process and part of the code in a white paper.[63] In 2014, they followed up with a survey of remote cyber-physical attacks and a widely

[60]Nilsson, D. K. and Larson, U. E. (2009). A Defense-in-Depth Approach to Security the Wireless Vehicle Infrastructure. *Journal of Networks.* Volume 4, No. 7, pp. 552–564, September 2009.

[61]Koscher, K., Czeskis, A., Roesner, F., Patel, S., Kohno, T., Checkoway, S., McCoy, D., Kantor, B., Anderson, D., Shacham, H., and Savage, S. (2010). Experimental security analysis of a modern automobile. In the *Symposium on Security and Privacy, IEEE*, pp. 447–462, Oakland, CA, USA, May 16–19, 2010.

[62]Checkoway, S., McCoy, D., Kantor, B., Anderson, D., Shacham, H., Savage, S., Koscher, K., Czeskis, A., Roesner, F., and Kohno, T. (2011). Comprehensive Experimental Analyses of Automotive Attack Surfaces. In *USENIX Security Symposium*, August 2011.

[63]Miller, C. and Valasek, C. (2013). Adventures in Automotive Networks and Control Units, Def Con 21.

publicized table ranking popular car models with regard to their (theoretical) susceptibility to such attacks.[64]

The cyber security of automobiles is now a significant concern in the industry and an active area of research globally. For example, one of the open competitions at the 2014 SyScan 360 conference held in Beijing, China, involved the remote hijacking of the Tesla Model S electric car with a grand prize of $10,000 for the team that would compromise remotely the doors and the engine. Although the latter proved too difficult to compromise, a team of students from Zhejiang University was able to remotely switch on the headlights, sound the horn, and open the doors and sunroof while the car was in motion[65] (T11). This was significant not because a particular car model was found to have security flaws, but because the organizers running this competition assumed that small teams of students had a sufficiently good chance to find such a flaw on a high-end modern car, exploit it, and demonstrate it within the time constraints of the conference. And they were right.

Such attacks on individual vehicles require elaborate intrusions and cannot easily cause large-scale disruptions. An incident in Austin, Texas that occurred in 2010 showed that large numbers of private cars can indeed be simultaneously affected by a much simpler cyber attack. A hacker gained access to a web-based vehicle-immobilization system that had been set up by a car dealer to disable a car's ignition system if the owner was late with the car payments. He changed customers' payment details and caused over 80 private cars to be simultaneously immobilized and their horns to be activated, causing many to miss work, be late for school, or have to pay for towing (T12). The person accused by the police was an ex-employee who had recently been laid off. It is unclear whether a web site flaw was exploited or if he simply used the password of an ex-colleague, but in either case this was a rare case of a cyber-physical attack that was solely based on misuse of an external web site.[66]

Cyber attacks are not unheard of in the somewhat related maritime industry either. Most are down to common malware infections, but there are also concerns about attackers locating specific containers by infiltrating a port's computers, or

---

[64]Miller, C. and Valasek, C. (2014). A Survey of Remote Automotive Attack Surfaces, Black Hat 2014, Las Vegas, Nevada, USA.

[65]Griffiths, J. (2014). *Zhejiang University team scoops 10,600 Yuan for hacking into Tesla Model S.* South China Morning Post, July 17, 2014.

[66]Mason, S. (2012). Vehicle remote keyless entry systems and engine immobilisers: Do not believe the insurer that this technology is perfect. *Computer Law & Security Review,* Elsevier, Volume 28, No. 2, pp. 195–200, April 2012.

Figure 2.2 Official US Navy photo of USS *Yorktown* CG-48 (www.navy.mil).

transmitting fake GPS signals to alter a ship's route,[67] altering a ship's automatic identification system (AIS) signals to misreport its location,[68] accessing Electronic Chart Display and Information Systems software to modify maps,[69] as well as pirates listening into AIS transmissions to locate potential victims. However, concrete and dependable information is particularly difficult to find, as it is an industry with very little experience in detecting and reporting cyber threats. There has also been a report on a cyber-physical attack that shut down a floating oil rig off the coast of Africa by tilting it to one side,[70] which has not been publicly confirmed but is not implausible.

Defense

Accidents related to malfunctions of the computer infra-structure are not uncommon in the defense sector, as military needs have always pushed for experimental technologies that may carry a higher risk of failure. An example was the US Navy's Smart Ship program, the testbed for which was the missile cruiser USS *Yorktown (CG-48)* (Figure 2.2). *Yorktown* was

[67]Thompson, I. (2013). Texas students hijack superyacht with GPS-spoofing luggage, The Register, July 29, 2013.
[68]Katsilieris, F., Braca, P., and Coraluppi, S. (2013). Detection of malicious AIS position spoofing by exploiting radar information. In Proceedings of *16th International Conference on Information Fusion (FUSION)*, pp. 1196–1203, IEEE, July 2013.
[69]Dyryavyy, Y. Preparing for cyber battleships – Electronic chart display and information system security, NCC group, 2014.
[70]Wagstaff, J. (2014). All at sea: global shipping fleet exposed to hacking threat, Reuters, April 23, 2014.

equipped with Microsoft Windows NT machines communicating with each other over fiber-optic cabling and running software that was designed to monitor and control key functions of the ship. By automating several tasks, the program had achieved a 10% reduction of crew required on the ship. In 1997, after a member of the crew entered a zero into a database field, the ship's software attempted to operate a division by zero and crashed[71] (D1). The failure gradually cascaded from system to system and eventually caused the propulsion system to fail, leaving *Yorktown* "dead in the water" for 2 hours and 45 minutes. Although there was no malicious intent and no unauthorized use of any kind, the software-based automation and interdependencies between control systems allowed an elementary error in software design to cause a missile cruiser to lose propulsion.

Government departments and companies in the defense sector have always been prime targets for hackers. Their strong security measures constitute an attractive challenge for ambitious individual hackers, while the sensitive data of national security that they hold are attractive to foreign state-sponsored hackers. Reports on cyber-physical attacks, however, are not common. An exception has been the field of unmanned aerial vehicles (UAV). In 2009, militants in Iraq were reported to have used off-the-shelf software to intercept live video feeds from US Predator UAVs[72] (D2). The software package that has been linked to this incident is SkyGrabber. It allows the recording of satellite feeds on a computer that is equipped with a digital satellite tuner card. The intelligence video captured by these UAVs was streamed to its operators in an unencrypted form, possibly because encryption would slow down the transmission. Without encryption, anyone able to intercept the signals would have access to the same images as the US forces that relied on them. On one occasion, US forces found several days' worth of UAV footage on an Iraqi laptop that they captured.

In 2011, US UAVs were again reported to have been targeted by cyber attacks. A virus that contained keystroke logging payload infected the computer network of the operators of Predator and Reaper UAVs[73] (D3). It is not known whether this

[71]Gotterbarn, D. (1999). Not all codes are created equal: The software engineering code of ethics, a success story. *Journal of Business Ethics*, Volume 22, Issue 1 pp. 81–89, October 1999.

[72]Gorman, S., Dreazen, Y. J., and Cole, A. (2009). *Insurgents Hack U.S. Drones*, Wall Street Journal, December 17, 2009.

[73]Shachtman, N. (2011). *Computer Virus Hits U.S. Drone Fleet*. Wired, October 7, 2011.

malware infection was intentional or not, and whether anyone benefitted by logging the keystrokes that are required to control a UAV in combat. The same year, Iranian television showed a captured RQ-170 Sentinel UAV claiming that it had been electronically hijacked and landed virtually intact by the Iranian army's electronic warfare unit[74] (D4). According to an Iranian engineer, it was the result of jamming its communication links and feeding it with spoofed GPS signals.[75] The claim has not been confirmed by sources outside Iran and is unlikely to be accurate, as the navigation of large military UAVs does not depend only on communication with the operators and GPS signals. Although the specific claim is highly questionable, a research group at the University of Texas investigated the feasibility of such an attack. Invited by the US Department of Homeland Security, the researchers demonstrated a sophisticated GPS spoofer of their design that is able to send fake GPS signals to a civilian UAV (D5). As a result, the UAV that depended on GPS was effectively hijacked and controlled remotely.[76]

A Discussion on the Cyber-Physical Security Incident Reports

Motivations

As Charles Perrow suggested in 1984, "normal accidents" are to be expected in a society that depends on complex technologies such as air traffic, dams, and nuclear plants.[77] Naturally, a large number of incidents reported are nothing more than system failures. The 2006 power outage that disrupted 112 trains in the United States was attributed to the failure of a single four-year-old computer.[78] The 2011 failure of the water pump in Illinois (W7) that was hastily reported as a Russian attack on a US public utility was again just a system failure. In fact, it was a predictable one considering the pump's history of failures.

---

[74]Cole, C. (2012). *The Drone War Briefing.* Drone Wars UK, January 2012.

[75]GPS spoofing is the process of generating false GPS signals so as to deceive a GPS receiver with regard to its location.

[76]Wesson, K. and Humphreys, T. (2013). Hacking Drones. *Scientific American,* Volume 309, No. 5, pp. 54–59, October 2013.

[77]Perrow, C. (1984). *Normal Accidents: Living with High-Risk Technologies.* New York: Basic Books.

[78]Karush, S. (2007). *Amtrak Blames Outage on Computer Flaw.* Associated Press, February 23, 2007.

Even when they are not the result of system failures but of human involvement, the vast majority of cyber-physical security incidents have been accidental. Especially the ones involving control systems tend to be the result of lack of understanding of the related interdependencies by their users or more crucially by their designers. The routine update that was designed to synchronize data between the control and corporate networks at the Hatch Nuclear Plant (E5) was an accident waiting to happen. The developer of USS *Yorktown's* (D1) database system who failed to provide the most basic of checks for division by zero must not have expected that such a simple error (albeit an unjustifiable one) would be able to cause cascading failures that would shut down the ship's propulsion.

Very often cyber-physical security incidents are the result of indiscriminate malware infections. This is particularly common for systems that are connected to the Internet or are based on off-the-shelf hardware, operating systems, and applications. In fact, an infected USB memory stick, smartphone, or laptop can allow malware to enter an industrial control network or damage medical equipment even if these are not connected to the Internet. Such systems tend to be more vulnerable to common malware than personal computers because of the length of their service. A SCADA system in a power station may be in use for more than two decades and a MRI machine in a hospital at least 10 years. They are designed based on proven operating systems, which were already a few years in production at the time, and are too expensive to replace often. After so long, support for the operating system has probably ceased and security threats have changed. While a personal computer can be kept secure with regular operating system upgrades, security patches, and antivirus updates, SCADA systems and medical machines are often some generations behind in terms of security protection.

For incidents that can be classified as system failures without human involvement or as accidents with human involvement there is clearly no motivation behind them. For indiscriminate malware infections one could argue that the motivation of their designers was to cause maximum damage worldwide, but again the fact that they infected cyber-physical systems too was probably unexpected and unlikely to have been their main aim. Beyond these accidents or untargeted security incidents, there are an increasing number of attacks that are targeted. Very often the only motivation is curiosity, satisfaction through intellectual challenge, or bragging rights. When this is the case, it is rare that actual physical damage will be caused. Taking a screenshot that proves the exploit and sharing it online may be enough. In fact, on occasion the perpetrator may even report the vulnerabilities discovered, so that defense measures can be implemented in the future. Attacks motivated by curiosity are often opportunistic. In the past, cyber-physical systems, such as water pumps, would be protected to an extent by their obscurity. Lately, the publicity that such attacks have gained and the availability of tools such as Shodan that make them visible to everyone, have turned pumps at obscure water facilities into attractive targets for curious hackers. The specific target may not hold any significance for the hacker. What matters is the thrill of proving that one has the skills to damage a critical physical system from the other side of the world.

In other cases, the motivation behind a targeted attack is more sinister. The 2000 Maroochy attack (W2) in Australia, the 2007 attack that diverted water from the Sacramento River (W5), and the 2010 remote immobilization (T12) of over 80 cars in Austin, Texas were most probably motivated by revenge. The first one's perpetrator had just been denied employment for the second time, while the other two had just been laid off. Although none were employed by the organizations they targeted at the time of the attacks, they were all insiders, as they had inside information about their computer systems and security practices. They had experience working with their target's actual systems and knew not only how to operate them but also how to maximize the impact that they could cause, whether through a SCADA system controlling a water pump or through a web site remotely linked to immobilization devices on hundreds of cars.

Undoubtedly the most significant of all cyber-physical security incidents was the Stuxnet attack (E8) on the Iranian nuclear facility. Its sheer complexity, the fact that it made use of four previously undiscovered exploits and was written in multiple different programming languages, yet it targeted a single and very specific type of industrial control equipment, makes it completely different from the usual malware found on the Internet. It was clearly not the work of a lone hacker or of a gang of cyber criminals, but an attack that only technologically advanced states could have organized. As the majority of computers infected with it were in Iran and its highest-profile victims were the centrifuges at Natanz, most security experts see it as a politically motivated attack. At the time, Iran's nuclear program was possibly the most significant political issue in the Middle East. Any possibility of disrupting it without triggering military action must have been seen as very attractive to political circles in the West. For this reason, it is often labeled as the first true cyber weapon.[79]

In parallel with all these incidents in the real world, there has also been a growing interest in the scientific community and among hacking enthusiasts who devise and demonstrate staged proof-of-concept attacks. The experiment that has contributed the most to raising public awareness on cyber-physical attacks is the Aurora Generator Test (E4), which was broadcast on CNN a few months after the Stuxnet attack. Since then, staged attacks on automobiles, implantable medical devices, and home automation devices have also gained media exposure and have sparked a series of new research initiatives.

Finally, it is important to note that in comparison to physical attacks with the same aim, a cyber-physical attack may require less preparation and less access to resources. Physical sabotage that would lead to the release of 800,000 liters of raw sewage, the derailment of four trams, or the immobilization of 80 cars would most likely not be within the capabilities of the same perpetrators who achieved impact of such scale via cyber means. At the same time, prosecuting someone for a cyber attack presents unique challenges that would not be applicable to prosecution for a physical crime. As the trial of the British teenager accused for the 2001 attack on the Port of Houston (T2) showed, it is not easy to attribute a cyber attack to a specific person without reasonable doubt. The prosecutors need to have sufficient evidence that it was the accused individual who was in control of the computer launching the attack and not another hacker who was remotely controlling it at the time.

Second Order Cyber-Physical Dependencies

Embedded systems, cyber-physical systems, and the Internet of Things are examples of environments where cyber-physical dependencies are direct: a physical process depends on the computer software and communication infrastructure that controls it. If the software or the communication fails, the physical process will be affected too. Throughout this book, we focus almost exclusively on these first-order dependencies and the immediate physical impact of a cyber attack (or, in Chapter 7, on the immediate cyber impact of a physical attack). Yet, most incidents in cyberspace have knock-on effects due to second-order dependencies.

[79]Langner, R. (2011). Stuxnet: Dissecting a cyberwarfare weapon. *Security & Privacy, IEEE*, Volume 9, No. 3, pp. 49–51, May–June 2011.

In some cases, these dependencies are well known. The safe operation of aircraft depends on the uninterrupted operation of air traffic control centers, which in turn depends on the uninterrupted operation of their communications or computer software. The risks associated with these dependencies are known. For instance, in December 2014, a failure of a flight data server at the United Kingdom's national air traffic control center caused hundreds of aircraft across the country to be grounded and the airspace over London to be closed for 1 hour, because the safety of flights could not be guaranteed.[80]

In other cases, cyber-physical dependencies are anything but obvious. The electric racing cars of the Formula E championship are advanced cyber-physical systems with complex onboard networks and software, but an adversary targeting these to affect a car's performance is a rather implausible scenario for the foreseeable future. However, the championship organizers have introduced a unique feature called FanBoost, which is a 90 bhp engine boost voted by fans through social networks to be made available for 2.5 seconds to the drivers of their choice. A breach of security in a social network is much more plausible than an incredibly elaborate attack on the cyber-physical elements of a racing car, yet the impact is still firmly in physical space. To protect the races from fake social network accounts and fake votes, the organizers hired an independent company to validate the online voting process.

A conventional cyber attack can cause physical disruption by affecting the business processes of an organization. For example, in manufacturing it is much more common for production to be disrupted due to malware in the business networks than due to a successful attack against its industrial control systems. In August 2005, a worm called Zotob caused computer outages at Caterpillar Inc., Boeing, and 13 of DaimlerChrysler's manufacturing plants, with the latter remaining offline for almost an hour.[81] When the Sasser worm infected major airlines in 2004, they were unable to issue tickets or check in passengers and were forced to cancel flights.[82] In 2008, when the municipal court system in Houston, Texas was hit by malware, court

---

[80]Farmer, B. (2014). Flights in chaos across UK as air traffic control computers fail. The Telegraph. December 12, 2014.

[81]Government Accountability Office (2007). *Critical Infrastructure Protection: Multiple Efforts to Secure Control Systems Under Way, but Challenges Remain (GAO-07-1036).* Washington, DC, USA.

[82]Gercke, M. (2012), Legal Responses to Terrorist Use of the Internet. *Enhancing Cooperation in Defence Against Terrorism*, Tokgoz, K. (ed.), IOS Press, Volume 99, pp. 19–34.

proceedings were suspended and local police temporarily stopped making arrests for minor offenses.[83] Most notably, in 2009, the Conficker worm infected the French Navy's computer network, forcing several airbases to ground their aircraft because they could not download their flight plans.[84] In all these cases, although no cyber-physical system was affected, routine physical operations of organizations were disrupted due to untargeted malware infections of their business networks. A military aircraft cannot be sent to a routine flight if its flight plan cannot be accessed, and a civilian aircraft cannot take passengers if they cannot be issued tickets or they cannot be checked in.

In the past, when most people used to be connected to the Internet via dial-up modems, malware could easily make a computer initiate calls to a specific telephone number. Most such malware would aim to incur charges to premium rate numbers,[85] but the Firkin worm,[85] discovered in 2000, would call instead 911, which is the telephone number for emergency services in North America. Firkin was not particularly widespread and is unlikely to have caused significant disruption to emergency services. Since then, malware that initiate their own phone calls have reappeared in smartphones and Voice over IP services, but none has been reported to aim for disruption of a physical process. They are again linked to premium rate charges.

Another example of physical disruption achieved partly via cyber means is the rush-hour protest organized by the hacking group Anonymous at underground stations in San Francisco in 2011. The unexpected overcrowding forced police to shut down several of these underground stations due to safety concerns. The disruption had been organized in a manner similar to the group's usual denial of service attacks on web sites. After two days of cyber-attacks, instead of launching an attack against an IP address provided by the group, their supporters had been asked to physically go to specific stations and participate in parallel protests across the underground network.[86] Technically, this event was nothing more than a public protest that was organized via social media, just like every other event

[83]Walker, J. J. (2012). Cyber Security Concerns for Emergency Management. *Emergency Management*, Dr. Burak Eksioglu (Ed.), InTech, pp. 39–58.
[84]Willsher, K. (2009). *French fighter planes grounded by computer virus.* The Telegraph, February 7, 2009.
[85]CERT (2000). *911 Worm.* Incident Note IN-2000-03, April 4, 2000.
[86]Williams, C. (2011). *Authorities face Anonymous protests over San Francisco mobile network shut down.* The Telegraph, August 15, 2011.

nowadays. What makes it noteworthy is that the group of hackers behind it saw it as complementary to their usual cyber attacks. It was the speed and reach of communication provided by their Twitter account and their long list of followers that made disruption of such scale possible, even though it did not involve the misuse of any computer system.

In some ways, the San Francisco disruptions by Anonymous were reminiscent of an article by Byers, Rubin, and Kormann,[87] who observed that "in the physical world, attacks do not scale well, but as soon as a physical world process is moved online, malicious parties can potentially exploit vulnerabilities in an automated and exhaustive fashion." In that article, they presented a cyber attack that could lead to immense amounts of junk mail sent to the same individual. The approach was relatively simple. The hacker would need to develop a software tool that would look for web sites that provide online forms where one could request free printed brochures to be sent by post. Then, by automating the process of filling in these forms, a malicious user would order immense amounts of junk mail to be directed to a single person's mailbox. By further automating the same attack against a large number of individuals in the same area, this approach could theoretically affect the infrastructure of the post office. Such an attack is particularly difficult to defend against, because what follows after it is launched is semiautomated. There could be thousands of senders, all of which would be unaware of their participation in the attack and would be located in different geographical areas.

The Impact of Cyber-Physical Attacks

As cyber-physical incidents involve the misuse of a cyber process to affect a physical one, they have an impact in both cyberspace and physical space. What makes them distinguishable from other types of cyber security incidents is their impact in physical space. In many cases, the availability of a physical process may depend on the availability of the computer on which it depends. During the 1999 Bellingham pipeline incident (E2), the slowing down of the SCADA system prevented the engineers from alleviating effectively the impact of the pressure build up. The service of remotely controlling the pumps had become unavailable. The specific case was an accident, but the

---

[87]Byers, S., Rubin, A. D., and Kormann, D. (2004). Defending against an Internet-based attack on the physical world. *ACM Transactions on Internet Technology (TOIT)*, Volume 4, No. 3, pp. 239–254.

loss of availability of the device could have been the result of a malicious denial of service attack, as in the case of the Port of Houston in 2001 (T2). The availability of a physical service can also be affected by malware, sometimes targeted but more often not. In addition to disabling thousands of personal computers worldwide, the 2003 Slammer epidemic rendered unavailable 13,000 Bank of America ATM machines, the electronic check-in kiosks of Continental Airlines,[88] and the safety display at Davis-Besse nuclear power plant (E3). As a result, the bank's customers could not withdraw money and the airline had to cancel flights. The impact on the power plant would have been more severe if it were not already shut down for maintenance at the time of the infection. Technically, Slammer did not carry a malicious payload, but it was causing infected machines to scan for other machines to infect, and in the process was overloading their networks.

In the context of cyber-physical security, it is important to note that the loss of the availability of a physical process is not always the result of the loss of availability of the computer system on which it depends. The security breach that immobilized the 80 cars in Houston (T12), rendering them unavailable to their owners, did not involve a denial of service attack or other breach of the availability of an associated computer system. Instead, the hacker had gained access to a car dealer's web system and had altered the data related to each owner's payments. So, it was a breach of authentication followed by a breach of data integrity in cyberspace that led to prevented actuation in physical space.

Instead of simply rendering a physical system unavailable, cyber-physical attacks may try to hijack it. The Polish teenager who attacked the trams in Lodz (T8) was able to control them and steer them against the will of their drivers, and University of Texas researchers achieved the same result for a civilian UAV (D5) by manipulating the GPS signals on which it relied. Such a cyber-physical attack can directly cause physical damage. The Aurora Generator Test (E4) physically destroyed a generator by bringing it out of phase with carefully timed commands. An attack can also cause injuries and even fatalities, for example by making an implantable medical device deliver a lethal electric shock to its user (H3) or by manipulating a car's braking system (T9). The potential of some cyber-physical attacks to cause

[88]Billo, C. and Chang, W. (2004). *Cyber warfare: An analysis of the means and motivations of selected nation states.* Dartmouth College, Institute for Security Technology Studies.

damage that in the past would be possible only with a conventional kinetic (armed) attack has led some researchers to refer to them as cyber-kinetic or kinetic cyber attacks.[89] The term is applicable only for the cyber-physical attacks that purposely affect actuation with the intention of causing physical damage.

The scale of the impact also varies, and partly depends on the motivation of the perpetrator. An attack motivated by mere curiosity may be limited to a successful intrusion and to causing minor disruption or no physical damage at all. On the other hand, attacks motivated by revenge usually aim to maximize the physical damage inflicted on the target organization. For untargeted worm infections, the usual aim is to maximize the number of systems affected, regardless whether they are cyber-physical systems or simple personal computers. For targeted attacks, such as Stuxnet, the aim is to disrupt or damage a particular system or organization. Although it infected thousands of machines worldwide, Stuxnet's extremely complex and potent payload caused damage only on the system that was its intended target. All other infected machines remained unaffected.

Cyber-physical systems are often designed to automate processes. As a result, a security incident that directly affects one may have a cascading effect on other processes. The Hatch Nuclear Plant (E5) shutting down was an automated routine triggered by an erroneous safety report of low water level. Similarly, the failure of the computer running USS *Yorktown's* (D1) database propagated from system to system and eventually reached the ship's propulsion. This cascading effect can also be observed between different sectors. A failure in the energy sector in particular can affect all other sectors. During a blackout, the local mobile communications transmitter will probably be up and running thanks to back-up power, but communication between mobile phone users will still be available only for as long as their batteries last. Even if the telephone back-up system is operational, payphones will still be practically useless if their keypads are run by mains power, which is what happened during the 2003 blackout in New York.[90]

[89]Applegate, S. D. (2013). The Dawn of Kinetic Cyber. In the *5th International Conference on Cyber Conflict (CyCon), IEEE*, pp. 1–15, Tallinn, Estonia, June 4–7, 2013.

[90]Fisk, D. J. (2004). Engineering complexity. *Interdisciplinary Science Reviews*, Volume 29 Issue 2, pp. 151–161, June 2004.

Summary

Until the beginning of the twenty-first century, reports on cyber-physical security incidents were rare. Albeit fascinating, the oft-repeated story of CIA cyber sabotage during the Cold War that caused a "monumental" pipeline explosion in the Soviet Union (E1) remains unconfirmed. The most notable cyber-physical security incidents that were reported in the 1990s were accidents, such as the ruptured pipeline in Bellingham, Washington (E2). Only a few of them were intentional and could be categorized as attacks, with a perpetrator, a motive, and a target. Still, most were low-impact hacker intrusions motivated by curiosity rather than by malicious intent. The event that changed people's perception on cyber-physical attacks and their potential impact took place in Queensland, Australia in 2000 (W2). A man who had been recently denied employment at a local council gained remote access to the brand new SCADA infrastructure that was operating pumping stations. Over a period of two and a half months he caused unprecedented environmental damage by releasing 800,000 liters of raw sewage into public waterways. Since then, SCADA systems have been repeatedly attacked by hackers and have been infected by both targeted and untargeted malware.

Our increasing dependence on SCADA and other cyber-physical systems has made such security incidents increasingly common. Of particular interest is the energy sector. The footage from the Aurora Generator Test experiment (E4) that showed a $1 million diesel generator being destroyed by a few lines of remotely run commands made cyber-physical attacks a matter of intense public interest. A coordinated attack against power generators or the smart grid could cause a blackout that would naturally affect every other sector, which has made the security of the energy sector a key concern for every nation's critical infrastructure. This experiment and a few other high-profile incidents were followed by the discovery of Stuxnet (E8), one of the most significant pieces of malware in history. Stuxnet was unique in that despite its impressive complexity, destructive potential, and the fact that it infected thousands of computer systems worldwide, it caused virtually no damage to anything other than the centrifuges of an Iranian nuclear facility at a time that Iran's nuclear program was a key political issue in the Middle East. Being highly targeted and highly effective, Stuxnet is often considered the first cyber weapon and has become a point of reference for security professionals, scientists, policy makers, and political and military analysts.

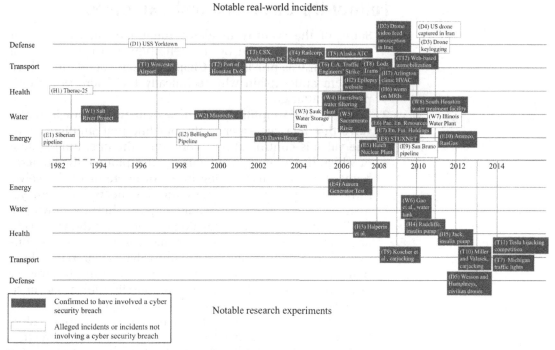

Figure 2.3 Historical timeline of publicly reported cyber-physical security incidents. The upper half contains notable real-world incidents and the lower half contains notable research experiments. Confirmed cyber-physical attacks are highlighted with a dark background.

Since Stuxnet, reports on cyber-physical attacks have multiplied. A history of publicly reported incidents illustrates a remarkable variety of motives and attack approaches in cyberspace with a direct impact in physical space. Public spending on security of critical national infrastructures against security threats has also increased globally and researchers have extended the breadth of potential targets by staging attacks against implantable medical devices, private cars, autonomous vehicles, building automation devices, and other cyber-physical systems. Causing physical damage or injury with a cyber attack is now seen as a reality, not merely a possibility.

Figure 2.3 shows a timeline of the publicly reported incidents that were discussed in this chapter. Notable incidents confirmed to have been the result of a cyber security breach, whether real-world ones or research experiments, are highlighted with a dark background.

Follow-Up Questions and Exercises

1. Some of the security incidents mentioned in this chapter would not be covered by the definition of a cyber-physical attack that was provided in Chapter 1. Can you identify three of them and explain why technically they were not cyber-physical attacks?

2. Consider the simplified case of a dam with a single outlet valve that releases water to the pipeline that supplies a city. The valve is controlled by a computer, the operating system of which has a known vulnerability. If exploited, the vulnerability allows any user to log in as an operator of the valve. Although a patch exists, the dam's engineers have not yet installed it, because that would require shutting down the facility for a few hours. They do not think that the valve is in any danger, since the computer that controls it is not connected to anything other than the valve. Their rationale is that since the computer is not connected to the Internet or any other network, it would not be possible for a hacker to damage it or hijack its control. Is their rationale valid?

3. The Conficker worm was first detected in November 2008. Shortly after, Microsoft released a patch to prevent infection and a removal tool. Why do you think the worm has continued infecting critical medical devices several years later?

4. Consider the simplified scenario of two cities that are connected by a railway line and two busy highways. One highway includes a long tunnel through the mountains. Can you think of three different approaches with which a hacker could create a traffic jam on either highway? Discuss the difficulty and likelihood of occurrence of each approach.

5. Assuming that Stuxnet's sole objective was to delay the Iranian nuclear program by damaging centrifuges, why would it be allowed to infect thousands of other computers worldwide? Suggest three likely reasons.

6. Identify a real-world cyber-physical security incident reported to have occurred after the publication of this book. Discuss the likely motivation behind it, whether it was a targeted attack or not, and its impact in physical space.

7. Identify a notable cyber-physical security experiment that has not been included in this chapter. Describe the technical approach used by the researchers in cyberspace and its impact in physical space.

8. Which of the following statements is correct?
   a. A nonkinetic attack is one that aims to cause physical damage or injury.

   b. An artillery strike against an enemy's computer and communication infrastructure is a nonkinetic attack since its ultimate aim is to affect cyberspace rather than physical space.

   c. A cyber attack cannot cause physical damage or injury.

   d. The Aurora Generator Test was a demonstration of a kinetic cyber attack.

9. Which of the following could be categorized as "normal accidents"?

   a. The Stuxnet attack against the centrifuges in Natanz

   b. The ruptured pipeline in Bellingham, Washington

   c. The hijacked trams in Lodz, Poland

   d. The 2011 failure at the Illinois water plant

3

CYBER-PHYSICAL ATTACKS ON IMPLANTS AND VEHICLES

Chapter Summary

For reasons of performance, functionality, energy efficiency, and convenience, modern cyber-physical systems are highly automated and heavily dependent on a variety of sensing, computational, and communication technologies. These advantages, however, come at the expense of security. In this chapter, we explore the cyber-physical vulnerabilities of implantable insulin pumps and cardioverter defibrillators, which are critical for the health of their wearers; unmanned aerial vehicles, which are highly complex and expensive systems used in a wide range of civilian and military applications; as well as common automobiles. We discuss different attack mechanisms and their impact on each system. Some attacks require exceptional technical skills and have been successfully carried out only in proof-of-concept demonstrations by research teams. Others are much simpler and exploit the fact that for several years designers of cyber-physical systems have placed little or no emphasis on security.

Key Terms: Cyber-physical attack; implantable medical device; unmanned aerial vehicle; automobile; GPS

To understand the cyber-physical vulnerabilities of a system, one first needs to understand its architecture and the technologies upon which it relies. We begin our case studies of cyber-physical systems with implantable medical devices (IMDs), which are small-scale and relatively simple, featuring one sensor and one actuator (or very few of each) and some form of wireless communication. Their strict requirements for small size, low weight, and energy efficiency have always been seen as more important than any security requirement. This is understandable. What is less understandable is the extent to which security has often been ignored in the design process of devices that perform critical health functions. Limited emphasis on security can also be seen in larger-scale cyber-physical systems, such as unmanned aerial vehicles (UAVs) and automobiles. We use UAVs as a case study for discussing the vulnerabilities arising from extensive reliance on external communications with other systems. Then, we move on to the case of the automobile, which we present in more detail. Being arguably the most complex cyber-physical system that is affordable and available to the average family, it is an excellent example of a system designed to provide safety and comfort through an impressive number of on-board computers, sensors, and communication systems working together. Ironically, this complexity and automation can be exploited by cyber-physical attacks that can affect both the safety and the comfort of driver and passengers. Let us start, though, with the simpler IMDs.

Implantable Medical Devices

Implantable medical devices (IMDs) perform vital functions for several types of medical conditions. Cochlear implants, gastric stimulators, neurostimulators, insulin pumps, pacemakers, cardioverter defibrillators, and other IMDs are placed fully or partly within the patient's body. Because removing these devices to reconfigure them or collect data from them would usually be impractical, IMDs increasingly provide wireless communication features. Some are even able to adapt and optimize their configuration autonomously, based solely on sensors that measure the patient's condition. Naturally, such features have been met with enthusiasm by the medical community and by patients, since they make IMDs more practical and more effective. However, as with all wireless computerized devices, the operation of IMDs, and consequently the health of their users, can be severely affected by cyber security attacks.

The public's interest in information security in the health sector has traditionally revolved around data privacy. While this usually relates to the storage and sharing of health records, it is also true for IMDs, since their sensor readings generate sensitive personal data directly from the user's body. In most cases, these readings are transmitted in an encrypted manner. So, in order to access them, an attacker would need first to capture the network traffic sent from the sensor and then to carry out some form of cryptanalysis offline.

Beyond attackers that aim to gather information and are usually referred to as passive attackers, there is also an increasing threat of active attackers that may try to interfere with the operation of medical devices and possibly harm the patient.[1] A generic approach that can disable or degrade the performance of a device is to cause electromagnetic interference near it. Another approach is to intercept routine communication from and to a device, attempt to analyze the communication protocol, and after learning how it operates, try to communicate directly with the device and effectively control it.

In this section, we will provide a brief description of the architecture of two common IMDs and discuss relevant cyber-physical security threats. We have chosen insulin pumps, which are typically open-loop IMDs, and implantable cardioverter defibrillators as representative of closed-loop IMDs. An open-loop IMD is one where the patient is allowed to control the actuation of the device (e.g., the pump), usually with a remote control device, while a (usually fully-implanted) closed-loop IMD is one where there is normally no human input and sensor measurements dictate an automated actuation.[2]

Insulin Pumps

An increasing number of people suffering from diabetes, especially children with Type 1 diabetes, wear insulin pumps. These are small devices that sit partly inside and partly outside the body and are designed to deliver insulin from a reservoir into the layer of fat just below the skin. Their aim is to simulate the operation of the pancreas by controlling the level of glucose in the body. The principle is far from new, as the first prototype was demonstrated over 50 years ago, but lately these devices have become more practical and more popular. The wearers can

[1]Arney, D., Venkatasubramanian, K. K., Sokolsky, O., and Lee, I. (2011). Biomedical devices and systems security. In *Engineering in Medicine and Biology Society, EMBC, 2011 Annual International Conference of the IEEE*. IEEE, pp. 2376–2379.
[2]Burleson, W., Clark, S. S., Ransford, B., and Fu, K. (2012). Design challenges for secure implantable medical devices. In *Proceedings of the 49th Annual Design Automation Conference*. ACM, pp. 12–17.

typically use a simple digital interface to determine the amount of insulin to be delivered and can program its delivery at specific times of the day, such as while they are sleeping. A faulty device that would deliver less or considerably more than the required amount of insulin without the knowledge of the wearers could severely affect their health and in some cases be life-threatening. The design of such devices has traditionally focused on reducing the chance of a mechanical or electronic fault. Yet, as has been shown repeatedly in recent years, insulin pumps can also be targets for intentional cyber-physical attacks.

Let us consider the conceptual design of a typical wireless insulin pump. This includes the pump, a continuous glucose monitor, and a remote control. The continuous glucose monitor is effectively a sensor that measures the level of glucose in tissue fluid and reports it wirelessly to the pump, which releases insulin based on its settings and the sensor measurements. The remote control is for the user to change the pump's settings, configure the amount of insulin, program the timing of the delivery, and operate the pump. Depending on the architecture of the particular system, it may be a separate device or embedded on the same device that houses the controller of the pump, the display, and the insulin reservoir (Figure 3.1). An insulin pump is an open-loop system, whereby the user sees the glucose level on the display and operates the pump when needed, but there is intensive research effort worldwide for the development of practical closed-loop "artificial

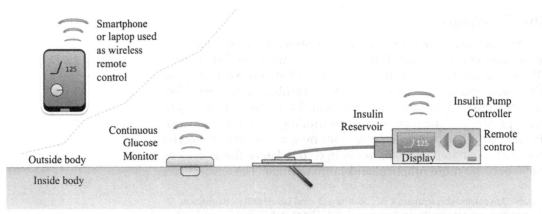

Figure 3.1 A continuous glucose monitor measures the level of glucose in tissue fluid and reports it wirelessly to the pump, which releases insulin based on its settings and the glucose measurements. The insulin reservoir, the pump controller, the display, and the remote control are housed within the same device typically attached at the abdomen. The patient can also use a smartphone to monitor the whole process.

pancreas"[3] systems, where the process is fully automated and involves no human action.

For the whole system to operate correctly, the continuous glucose monitor needs to measure the correct level of glucose and successfully report it via a wireless channel. For as long as there is enough insulin in the reservoir, the process can be pre-programmed and can run without much intervention from the wearer. As there have been thousands of adverse events involving insulin pumps and an error in the delivery of insulin can cause life-threatening hyperglycemia or hypoglycemia,[4] these devices are designed with an emphasis on safety. Security is seen as less important and in most cases can be considered simplistic. For the insulin pump hijacked by Li, Raghunathan, and Jha[5] in 2011, communication between the continuous glucose monitor and the pump, as well as between the remote control and the pump was authenticated with a six-digit hexadecimal PIN code. Often these digits can be found printed on the back of the devices. So, if someone had physical access to them and could read the code on the devices, perhaps prior to a patient wearing them, then they would be able to generate their own messages from and to the pump. In fact, as has been shown repeatedly, it is also feasible to read the PIN while the pump is in operation by intercepting the messages it sends and receives. Very often these are sent in plaintext.

Even if the attacker does not manage to gain access to the PIN, it is still feasible to affect the operation of the pump. An attack that was demonstrated by the same researchers is a replay attack that involves capturing two packets (let us call them P1 and P2) sent from the continuous glucose monitor to the pump and then resending them to the pump in an alternating manner (P1, P2, P1, P2, P1…). The networking protocol used by the specific pump uses a sequence counter to identify packets. As a security precaution, it blocks a packet that has the same sequence counter as the immediate previous one. However, if the attacker alternates between two packets as in this example, then the system will never see two consecutive

---

[3]Cefalu, W. T. and Tamborlane, W. V. (2014). The artificial pancreas: are we there yet? *Diabetes care*, Volume 37, No. 5, pp. 1182–1183.

[4]Paul, N., Kohno, T., and Klonoff, D. C. (2011). A review of the security of insulin pump infusion systems. *Journal of diabetes science and technology*, Diabetes Technology Society, Vol. 5, No. 6, pp. 1557–1562.

[5]Li, C., Raghunathan, A., and Jha, N. K. (2011). Hijacking an insulin pump: Security attacks and defenses for a diabetes therapy system. In *e-Health Networking Applications and Services (Healthcom), 2011 13th IEEE International Conference on,* IEEE, pp. 150–156, June 2011.

packets with the same counter and will always think that they are new legitimate packets. The result of this is that the pump will keep receiving out-of-date information on the level of glucose. To capture signals from the pump's network and generate fake compatible signals, the researchers used an off-the-shelf software radio board. The approach is not trivial but is well within the capabilities of an engineering student or radio communications enthusiast.

If the attacker manages to access the PIN, then the main authentication mechanism of the system has been compromised and there are several attacks that can be performed. The most obvious and possibly most dangerous one is to generate and send to the pump packets with fake sensor readings, forcing it to perform an undesired action. If a fake high glucose level is reported, the pump will automatically deliver a dose to lower it, causing the real glucose level in the body to drop to a dangerously low value.

The attacks discussed above target the insulin pump directly. Lately, an increasing number of insulin pumps have allowed control through smartphone applications. This approach can be very convenient, as there is no need for a separate fully functional remote control, but has introduced indirect security threats. By including a smartphone in the system, the pump effectively inherits its security vulnerabilities.[6] If the smartphone is infected with malware, hijacked, or stolen, a malicious user can start issuing commands remotely to the pump, bypassing any security measure. The same is true for any other peripheral computer system that is allowed to control the insulin pump.

In summary, an attacker could attempt the following:

- Read real-time glucose levels by intercepting wireless communication from a continuous glucose monitor to pump or peripheral device, such as a smartphone or laptop
- Replay packets sent from continuous glucose monitor to pump, so that the pump operates based on measurements that are out of date
- Breach the device's authentication mechanism by reading the PIN either physically or by intercepting a network packet that contains it
- Analyze the communication protocol and contents of a captured packet and inject its own packet reporting fake glucose levels

---

[6]Paul, N. and Klonoff, D. C. (2010). Insulin Pump System Security and Privacy. In *USENIX Workshop on Health Security and Privacy*.

- Infect with malware and potentially hijack any peripheral device that is allowed to control or communicate with the pump or the continuous glucose monitor

Implantable Cardioverter Defibrillators

Implantable cardioverter defibrillators are devices used by patients that are at risk of having life-threatening abnormal heart rhythms. These devices can deliver small electrical pulses at a fast rate to regulate the heart's rhythm, just like pacemakers, but they can also deliver small or large electric shocks when required, for example to reset the heart's rhythm during an episode of arrhythmia. Similarly to insulin pumps, they include a sensor and an actuator. The sensor is the component that monitors the heart's rhythm, while the actuator is the pulse generator that delivers the electric shock. Both make use of electrodes fitted near the heart (Figure 3.2). Because defibrillators are expensive and fitting one requires an invasive operation, they are expected to be able to run for several years on battery and inside the patient's body.[7] During routine operation, the system runs based solely on the sensor readings and without human intervention. Unlike an insulin pump, where the sensor and the actuator are located at a different place inside

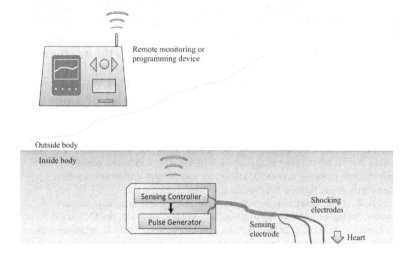

Figure 3.2 An implantable cardioverter defibrillator is a fully implanted closed-loop IMD, where a pulse generator is instructed to automatically deliver an electric shock when an abnormal heart rhythm is sensed.

[7]Burleson, W., Clark, S. S., Ransford, B., and Fu, K. (2012). Design challenges for secure implantable medical devices. In *Proceedings of the 49th Annual Design Automation Conference.* ACM, pp. 12–17.

the body of the patient and have to communicate wirelessly, here the sensing component and the pulse generator are housed within the same device. So, a hacker cannot realistically intercept the communication between these two. The only communication that can be intercepted is between the defibrillator and external devices used to alter its settings or to remotely monitor its operation.

A rather simple approach that has been shown to lead to hazardous incidents involving critical care medical equipment is to place near them two simple radio frequency identification (RFID) devices, a reader that generates an electromagnetic field and a tag that is activated when inside the field. The communication that is initiated between the two RFID devices causes electromagnetic interference that affects external pacemakers, syringe pumps, mechanical ventilators, and many other types of devices.[8] In particular for implantable pacemakers and defibrillators, electromagnetic interference has been shown to be feasible not only with RFID but also with electronic article surveillance devices and metal detectors.[9] On one occasion, a 72-year-old man received four shocks by his implantable defibrillator while standing next to a store's electronic antitheft system. The electromagnetic noise caused by the latter affected the sensor readings of the defibrillator, making them look as if the wearer had developed high heart rhythm and needed a shock to reset it. A nurse that noticed the incident pulled him away from the antitheft system and the man soon recovered.[10] Between 1987 and 2004, the Food and Drug Administration (FDA) received 109 reports on IMDs malfunctioning due to electromagnetic interference caused by security systems.[11]

The security of defibrillators, as well as of pacemakers, was first analyzed in detail by an interdisciplinary team of computing

[8]Van Der Togt, R., van Lieshout, E. J., Hensbroek, R., Beinat, E., Binnekade, J. M., and Bakker, P. J. M. (2008). Electromagnetic interference from radio frequency identification inducing potentially hazardous incidents in critical care medical equipment. *Jama*, Volume 299, No. 24, pp. 2884–2890.

[9]Irnich, W. (2002). Electronic security systems and active implantable medical devices. *Pacing and clinical electrophysiology*, Volume 25, No. 8, pp. 1235–1258.

[10]Santucci, P. A., Haw, J., Trohman, R. G., and Pinski, S. L. (1998). Interference with an implantable defibrillator by an electronic antitheft-surveillance device. *New England Journal of Medicine*, Volume 339, No. 19, pp. 1371–1374.

[11]Kainz, W., Casamento, J. P., Ruggera, P. S., Chan, D. D., and Witters, D. M. (2005). Implantable cardiac pacemaker electromagnetic compatibility testing in a novel security system simulator. *IEEE Transactions on Biomedical Engineering*, Volume 5, No. 23, pp. 520–530.

and medical scientists in 2008. Halperin et al.[12] found a series of potential security threats applicable to a popular commercial device, ranging from breach of privacy to allowing an unauthorized person to remotely deliver a life-threatening shock. It is important to note that replicating these attacks requires considerable technical know-how, especially with regard to radio frequency data communications, and is not possible for all commercial implantable defibrillators. The specific product that they worked on could communicate with its external programming device over short-range wireless at a frequency that was published by the manufacturer. They observed that inside the defibrillator there was a magnetic switch that would trigger a wireless transmission of the sensor readings when closed. For the specific model's switch to close, all that was needed was a sufficiently strong magnet to be placed in its proximity. (While this is a somewhat different use of a magnet, there have been several reports of magnets inside patients' headphones interacting with pacemakers and implantable cardiac defibrillators, causing asynchronous pacing and suspension of tachyarrhythmia detection and therapy if placed within 1.2 inches from them.[13]) The researchers started their analysis by capturing the wireless transmissions with laboratory equipment and converting the radio signals into streams of bits. Then, they methodically experimented with different transmissions, so as to understand how the communication protocol works. They concluded that neither the defibrillator nor its programming device encrypted the data they exchanged between them. As a result, an attacker could read the name of the patient, the date of birth, the patient history, and the name of the treating physician.

Having established that using a magnet could trigger the transmission of private data, which could then be captured and read in plaintext, they continued by building their own prototype device to transmit signals to the defibrillator. As their analysis of the communication protocol was not complete, they could not create from scratch their own signal that would be compatible with the device. So, they were limited to replaying a communication that they had previously recorded. Nevertheless, this is sufficient for launching replay attacks. By replaying previously

[12]Halperin, D., Heydt-Benjamin, T. S., Ransford, B., Clark, S. S., Defend, B., Morgan, W., Fu, K., Kohno, T., and Maisel, W. H. (2008). Pacemakers and implantable cardiac defibrillators: Software radio attacks and zero-power defenses. In *IEEE Symposium on Security and Privacy (SP 2008)*, IEEE, pp. 129–142.
[13]Lee, S., Fu, K., Kohno, T., Ransford, B., and Maisel, W. H. (2009). Clinically significant magnetic interference of implanted cardiac devices by portable headphones. *Heart Rhythm*, Volume 6, No. 10, pp. 1432–1436.

recorded communication, they were able to request from the defibrillator to identify itself (model and serial number), change the patient name, set its clock, reprogram its responses to cardiac events, and even deliver a shock. Of course, all these are replay attacks. They require that the attacker must have somehow captured the required communication before, perhaps while a physician was testing the equipment.

An easier attack starting from the physical space would be to simply leave a magnet near the defibrillator. This would cause a continuous transmission of data that would drain the battery of the device. The impact of battery exhaustion in this case would be severe because replacing it would require an invasive operation. The same effect could be achieved starting from cyberspace by continuously attempting to communicate with the device. As long as the device is configured to respond to requests wirelessly, even to reject them, continuous communication attempts can exhaust its battery.

Following the research of Halperin et al. and the work carried out independently and demonstrated at hacking conferences by Jerome Radcliffe and Barnaby Jack in 2011, the US Government Accountability Office published a report that recommended strengthening the security of implantable medical devices, including pacemakers and defibrillators.[14] During a televised interview, former US Vice President Dick Cheney revealed that as early as 2007, the threat of hackers attempting to assassinate him by hijacking his defibrillator had been assessed to be realistic (albeit "slim") and his doctors had disabled its wireless connectivity as a precaution.[15]

In summary, an attacker could attempt the following:
- Cause the defibrillator to start transmitting private data by using a physical trigger if one exists for the particular type (e.g., by placing a magnet in its proximity).
- Capture and record communication between the programming device and the defibrillator. Access private data, especially if transmitted without encryption.
- Replay previously recorded communication for identifying the device, changing its settings, requesting the transmission of cardiac data (thus bypassing the need for the magnet), and even inducing defibrillation.

[14]Government Accountability Office (2012). *Medical Devices – FDA Should Expand Its Consideration of Information Security for Certain Types of Device (GAO-12-816)*. Washington, DC, USA.
[15]Peterson, A. (2013). *Yes, terrorists could have hacked Dick Cheney's heart.* Washington Post, October 21, 2013.

- By replaying the corresponding communication signal (or with a physical trigger if one exists), continuously request transmission of data so as to drain the defibrillator's battery.
- Analyze the communication protocol, so as to be able to inject spoofed communication signals to the programming device or the defibrillator.

Vehicles

In the past, the relevance of vehicles to cyber security was limited to war-driving,[16] which is the practice of driving around town with a laptop and looking for wireless networks to map or to exploit, and war-flying, which is the same concept but instead of a car uses a private plane[17] or, more recently, a UAV.[18] Today, vehicles are attractive targets of cyber attacks by themselves. That is partly because, for their size, they are among the most complex and most difficult to secure cyber-physical systems. Whether the most advanced military or civilian UAVs or the most low-end automobiles, vehicles designed over the last two decades rely on an impressive number and range of on-board computers, sensors, and communication systems.

Unmanned Aerial Vehicles

Often referred to as drones, UAVs are aircraft that fly without a crew onboard. In the past, they would be controlled remotely by a human pilot on the ground, but they are now becoming increasingly autonomous, dependent less on human intervention and more on their own onboard sensors and computer systems. They are usually equipped with cameras for recording image and video over large geographical areas, which makes them particularly useful in archaeology, film making, agriculture, policing, wildfire detection, search and rescue, disaster relief, and other areas.[19] Since they do not carry a pilot onboard, they can be sent to operate in hostile environments that would be dangerous to human life. If designed with sufficient

---

[16]Berghel, H. (2004). Wireless infidelity I: War driving. *Communications of the ACM*, Volume 47, No. 9, pp. 21−26.

[17]Brewin, B. (2002). War flying: Wireless LAN sniffing goes airborne. *Computerworld*, August 30, 2002.

[18]Storm, D. (2010). War-flying with a Wi-Fi-sniffing drone. *Computerworld*, August 18, 2010.

[19]Bloss, R. (2014). Unmanned vehicles while becoming smaller and smarter are addressing new applications in medical, agriculture, in addition to military and security. *Industrial Robot: An International Journal*, Volume 41, No. 1, pp. 82−86.

autonomy, they can even be programmed to complete missions in remote areas that are outside the communication range of their operators. Specifically in a military context, UAVs are primarily used for aerial reconnaissance and surveillance, but can also be used for transporting supplies to troops and even for carrying out armed attacks. In this context one of their greatest advantages is endurance. Military UAVs can stay in the air for more than a day, waiting for a mission to be specified to them or loitering and gathering intelligence.

As with all complex cyber-physical systems and especially those that operate without direct human control, natural accidents involving UAVs are not uncommon. In 2010, a Fire Scout unmanned autonomous helicopter that was being tested by the US Navy lost communication and continued flying in the wrong direction and into a restricted airspace near Washington, DC. It had been programmed with an autopilot function, which should have ensured that it would return to base upon losing connection, but the autopilot malfunctioned. The Navy considered scrambling fighter jets to shoot it down because it could cause considerable damage if it fell in a populated area, but eventually ground control crew regained contact and returned it to base.[20] Unsurprisingly, the US Air Force has found that UAVs are the most accident-prone aircraft in its fleet, with 129 accidents recorded between 1997 and 2012.[21] While our focus here is on intentional attacks, accidents reveal weaknesses that can be exploited intentionally. For example, the Fire Scout incident above showed that a UAV with an unreliable autopilot system might fly in an undesirable manner if an attacker manages somehow to block communication with its pilot on the ground. Before discussing the security threats affecting UAVs, we will first describe the systems in which they operate and their usual architecture (see Figure 3.3 for some common types of communication involved).

A fairly typical unmanned aerial system would include the UAV, a ground control station, two communication links with the ground control, and a satellite link. The ground control station is where the human operators are housed. The one communication link is usually called Video Data Link (VDL) and is used to transmit the video captured by the onboard cameras. The VDL uses an antenna that is omnidirectional, which means

[20]Bumiller, E. (2010) Navy Drone Violated Washington Airspace, New York Times, 25 August 2010.
[21]McGarry, B. (2012) Drones Most Accident-Prone U.S. Air Force Craft: BGOV Barometer, Bloomberg, 18 June 2012.

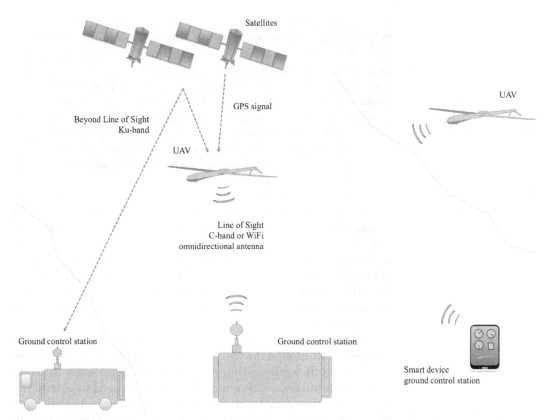

Figure 3.3 Some of the different types of communication involved in the operation of an unmanned aerial system. The example shows two UAVs that are able to communicate with each other, as well as three different ground control stations.

that it broadcasts the video feed in all directions. The other link is the Common Data Link (CDL), which is used by the pilots to operate the UAV remotely from the ground control station. It can also use an omnidirectional antenna, or it can use a directional one, which transmits only toward the ground control station.[22] The communication technology used may be based on C-band radio, satellites, or the familiar Wi-Fi, each with their own strengths and weaknesses that we will discuss later in this section. The UAV itself is a complex cyber-physical system that includes an avionic system and several sensor systems. Some are related to the missions it has been designed for, such as cameras for gathering intelligence, and others are used by the

[22]Yochim, J. A. (2010). *The Vulnerabilities of Unmanned Aircraft System Common Data Links to Electronic Attack*, Doctoral dissertation, Weber State University.

UAV's onboard flight control system. For example, gyroscopes help with the stabilization of the UAV, while radar mounted on the UAV's nose is used to avoid collisions by detecting objects in its path. Thanks to such systems and the software that controls them, UAVs can be designed to fly autonomously. This means that the pilot on the ground only needs to point to a specific destination on the map and the UAV then flies to it without a human controlling it. It may also be programmed to enter an autopilot mode, for example to return to base after a mission has been completed or when communication with the ground control station is lost.

Most UAVs, whether civilian or military, use satellite communication for GPS geolocation[23] and navigation. Satellite communication may also be used to control the UAV if a direct line-of-sight link is not available. While the general architecture of civilian and military UAVs can be similar, there is a significant difference in their use of GPS. Civilian aircraft rely on civilian GPS signals, while military aircraft can use military GPS signals. The latter are protected with encryption and are more resistant to interference.

Beyond this typical architecture, UAVs may also be designed to operate in groups, in which case they have to communicate with each other wirelessly and may depend on each other to complete a mission. This capability has been used to extend the communication range of UAVs, as by communicating with each other they can form networks. Even if only one of the UAVs is in communication range with the ground control station, they can all communicate with the latter through the network they have formed.[24] Each UAV would effectively become a node of an airborne ad hoc network. The capability of forming such networks has also been proposed for tracking ground targets in densely built-up areas[25] or fast-moving aerial targets such as enemy ballistic missiles.[26] A single UAV might soon lose sight of a faster

---

[23]Geolocation is the process of identifying an object's real geographic location. This can be achieved in many different ways, but the most common one for positioning at a global scale is to use a satellite-based technology such as GPS.

[24]Harris, S. (2011). Wireless system enables UAVs to communicate with operators, The Engineer, September 14, 2011.

[25]Kim, J. and Kim, Y. (2008). Moving ground target tracking in dense obstacle areas using UAVs. In *Proceedings of the 17th World Congress*, Volume 17, pp. 8552–8557, July 2008.

[26]Javaid, A. Y., Sun, W., Devabhaktuni, V. K., and Alam, M. (2012). Cyber security threat analysis and modeling of an unmanned aerial vehicle system. In *IEEE Conference on Technologies for Homeland Security (HST)*, IEEE, pp. 585–590, November 2012.

missile. If in a network though, it could report the missile's position to other UAVs that may be in its path, so as to collectively continue tracking it. Airborne networks of UAVs can also help establish network connectivity for users on the ground, where no other network infrastructure is available.[27] All these examples require an additional wireless communication link to allow a UAV to connect with another UAV directly.

The type of ground control station varies depending on the type and size of UAV. For a large military one, the ground control station may be a trailer housing a relatively large and expensive setup with specialized hardware and a personal computer workstation. For smaller ones, there is usually a portable ground control station, which includes a laptop, a radio antenna, and a hand controller for maneuvering it. A third option is to use a smart device ground control station, where the real-time monitoring of the flight characteristics, the display of image and video captured by the UAV, and even its actual maneuvering are done with a smartphone or tablet. This is most common for civilian UAVs, but has also been introduced to military ones. The US Department of Defense has already deployed such smart device ground control stations, allowing soldiers to operate surveillance cameras on military UAVs and share the intelligence collected by them in the battlefield.[28] Smart devices have the advantage of being very familiar to most military personnel. So, in addition to being less expensive, they also require less training than purpose-built ground control stations.

At a theoretical level, the effect of a cyber-physical attack involving a UAV seems relatively straightforward, since without a human pilot onboard it relies entirely on the information it receives from its onboard sensors and external communications. Disruption of communications would prevent its legitimate pilots from controlling it or receiving updates from it. Interception of its communications would allow an adversary to access the information it receives and transmits. If fed with false data from its sensors or communication links, it could be made to fly in an undesired manner or toward the wrong

---

[27]Asadpour, M., Giustiniano, D., Hummel, K. A., and Egli, S. (2013). UAV networks in rescue missions. In *Proceedings of the 8th ACM international workshop on Wireless network testbeds, experimental evaluation & characterization*, ACM, pp. 91–92, September, 2013.

[28]Mansfield, K., Eveleigh, T., Holzer, T. H., and Sarkani, S. (2013). Unmanned aerial vehicle smart device ground control station cyber security threat model. In *IEEE International Conference on Technologies for Homeland Security (HST)*, IEEE, pp. 722–728, November 2013.

destination. At a practical level, these attacks are not straightforward, but as researchers have shown they are feasible.

Depending on its application, a UAV may use different communication technologies. There are several variations, but a common one is to use Ku-band communication over satellite for UAVs that are not within line of sight, and C-Band or Wi-Fi for those within line of sight. The US military uses the Ku-band–based Tactical Common Data Link (TDCL), which can operate on both directional and omnidirectional antennas up to a range of 200 km and can achieve a data rate of up to 10.7 Mbits/s. It is used primarily to transmit data gathered by the UAV and is considered much more secure than C-band and Wi-Fi. However, it is also more easily affected by rain, snow, and other environmental conditions. UAV C-band and Wi-Fi communications typically use omnidirectional antennas, making them easier to intercept. The data rate of Wi-Fi depends on the variant used (11 Mbits/s for Wi-Fi b, 54 Mbits/s for a and g, and 600 Mbits/s for n).

Interference with the signal has always been one of the key threats to wireless communications. When this interference is deliberate, it is called jamming. A key aspect of electronic warfare,[29] jamming has been in widespread use since World War II, when it was employed to disrupt communications, radio broadcasting, radar, and radio-controlled missiles and torpedoes. Its principle is very simple. In our case, consider a UAV transmitting information over a radio link at a specific range of frequencies. If at the same time an adversary transmits random noise at the same radio frequencies and with greater power, then the ground control station will receive a mixture of both and will find it difficult to tell what part is the legitimate transmission from the UAV. A UAV that has lost communication with the ground control station will need to operate fully autonomously, often entering an autopilot mode and returning to base. This means that if adversaries aim to force a UAV to abandon its mission or fly in the direction of its base, they may achieve this relatively simply by jamming its communication with the ground control station.

As UAVs rely on GPS to tell their location and to be able to navigate without direct control from their pilots on the ground, the availability of the GPS signal is also critical. Authentic GPS

[29]Price, A. (1978). *Instruments of Darkness: The History of Electronic Warfare*. New York: Scribner.

signals are very weak. As Warner and Johnston put it, a GPS signal's strength measured at the surface of the earth is "roughly equivalent to viewing a 25-Watt light bulb from a distance of 10,000 miles."[30] Being so weak, they are particularly vulnerable to jamming. In fact, low-cost devices that can jam civilian GPS signals are sold legally (but not always used legally) in most parts of the world and are currently in widespread use. Car thieves plug them into the cigarette lighter and activate them to prevent tracking systems from transmitting their location. There have also been several cases of truck drivers using GPS jammers to prevent their bosses from knowing where they are.[31] In one such case, a truck driver drove near Newark Airport in New Jersey and unknowingly jammed the GPS signals on which the air traffic control system depended.[32] (See Box 3.1 for more information on how GPS works.)

Box 3.1 Global Navigation Satellite Systems

The only two satellite navigation systems that operate with a global coverage are the US's GPS and Russia's GLONASS; China's Beidou and the European Union's Galileo are scheduled to be globally deployed by 2020. Despite their differences in frequencies used and precision, they all operate based on the same principles. Here, we will describe only the GPS, which is the most mature and the one most commonly used globally.

GPS was originally a US Air Force project that was first conceived in 1960 for military operations but was later extended to civilian use. It became fully operational in 1995. GPS consists of the space segment, the control segment, and the user segment. The space segment currently comprises around 30 satellites that circle the globe every 12 hours at an altitude of 20,200 km. The orbit of each satellite is such that at any time every location on earth is in direct line of sight to at least four GPS satellites. Each satellite transmits radio signals that can be received by an increasingly diverse range of devices (GPS receivers), from car navigation devices to smartphones and watches. The control segment consists of a worldwide network of ground-based stations that track the satellites and provide corrections. The analysis of information collected from the satellites and the command and control of the whole system are performed by the master control station, which is located inside a US Air Force base in

(Continued)

[30]Warner, J. S. and Johnston, R. G. (2003). GPS spoofing countermeasures. *Homeland Security Journal.*

[31]Hambling, D. GPS chaos: How a $30 box can jam your life. New Scientist, March 6, 2011.

[32]Matyszczyk, C. Truck Driver has GPS jammer, accidentally jams Newark airport, CNET News, August 11, 2013.

Box 3.1 (Continued)

Colorado. Its primary aim is to ensure the integrity and accuracy of the system. Finally, the user segment consists of the GPS receivers and their users. The technical configuration of GPS differs for military and civilian users. Military GPS features provisions for authentication of the users, antijamming technologies, and greater accuracy than civilian GPS, and is intended for use by the armed forces of the United States and their allies, whereas civilian GPS is for everyone else. In the past, the accuracy of civilian GPS was artificially degraded on a global basis, but after a US presidential order in 2000 this is no longer the case. Having allowed civilian GPS to achieve accuracy of a few meters (as opposed to 50 meters previously), it became the obvious technology to integrate in any device that would benefit from geolocation.

GPS works based on trilateration, a complex process that involves receiving signals from three different GPS satellites and calculating the difference between the time they were sent by the satellites and the time they were received. Since $distance = speed \times time$ and the speed of a GPS signal is the speed of light, the GPS receiver can estimate its distance from each satellite. Using geometry, it can then estimate its actual position. A fourth satellite is used to crosscheck this estimation and correct any timing discrepancies.

Although most people are aware of the use of GPS in car navigation systems and smartphones, its vital role in every sector of a country's critical national infrastructure is less well known. GPS allows farmers to work even when visibility is low. It allows fishermen to track fish migrations and identify the best fishing locations. It is also integrated in the automatic identification systems that help track and manage vessels around busy seaways. In fact, GPS provides not only positioning and navigation, but also precise timing, which helps receivers to synchronize with each other. This is particularly important in the financial sector, where GPS is used to timestamp business transactions between different organizations in a consistent and accurate manner. GPS-based timing precision in the electric grid helps quickly respond to power outages, as knowing when an electrical anomaly occurred with sufficient precision helps estimate also where it occurred. As it is provided transparently, very reliably, and at no cost to the user, GPS is often considered an "invisible utility"[33] that organizations depend on without always knowing it. Yet, as Warner and Johnston aptly remarked in as early as 2003, the "civilian GPS signal was never intended for critical or security applications, though that is, unfortunately, how it is now often used."[34] In 2012 to 2013, the US Department of Homeland Security conducted a study on the potential impact of naturally occurring, unintentional, as well as intentional GPS disruptions in four key sectors, and concluded that the US critical infrastructure is "increasingly at risk from a growing dependency on GPS for positioning, navigation, and timing."[35]

---

[33]Hambling, D. GPS chaos: How a $30 box can jam your life. New Scientist, March 6, 2011.
[34]Warner, J. S. and Johnston, R. G. (2003). GPS spoofing countermeasures. *Homeland Security Journal*.
[35]Department of Homeland Security (2012), National Risk Estimate: Risks to U.S. Critical Infrastructure from Global Positioning System Disruptions. Factsheet.

The type of attack that has received the most attention in relation to UAVs is GPS spoofing. In the context of cyber security, spoofing[36] is the process of purposefully providing false information. GPS spoofing, in particular, refers to the generation of fraudulent GPS signals that cause the receiver (the UAV in this context) to determine its location incorrectly. This is easier for civilian GPS signals, which lack any form of security, than for military GPS signals, which use encryption. A straightforward way to achieve GPS spoofing is to use a GPS simulator. This is a commercially available but usually expensive device, which is used for research and for evaluating the performance of GPS receivers. In 2002, Warner and Johnston[37] rented such a simulator for $1,000 per week, amplified its signal with additional hardware equipment of a total cost of about $400 and managed to cause two handheld GPS receivers to believe they were at a location different than where they actually were. Such an attack would certainly confuse a civilian UAV but would be easy to detect and unlikely to lead to actual control of it. A legitimate operator of the UAV would notice the sudden jump in reported location or the unexpected change in direction it would trigger.

More recently, a team of researchers from the University of Texas at Austin and Northrop Grumman Information Systems led by Todd Humphreys took on the task of proving the concept of hijacking a UAV via GPS spoofing.[38] To achieve seamless control without raising alarms, any fraudulent GPS signals sent to the UAV would need to align precisely with the authentic GPS signals that its antenna was receiving up to that point. This is far from straightforward and unlikely to be within the capabilities of the average hacker. To achieve it, the team designed a custom-made device that combined a GPS spoofer and a GPS receiver based on software-defined radio. While the technical development required is complex, the principle behind their attack approach is relatively simple. The receiver observes the authentic GPS signals received by the UAV and the spoofer tries to produce fraudulent GPS signals that look similar, in the sense that if picked up by the UAV at that time they would provide it

---

[36]Felten, E. W., Balfanz, D., Dean, D., and Wallach, D. S. (1997). Web spoofing: An internet con game. *Software World*, Volume 28, No. 2, pp. 6–8.

[37]Warner, J. S., and Johnston, R. G. (2002). A simple demonstration that the global positioning system (GPS) is vulnerable to spoofing. *Journal of Security Administration*, Volume 25, No. 2, pp. 19–27.

[38]Shepard, D. P., Bhatti, J. A., Humphreys, T. E., and Fansler, A. A. (2012). Evaluation of smart grid and civilian UAV vulnerability to GPS spoofing attacks. In *Proceedings of the ION GNSS Meeting*.

with the same navigation solution (the same coordinates and time). To reduce the chances of being detected, the attack starts with the spoofer transmitting these fraudulent signals at a low power rate and slowly increasing it. At some point, when the fraudulent signals are considerably more powerful, to the extent that they start jamming the authentic ones, they are the ones that the UAV starts depending on to determine its navigation solution. From then on, the attacker uses the spoofer to effectively control the UAV by gradually changing its navigation solution. For example, by making the UAV think that it is west of its intended destination, the spoofer makes it fly toward the east. So, what Humphrey's team showed is that it is indeed feasible to steer a civilian UAV by manipulating its perception of its own location. Achieving the same result on military UAVs that would be guided by encrypted GPS, though, would be much more difficult, because the attacker would also need to compromise the secret keys involved. It is worth noting that in many cases military systems are designed to temporarily revert to less secure secondary communication and navigation technologies, including civilian GPS, when the primary ones are not available. Nevertheless, they typically use more than one technology to estimate their location. So, an attack affecting one is unlikely to be sufficient.

A special case of spoofing is GPS meaconing,[39] where instead of synthesizing a fake GPS signal, the attacker captures a legitimate GPS signal and rebroadcasts it with a slight delay. As the receiver estimates distance from the satellite based on the time it takes for the GPS signal to arrive, a delay of even a few microseconds is enough to introduce a large error in the calculation and make the receiver think it is at a location different from the actual one.

Beyond GPS jamming, spoofing, and meaconing, researchers from Carnegie Mellon University and Coherent Navigation have recently demonstrated the feasibility of broadcasting fake GPS messages that aim not to mislead GPS receivers regarding their location but to affect the operation of their software by identifying and exploiting flaws in their design.[40] Possibly the first and simplest such GPS-borne cyber attack was their Middle-of-Earth attack, where a fake GPS signal fraudulently reports a position in the middle of the earth, which corresponds to a

[39]Papadimitratos, P. and Jovanovic, A. (2008). Protection and fundamental vulnerability of GNSS. In *IEEE International Workshop on Satellite and Space Communications (IWSSC)*, pp. 167–171, October 2008.

[40]Nighswander, T., Ledvina, B., Diamond, J., Brumley, R., and Brumley, D. (2012). GPS software attacks. In *Proceedings of the 2012 ACM conference on Computer and communications security*, ACM, pp. 450–461, October 2012.

value of zero for one of the spatial axes that determine the position. When receiving such a signal, a type of GPS receiver, which was tested by the researchers (and used in critical services worldwide), was unable to process the information, presumably because of some division by zero, and entered an infinite cycle of reboots. Every time it would fail to process the zero value received, it would reboot, then attempt again to process the same zero value and reboot again until someone would manually shut down the device. The same researchers went on to demonstrate a series of more sophisticated attacks exploiting the manner in which GPS receivers handle dates, map updates, connect to networks, and so on. They found that GPS receivers operate based on common operating systems, such as Linux and Microsoft Windows, and have a series of security flaws that can be exploited by malicious users broadcasting carefully crafted GPS signals. Some of the cyber attacks demonstrated led to permanent damage of the GPS receivers.

The satellites themselves can also be targeted by cyber attacks. The 2011 annual report to Congress on the US–China trade and economic relationship[41] confirmed that adversaries have previously hijacked at least two US government satellites. According to the same report, Chinese military writings have advocated such activities and have specified the ground-based control stations of satellites as targets. As these stations are often connected to the Internet for "data access and file transfers,"[42] they are vulnerable to malware and other common Internet-borne threats. Unauthorized users can potentially take over remotely a control station's computers that have been infected with malware. Control of these computers effectively allows control of the corresponding satellites.

The capability of some types of UAVs to operate in groups and form networks creates additional cyber threats. Because they usually need to cover large geographical areas, such UAVs have relatively long communication range. So, it is theoretically possible for adversaries to fly rogue UAVs of their own in the vicinity undetected and attempt to connect them to their enemy's network.[43] As a result, smaller UAVs that do not have

[41]U.S.-China Economic and Security Review Commission (2011). 2011 Report to Congress of the U.S.-China Economic and Security Review Commission, November 2011.

[42]Tsiao, S. (2008). The enduring legacy of the 'invisible network', News and Notes, NASA History Division, Volume 25, No. 3, pp. 1–6, August 2008.

[43]Javaid, A. Y., Sun, W., Devabhaktuni, V. K., and Alam, M. (2012). Cyber security threat analysis and modeling of an unmanned aerial vehicle system. In *IEEE Conference on Technologies for Homeland Security (HST)*, IEEE, pp. 585–590, November 2012.

enough processing power to operate strong mechanisms for the authentication of communications in their network can be vulnerable to the usual security threats seen in wireless networks.[44] For example, rogue UAVs can pose as legitimate nodes of the UAV network (masquerading attack), capture communication and fraudulently retransmit it later (replay attack), or make independent connections to two UAVs and make them think they are communicating with each other directly, while they are in fact communicating through the rogue UAV, which in the process is eavesdropping (man-in-the-middle attack). It has been suggested that such rogue UAVs could also carry jamming equipment,[45] in order to disrupt communications to UAVs possibly more effectively than ground-based jammers would.

Of particular interest is the relatively new Automatic Dependent Surveillance-Broadcast (ADS-B) technology, with which aircraft broadcast their position, heading, and velocity every second. When using an ADS-B system, pilots are able to view surrounding aircraft, receive weather reports, information regarding the terrain, and reports about hazards in the area. In the European Union, most aircraft will be required to carry ADS-B by 2017 and in the United States by 2020. ADS-B is seen as critical for integrating UAVs into national air spaces, primarily because it helps track other aircraft in the vicinity and avoid collisions. For safety reasons, all nearby aircraft need to be able to quickly and easily understand the information transmitted, so there is no encryption specified. There is also an implicit trust that the ADS-B information transmitted from an aircraft is legitimate. Kim et al. have observed that the lack of encryption and the possibility of transmitting false ADS-B information can lead to new security threats involving UAVs.[46] Both the injection of false data and the jamming of ADS-B transmissions would affect the survivability of the UAV, as they would prevent it from sensing (or being sensed by other aircraft) and avoiding other aircraft that are en route for collision.

In cases where some or all of a UAV's functions can be operated through some type of smart handheld device, the latter may

[44]Han, D., Wang, S., and Zhang, L. (2011). Authentication Service for Tactical Ad-Hoc Networks with UAV. In *Computing and Intelligent Systems*, Springer Berlin Heidelberg, pp. 464–469.

[45]Bhattacharya, S., and Basar, T. (2010). Game-theoretic analysis of an aerial jamming attack on a UAV communication network. In *American Control Conference (ACC)*, IEEE, pp. 818–823, June 2010.

[46]Kim, A., Wampler, B., Goppert, J., Hwang, I., and Aldridge, H. (2012). Cyber attack vulnerabilities analysis for unmanned aerial vehicles. *The American Institute of Aeronautics and Astronautics*, Reston, VA, USA.

introduce its own vulnerabilities to the system. Mansfield et al. have argued that conventional flooding attacks or specialized attacks that would rapidly exhaust the device's battery would prevent the user from operating the UAV or sharing the information gathered by it.[47] Civilian UAVs especially are not expected to operate at the same high level of security that military ones would. A smart device controlling a military UAV would not be used for other purposes, but for a civilian UAV, it might be the pilot's own smartphone controlling it. So, if the pilot installs applications from untrustworthy sources, malware might be introduced, which could affect the smartphone and consequently the control of the UAV and the confidentiality of its communications.

Finally, military UAVs have significant supply chain security risks.[48] As several countries are investing heavily in them and more than 40% of the US Department of Defense's aircraft are UAVs,[49] they are prime targets for espionage and sabotage. Access to the designs of a UAV would allow an enemy state to analyze its existing security measures and concentrate on attacks that would have a good chance of overcoming them. In fact, it is also conceivable that a foreign agent would attempt to introduce security vulnerabilities to their components in the design, implementation, or production phase. A country's department of defense usually has good controls in place for vetting its suppliers and ensuring that they are highly trusted. Regarding their suppliers' suppliers though, there is much less control. This problem is particularly prevalent in the software industry, since software development is rarely free of defects and it is not easy to detect defects that are inserted intentionally.[50] UAV systems are based in part on commercial off-the-shelf software and hardware components.[51] As a result, it

[47]Mansfield, K., Eveleigh, T., Holzer, T. H., and Sarkani, S. (2013). Unmanned aerial vehicle smart device ground control station cyber security threat model. In *IEEE International Conference on Technologies for Homeland Security (HST)*, IEEE, pp. 722–728, November 2013.

[48]Dominy, J. R., Arnold, S. A., Frank, F. R., Holzer, J. R., and Richmann, J. N. (2012). *Exploratory Analysis of Supply Chains in the Defense Industrial Base* (No. IDA-D-4308). Institute for Defense Analyses, Alexandria, VA.

[49]Blackhurst, R. (2012). The air force men who fly drones in Afghanistan by remote control. The Telegraph, September 24, 2012.

[50]Ellison, R. J., Goodenough, J. B., Weinstock, C. B., and Woody, C. (2010). *Evaluating and mitigating software supply chain security risks* (No. CMU/SEI-2010-TN-016), Carnegie-Mellon University, Software Engineering Institute.

[51]Baldwin, K., Miller, J. F., Popick, P. R., and Goodnight, J. (2012). The United States Department of Defense revitalization of system security engineering through program protection. In *IEEE International Systems Conference (SysCon)*, IEEE, pp. 1–7, March 2012.

may be easier for an enemy state to infiltrate the network of the supplier of a contractor known to develop components for military UAVs than to breach the security of their encrypted communications during an actual military operation.[52] Identifying contractors and their suppliers is often straightforward. Companies tend to publish the list of their partners on their web sites so as to enhance their reputation and attract new business.

The large variety of technologies involved and the nature of the missions for which they are designed make UAVs very attractive cyber-physical attack targets. In summary, an attacker could attempt the following:

- Jam the communication links between the UAV and the ground control station
- Jam, meacon, or spoof the GPS signals that the UAV relies on for navigation
- Broadcast carefully crafted GPS signals that can damage the GPS receiver on the UAV
- Infect with malware the ground control station, especially if the latter is connected to the Internet
- Fly rogue UAV in the vicinity of target group of UAVs and connect to their network in order to eavesdrop on their communications or inject false information
- Jam or spoof ADS-B transmission, so as to compromise the UAV's ability to track or be tracked by other aircraft and avoid collisions
- Introduce malware to smartphones and tablets used as handheld smart device ground control stations
- Infiltrate a contractor's network to introduce vulnerabilities to a UAV's components or steal design documents and analyze its security

Automobiles

Over the last two decades, the automotive industry has been steadily replacing mechanical parts with software and electronic components that communicate with each other to monitor and control an automobile's state. This has allowed the introduction of several new technologies that would have previously been infeasible or too expensive to develop. A communication network allows information collected from multiple sensors to be shared with multiple other components and to be reused where

[52]Giray, S. M. (2013). Anatomy of unmanned aerial vehicle hijacking with signal spoofing. In *6th International Conference on Recent Advances in Space Technologies (RAST)*. IEEE, pp. 795–800, June 2013.

appropriate. It also replaces the large number of cables and harnesses that were previously needed in a vehicle, and as a result it helps reduce both weight and cost. However, the heavy reliance on software and network technologies introduces new concerns, as automotive designers now have to consider not only accidental failures of equipment, but also intentional cyber-physical attacks targeting the software and the networks. Before discussing these security threats, we first need to describe the functionalities and the different information and communication technologies in an automobile's architecture (Box 3.2).

Box 3.2 Electronic Control Unit (ECU)

ECUs are digital computers embedded in modern automobiles to support a variety of functionalities. They receive measurements gathered from multiple sensors, process them, and based on these generate signals that control various systems in the vehicle, either on their own or through communication and cooperation with other ECUs. An ECU operates on the same basic principles as a personal computer. It has a processor, memory, and communication chips to allow it to connect to networks in the vehicle. A modern automobile has at least 15 and some times over 90 ECUs typically grouped on two or more networks.[53]

What each ECU does depends on the software[54] it runs and the sensors and actuators to which it is connected. Sensors collect measurements while actuators control various devices around the vehicle. The software on the ECU processes the measurements and determines what commands to send to the actuators. Possibly the most important ECU is the Engine Control Module (ECM).[55] The ECM communicates with a large number of sensors measuring the position of the throttle, the water temperature, the amount of air sucked into the engine, the level of oxygen in the exhaust, and other information, processes the information, and then sends commands to the actuators that adjust the fuel mixture and the ignition timing in the engine. This is the primary mechanism used by manufacturers to regulate fuel economy and ensure that the pollutants emitted are within acceptable limits. Other ECUs are responsible for the ABS braking, cruise control, power steering, airbags, the windows, the lights, and pretty much every other functionality.

Just like every other type of computer, ECUs may fail. This is usually due to physical damage (corrosion, moisture, etc.) but can also be due to flaws in the software. The latter are remarkably rare considering the complexity of automotive software, since a high-end automobile may contain close to 100 million lines of software code, as opposed to 1.7 million lines on the F-22 Raptor jet fighter[56] and 50 million lines for CERN's Large Hadron

(Continued)

---

[53]Some examples: A 2014 Dodge Viper has 19, a 2010 Toyota Prius has 23, and a 2014 Range Rover has 98 ECUs.
[54]To be more precise, an ECU runs firmware, which is software that is permanently placed into the hardware.
[55]The ECM rather confusingly is very often referred to as Engine Control Unit (ECU).
[56]Charette, R. N. (2009). This car runs on code. *IEEE Spectrum*, Volume 46, No. 3.

Box 3.2 (Continued)

Collider.[57] To correct software flaws, manufacturers occasionally recall vehicles to update the ECU software. There are security measures (usually some weak cryptographic method) in place to ensure that only the manufacturers can install such updates, but these measures are routinely bypassed in the "tuning community." These are enthusiasts who try to improve the performance characteristics of their vehicles and remove electronic limitations set by the manufacturers by installing their own modified software on the ECM. There is certainly no malicious intent there, but in the same manner an attacker can bypass the security of a target vehicle's ECM and install modified software with intentional flaws. At the same time, every ECU is a node of at least one communication network inside the vehicle, and this makes it potentially vulnerable to network security threats too.

A modern automobile is expected to feature an impressive range of functionalities. Based on a classification provided by Volvo's scientists,[58] they include feedback control systems, discrete control systems, diagnostics, infotainment, and telematics. A typical example of feedback control is cruise control, which varies the rate of fuel in the engine based on the difference between the actual speed measured by sensors and the target speed that has been set by the driver. Discrete control refers to switching devices between a discrete number of states, such as turning lights on or off and changing the setting of the windshield wipers. Diagnostic functions support maintenance by detecting faults in the vehicle's components and by reconfiguring and updating their software. Infotainment may include music players, television screens for the rear seats, and other information and entertainment functions; telematics typically includes satellite navigation, company fleet management, and any other functions related to tracking the movement and condition of vehicles.

All these functionalities have different communication requirements, and as a result a modern automobile has to rely on several different network technologies. The Society for Automotive Engineers has classified these into four classes:[59] Class A refers to low-rate and low-cost networks, such as the Local Interconnect Network (LIN).[60] LIN operates based on a

[57]McCandless, D. (2014). *Knowledge Is Beautiful: A Visual Miscellaneum of Compelling Information*. HarperCollins.
[58]Axelsson, J., Fröberg, J., Hansson, H., Norström, C., Sandström, K., and Villing, B. (2003). Correlating Business Needs and Network Architectures in Automotive Applications – A Comparative Case Study. *Proceedings of FET'03*, pp. 219–228.
[59]Navet, N., Song, Y., Simonot-Lion, F., and Wilwert, C. (2005). Trends in automotive communication systems. *Proceedings of the IEEE*, Volume 93, No. 6, pp. 1204–1223.
[60]Specks, J. W. and Rajnák, A. (2000). LIN-protocol, development tools, and software Interfaces for local interconnect networks in vehicles. *VDI-Berichte*, pp. 227–250.

master–slave model, with one node acting as the master and up to 16 as the slaves, the latter transmitting information only when the master asks. Operating at a maximum rate of only 20 kbit/s, LIN is used to control noncritical functions, such as windshield wipers, lights, seat position, door locks, cruise control, and the sunroof. Its primary advantage is the relatively low cost.

Class B networks have a slightly higher data rate but again are used for noncritical components, while Class C networks provide higher speeds to ensure reliable real-time communication with components that require constant monitoring. Developed in the 1980s by Bosch, the most commonly used standard for Class B and Class C networks is CAN bus.[61] CAN, which stands for Controller Area Network, is a networking protocol designed for the interconnection of real-time control units, especially ECUs in vehicles. A bus is a type of network where multiple nodes share the same communication medium (e.g., a single wire), only one node can transmit information at a time, and every other node on the bus receives all information transmitted even if not specifically directed to it. Figure 3.4 shows a simplified automobile network with two CAN buses and a gateway device connecting them. The Class B low-speed body control CAN bus is used to communicate with the doors, instruments, and lights, and the Class C high-speed powertrain CAN bus is used to communicate with the engine, the suspension system, and the brakes. Each of these buses is usually only

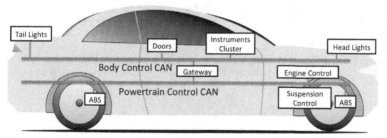

Figure 3.4 A simplified automobile network with two CAN buses connected with a gateway: The low-speed body control CAN bus is used to control noncritical components, such as the doors, instruments and lights, while the high-speed powertrain CAN bus is used to control critical components, such as the engine, suspension system, and brakes.

---

[61]Kiencke, U., Dais, S., and Litschel, M. (1986). Automotive serial controller area network. *Training, 2014*, pp. 5–19.

a pair of twisted wires.[62] The gateway's role is to exchange messages between the two buses, when an ECU on one bus requires information that is collected by an ECU on the other.

Class D networks have been introduced more recently. They require high data rates (at least 1 Mbit/s), especially for multimedia applications, but also for x-by-wire technology (see Box 3.3). The former is usually based on the 24.8 Mbit/s Media Oriented System Transport (MOST)[63] and Bluetooth,[64] whereas

Box 3.3 X-by-Wire Technology

In recent years, there has been an increasing adoption of x-by-wire systems,[65] where previously hydraulic and mechanical systems such as the steering, shifting, braking, and throttle control have been replaced by sensors and computers. A conventional throttle works with a direct mechanical link to the accelerator pedal, but a throttle-by-wire system works with a sensor on the accelerator pedal continuously measuring by how much it is pressed and communicating this information to the throttle over a network. Similarly, a steer-by-wire system measures the rotation of the steering wheel and communicates it to the vehicle's wheels over the in-vehicle network, as shown in Figure 3.5.

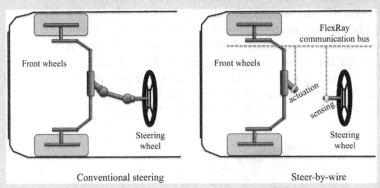

Figure 3.5 A simplified diagram of conventional steering versus a steer-by-wire system that uses a FlexRay communication bus.

[62]In CAN, it is the difference of voltage between the two wires of a twisted pair that determines whether a logical 0 or a logical 1 is transmitted. Being twisted together reduces the impact of external electromagnetic interference, as both wires would be affected equally by it and their difference in voltage would remain relatively unaffected.
[63]Grzemba, A. (2011). *MOST: the automotive multimedia network; from MOST25 to MOST150.* Franzis.
[64]Haartsen, J. (1998). Bluetooth – The universal radio interface for ad hoc, wireless connectivity. *Ericsson review,* Volume 3, No. 1, pp. 110–117.
[65]Wilwert, C., Navet, N., Song, Y. Q., and Simonot-Lion, F. (2005). Design of automotive X-by-Wire systems. *The Industrial Communication Technology Handbook.*

Table 3.1 Common Network Types Used in a Modern Automobile

Network Type	Speed	Medium	Typical Applications
LIN	20 kbit/s	Single wire	Windshield wipers, interior light, seat position, mirror
Low-speed CAN	125 kbit/s	Two wires twisted together	adjusters, door locks, cruise control, sunroof, rain sensors, windows, climate control, sunroof, alarm systems, instrument cluster, parking sensors, headlights and tail lights
High-speed CAN	1 Mbit/s	Two wires twisted together	ABS, engine control, suspension, stability control, air bags, x-by-wire
FlexRay	10 Mbit/s	Two wires twisted together or optical fiber	
MOST	24.8 Mbit/s	Optical fiber	Infotainment, digital radio, navigation, speakers
Bluetooth	1 — 24 Mbit/s	Wireless	Telematics, external devices
RFID	Varies	Wireless	Immobilizer

the latter is typically based on FlexRay, the intended successor to CAN. CAN is sufficient for soft real time systems, where a delay in the communication of information from or to a component could degrade its performance but not harm it. Like CAN, FlexRay also runs on a bus but can support much higher data rates (up to 10 Mbit/s). For this reason, it is preferable for hard real-time systems, where any delay could potentially cause damage. Table 3.1 shows an overview of the communication protocols used for the various systems found in a modern automobile.

Removing mechanical and hydraulic components helps reduce the weight of the vehicle. As a result, x-by-wire technologies are particularly important for electric and hybrid vehicles, where the emphasis on energy efficiency is greater than in conventional combustion engine ones. However, removing these components also means that the ability to control critical functions, such as steering and braking, depends almost entirely on the well being of the network that supports them. If the network is overloaded or disrupted by a cyber attack, the driver will not be able to steer the vehicle or brake.

CAN is a relatively simple protocol. Messages exchanged over CAN do not carry a source or destination address. Every message is broadcast to all network nodes that are on the same bus. The recipients of a message independently decide whether it is for them or not, and there is no provision to ensure that it is legitimate, which node is the sender of the message, and whether it can be trusted. As it operates on a bus, where messages are sent directly to each recipient without having to go through intermediary nodes, if some nodes fail the rest are not affected and can continue communicating. However, the fact that all nodes share one communication medium means that only one can transmit at a time. If two try to transmit at the same time, the one with the lowest priority will have to wait.[66] The priority is determined by a numerical identifier, which is reported by the nodes themselves (the lower the number, the higher the priority). In effect, CAN operates based on trust. It trusts that the node communicating through the bus is a legitimate node of the network, will report the correct identifier, and will transmit legitimate messages. The ISO 11898 standard[67] that describes how CAN should be implemented specifies a number of precautionary measures that would limit the impact of a failure of the in-vehicle network, whether accidental or the result of a cyber attack. However, these are not always implemented by the manufacturers.

On the single type of automobile on which they experimented, Koscher et al. identified several deviations.[68] The standard specifies that the "disable CAN communications" command has to be rejected when the vehicle is moving, the engine control module should not be allowed to be programmed if the engine is running, the gateway should be possible to program only from devices on the high-speed CAN bus and not by devices on the low-speed CAN bus, and so on. None of these measures were implemented by the specific manufacturer and it is unclear to what extent other manufacturers do implement them.

---

[66]In computer networks, this access control protocol is referred to as Carrier Sense Multiple Access with Collision Detection and Arbitration on Message Priority (CSMA/CD + AMP). Every node continuously listens to the bus and can start transmitting only if the bus is idle (no node transmitting). If simultaneously another node has also started transmitting, the one with the lower priority halts and waits for the high-priority one to stop and the bus to become idle again before restarting.

[67]ISO (2003). ISO 11898-1: 2003-Road vehicles–Controller area network. *International Organization for Standardization, Geneva, Switzerland.*

[68]Koscher et al. (2010). Experimental security analysis of a modern automobile. In the *Symposium on Security and Privacy, IEEE,* pp. 447–462, Oakland, CA, USA, May 16–19, 2010.

With CAN based largely on trust that all nodes are legitimate and manufacturers omitting many of the security precautions specified by the standard, an automobile's network presents multiple avenues for cyber-physical attacks. For example, an attacker gaining physical access to one of the vehicle's buses can introduce an additional node and use it to abuse the network. Until recently, CAN bus communication on almost all automobiles was unencrypted. So, in these automobiles, a rogue ECU[69] can generate spoofed messages reporting fake sensor readings or requesting potentially unsafe actions by other ECUs. Even if communication is encrypted and the rogue ECU cannot read the messages transmitted through the network or create its own spoofed ones, it is still in a position to abuse the network. As all nodes on the same bus receive all information, the rogue ECU could be used to record the messages that correspond to particular commands sent by other ECUs and replay them at a later time. A relatively benign example demonstrated by Hoppe and Dittman[70] is to prevent the actuation of electric windows by simply replaying a previously recorded "close window" message every time an "open window" message is detected on the bus. This is by no means trivial, but it can be achieved by triggering an action and using a CAN bus sniffer[71] to observe the messages that are sent on the bus at that time.

To extend such attacks to almost all functions of an automobile, fuzzing (or fuzz testing) can be particularly effective. Traditionally, fuzzing[72] has been used to automate the discovery of security vulnerabilities in a piece of software by bombarding it with random data inputs and observing whether it will crash or fail in some manner. In the context of automobile hacking, fuzzing involves the attackers transmitting random messages through the bus and observing any changes in the state of the automobile. Because the size of a CAN message (and consequently the number of all possible different CAN messages) is relatively small, by continuously testing different random

[69]A rogue ECU may be one of the vehicle's original ECUs, which has been tampered by the attacker, or an electronic device that is able to receive and transmit messages over a CAN protocol and has been physically connected to the bus by the attacker.
[70]Hoppe, T. and Dittman, J. (2007). Sniffing/Replay Attacks on CAN Buses: A simulated attack on the electric window lift classified using an adapted CERT taxonomy. In *Proceedings of the 2nd Workshop on Embedded Systems Security (WESS)*.
[71]A sniffer is a software package that runs on a computer connected to a network and is able to intercept and record messages transmitted through it. Researchers may choose to build their own for more flexibility (e.g., carshark), but there are already several commercial and open-source ones that can be used.
[72]Takanen, A., Demott, J. D., and Miller, C. (2008). *Fuzzing for software security testing and quality assurance*. Artech House.

messages one will sooner or later stumble upon one that is valid. Fuzzing can reveal the messages that disable the engine, lock individual brakes, or even prevent braking. Koscher et al.[73] have demonstrated several of these attacks experimentally with an automobile cruising at 40 mph on a runway (and the rest on jack stands). They reported that despite all safety precautions and the short duration of the experiment, it was still a frightening experience for the driver, who could not activate the brakes by pressing the brake pedal. At a higher speed, selectively locking the brakes on one side could have an even more dramatic effect, as the vehicle could veer uncontrollably toward that direction.

Another significant type of attack involves a rogue ECU exploiting CAN's priority system to lead to some form of denial of service. Messages sent with a low identifier have priority over any other communication on the same bus, but these identifiers are reported by the ECUs themselves. So, a rogue ECU can block valid CAN messages sent on the same bus by transmitting its own meaningless messages at a higher priority.[74] These illegitimate messages will be discarded by every node that receives them, as they do not contain any useful information, but in the process they occupy the bus and no other node can transmit until the rogue ECU stops sending them. Unless the manufacturer has implemented some proprietary extension of the CAN protocol that prevents such a situation from occurring, this can continue indefinitely (for more details, see Box 3.4).

Note that unlike other communication protocols, such as the Internet Protocol, there is no field in the standard CAN frame to specify who the sender or the intended recipient of a message is. This is because CAN has been designed for real-time systems where this additional information would introduce more overhead and processing delays, but also because multiple devices often need access to the same information. For example, a frame containing a measurement from a speed sensor is useful at the same time to the tachometer on the instruments cluster, the cruise control system, and the ABS. However, the lack of any provision in the frame structure to declare who the sender is means that a rogue device connected to the same network can start sending messages as if it is a legitimate node. Since

[73]Koscher, K., Czeskis, A., Roesner, F., Patel, S., Kohno, T., Checkoway, S., McCoy, D., Kantor, B., Anderson, D., Shacham, H., and Savage, S. (2010). Experimental security analysis of a modern automobile. In the *Symposium on Security and Privacy, IEEE*, pp. 447–462, Oakland, CA, USA, May 16–19, 2010.
[74]Wolf, M., Weimerskirch, A., and Paar, C. (2004). Security in automotive bus systems. In *Proceedings of the Workshop on Embedded Security in Cars*, November 2004.

Box 3.4 CAN Frame Structure

CAN is a communication protocol that uses frames to exchange messages between devices. Each frame is a sequence of 0 and 1 bits that are sent one after the other, carrying—in the data section—information collected from sensors, commands to particular systems in the vehicle, and so on. In addition to the actual message, which can be up to 64 bits long, each frame contains 44 bits of overhead, which is information related to the actual delivery of the message. For example, there is an identifier that is 11 bits long (29 bits in the Extended CAN protocol) and a code that helps the recipients of a message detect whether there was an error in the transmission. The precise structure of the standard CAN frame is shown in Figure 3.6.

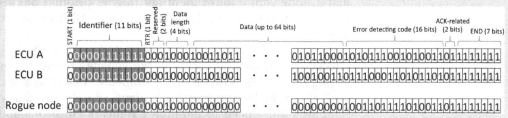

Figure 3.6 The structure of the standard CAN frame with up to 64 bits of data and 44 bits of overhead (identifier, error detecting code, etc.).

the rogue device does not need to declare who the recipient is, it also does not need to know and specify legitimate devices that are already connected to the network. It only needs to start transmitting and they will all receive the messages it sends. For the same reason, the rogue device will also be able to read all messages transmitted by any other node on the bus.

When two nodes (e.g., two ECUs) transmit at the same time, the one with the higher identifier has the lower priority. In Figure 3.6, ECU A and ECU B simultaneously start transmitting, one bit at a time. Note that the first 10 bits are identical (0 000011111), but the next bit coming from ECU A is a 1, but from ECU B it is a 0. At that point, ECU A realizes that another node with a lower identifier must be transmitting at the same time,[75] so it stops and waits for a predefined length of time before it tries

[75]CAN is usually implemented on a pair of twisted wires. Difference between the voltages of the two wires denotes a logical 0 (in CAN terminology, the "dominant bit"), while the same voltage on the two wires denotes a logical 1 (the "recessive bit"). By sensing a difference in the voltage of the two wires, ECU A determines that a 0 must have been transmitted where it was expecting the 1 that it transmitted itself. This indicates that an ECU with a 0 (lower identifier and thus higher priority) must be transmitting at the same time.

again. The standard CAN protocol does not provide any mechanism to dynamically assign these identifiers in a secure manner. In practice, every node specifies an identifier based on how urgently its messages need to be broadcast. These identifiers have to be unique so as to prevent a situation where two messages corrupt each other by occupying the bus at the same time, but there is no mechanism to prevent a rogue node from declaring any identifier it wants. In Figure 3.6, the rogue node has declared an identifier of all zeros. This means that any frame it transmits will have higher priority than all other nodes in the same network. Any other nodes beginning to transmit will see that a node with a lower identifier (higher priority) has already started transmitting on the bus and they will back off until it finishes.

For a rogue device to be connected to a CAN bus, the attacker needs to have access to the vehicle's network, possibly through the (US) OBD-II or (European) EOBD connector.[76] OBD-II and EOBD are practically identical onboard diagnostics standards introduced to monitor a vehicle's emissions and fuel economy. For the sake of simplicity we will refer to them as OBD connectors. Usually, the OBD connector provides access to one of the vehicle's buses and can be used to collect information from most of the vehicle's systems, not only related to fuel economy and emissions. The owner or a mechanic can plug in a reader device to detect errors and measure the vehicle's performance. Usually located just under the dashboard, somewhere above the pedals, the OBD connector is required by law to be accessible without tools. As a result, an attacker physically entering the vehicle can quickly locate it, plug in a laptop using some form of OBD-to-USB cable, and gain access to its CAN bus. Since it is unlikely that the owner would look under the dashboard before driving off, the attacker could connect a rogue device to the OBD connector and program it to perform a malicious action when a predefined set of conditions is met, effectively creating a vehicle virus. Nilsson and Larson first introduced this concept with simulated attacks programmed to trigger on a door lock message,[77] but it can be generalized to any message read on the bus. For example, the device could monitor the vehicle's speed, wait for it to be high enough, and then send a spoofed command to the brakes, or it may try to overwhelm the bus with a

[76]Geraldo, G. (2006). Differences between On Board Diagnostic Systems (EOBD, OBD-II, OBD-BR1 and OBD-BR2). *Training*, Volume 2006, pp. 3–15.
[77]Nilsson, D. K. and Larson, U. E. (2008). Simulated attacks on CAN buses: vehicle virus. In *IASTED International Conference on Communication Systems and Networks (AsiaCSN)*, pp. 66–72, April 2008.

Malware infects dealership's laptops used by mechanics

Figure 3.7 It has been suggested that an adversary can attack several vehicles by targeting the laptops of mechanics at a dealership.

flood of fake high priority messages to prevent legitimate ECUs from transmitting.

Up to now, all automotive attacks discussed in this section require a physical security breach to have occurred first. This may be feasible in some cases, but an attacker who has such level of physical access would realistically choose a conventional physical attack, such as simply cutting cables, over an elaborate cyber-physical attack. It has been argued that one could potentially affect several vehicles by compromising the personal computers of a dealership.[78] When required to program an ECU (such as a reset to factory defaults after a failure), a mechanic typically would use a Windows-based laptop interfacing with a diagnostic device, which in turn is plugged into the OBD connector and sends commands to the ECU. Theoretically, an adversary could infect the laptop with malware and use it to manipulate the programming process for all vehicles under service (Figure 3.7).

Although technically feasible, scenarios such as the dealership-targeting malware are rather far-fetched. A cyber-physical attack on an automobile is truly practical only if it can be launched remotely, preferably from a distance of at least a few meters, and possibly while the vehicle is moving. To achieve this, an attacker needs to target one of its several wireless communication systems. Take, for example, the tire pressure monitoring system (TPMS), which uses a wireless network of sensors fitted into the back of the valve of each tire to measure and periodically broadcast air pressures and temperatures. This information is received by the antenna of an ECU responsible for the tire pressure monitoring and is displayed on the dashboard. However, the signals from these sensors may also be received by an adversary's antenna within a range of a few meters. A research team from the University of South Carolina and Rutgers University was the first to demonstrate how this

[78]Checkoway, S., McCoy, D., Kantor, B., Anderson, D., Shacham, H., Savage, S., Koscher, K., Czeskis, A., Roesner, F., and Kohno, T. (2011). Comprehensive Experimental Analyses of Automotive Attack Surfaces. In *USENIX Security Symposium*, August 2011.

system can be exploited remotely.[79] In addition to eavesdropping from a distance of up to 40 m and decoding the information transmitted from these sensors,[80] they also built a prototype device that feeds the tire pressure monitoring ECU with wireless signals containing fake sensor measurements. In the absence of a mechanism to authenticate the sensor-to-ECU communication, a few spoofed messages reporting a low tire pressure are enough to trigger a warning light on the target vehicle's dashboard. It is also possible to target the battery consumption of these sensors. Mechanics troubleshoot TPMS with commercially available trigger tools that send activation signals to the sensors. An attacker using such a tool can keep activating these sensors remotely, asking them to report their measurements constantly, rather than at the usual rate of once every one minute or so, and in the process draining their batteries. Attacks against a noncritical system such as the TPMS are scientifically interesting but unlikely to cause anything more than inconvenience. The driver will pull over, physically check the tires, determine that TPMS has malfunctioned, and then drive off—unless the whole point of the attack was to trick the driver to stop, of course.

A more practical approach might be to target one of the third-party telematics units installed in automobiles by their owners to monitor their driving and their vehicle's location and performance. They usually consist of diagnostic software and a small device that is plugged into the OBD port, and can transmit real-time data from the vehicle to the owner's personal computer or smartphone directly (via Wi-Fi or Bluetooth) or to remote servers via a cell phone technology, such as general packet radio service (GPRS), from where they are made available to the owner through the Internet. This remote access to data that would otherwise be collected via physical access to OBD extends the range of a possible attack. If a particular system's software can be updated remotely (e.g., over GPRS), the security of this process becomes critical. If there is no encryption or authentication, as in the case of the early version of the Zubie telematics device analyzed by Argus Cyber Security

---

[79]Ishtiaq Rouf, R. M., Mustafa, H., Taylor, T., Oh, S., Xu, W., Gruteser, M., Trappe, W., and Seskar, I. (2010). Security and privacy vulnerabilities of in-car wireless networks: A tire pressure monitoring system case study. In *19th USENIX Security Symposium*, pp. 11–13, Washington, DC, February 2010.

[80]Since these sensors transmit only once every minute or so, an eavesdropping attack by a stationary attacker would realistically work only on a stationary vehicle. Assuming that the attacker would be standing by the roadside, a moving vehicle would pass and be out of range before the sensors could report any information possible to be eavesdropped on.

researchers in 2014,[81] a rogue mobile server can masquerade as a legitimate Zubie update mobile server and introduce malware into the device in the form of a software update. From then on, the attackers can generate their own CAN messages, effectively controlling the car. Such after-market telematics devices are rapidly becoming both more popular and more powerful. For instance, DroneMobile comes with a smartphone app that is able to turn the engine on and off, control the car's windows, and unlock the trunk remotely. The result of this is that the security of the CAN network effectively relies on the security of an external Internet-based service and of the devices from which it can be accessed.

Another function of an automobile that can be targeted by hackers is its immobilization system. Immobilizers are anti-theft devices that ensure that one cannot start up a vehicle's engine without an authentic key. They achieve this thanks to cryptography and a transponder hidden inside the plastic part of the key. A transponder (transmitter-responder) is a small RFID device that transmits a radio signal with a distinct identification code when the key is inserted in the ignition lock cylinder.[82] The signal is received by the immobilization system and the code is compared to the one expected for the specific vehicle. In early models, this was enough to allow the engine to start, but now there is an additional step with some form of cryptographic interrogation where the immobilizer tries to establish that the transponder of the physical key inserted contains the correct secret key. Having become mandatory in many parts of the world, including Europe, Canada, and Australia, immobilizers reduced the number of thefts of new vehicles, as the hot-wiring techniques that we used to see in movies are now largely ineffective. Because losing one's transponder-equipped key can be a major inconvenience (and expensive), there are numerous web sites providing advice on how to physically bypass the security of specific immobilization systems, sometimes by swapping components, entering a PIN, and using a simple mechanical key (where the manufacturer allows it), and even "a series of presses and pulls of the emergency brake"[83] for some models. Beyond such physical bypass techniques that may or may not have been intentionally introduced by the manufacturers, the cryptographic mechanisms used by

---

[81]Fox-Brewster, T. (2014). Zubie: This Car Safety Tool 'Could Have Given Hackers Control Of Your Vehicle'. Forbes, November 7, 2014.

[82]If one wraps the plastic part of the key in aluminum foil, the immobilization may not manage to read the signal and in that case the engine will not start.

[83]Stone, B. Pinch my ride. Wired, August 2006.

Box 3.5 Transponder Secret Key Length

In the 1880s, Auguste Kerkhoff set as a principle of a cryptographic system that "it must not be required to be secret, and it must be able to fall into the hands of the enemy without inconvenience"[84]; in the 1940s, Claude Shannon suggested the assumption that "the enemy knows the system being used."[85] Even if potential adversaries know the inner workings of a security system, they will not be able to read the messages exchanged with it if they do not know the secret key. So, it is generally accepted that it is the secret key that should ensure security. A short secret key can be broken easily by a brute force attack, where a computer tests all possible keys until it finds the right one. The larger the key the longer it will take the computer to break it. Some time ago, a key length of 40 bits would be beyond the capabilities of most computers and would be considered sufficient, but as computing power steadily increases, most cryptographic systems now use keys of a minimum of 128 bits. In broad terms, every bit added to a key doubles the difficulty of breaking it.

The Texas Instruments DST 40 transponder used in many automobiles built after 1999 uses a 40-bit secret key. But since this has been shown to be too short by researchers from John Hopkins University and RSA Laboratories,[86] it is gradually being replaced with a newer 80-bit version. Today, more popular transponders are the NXP Hitag2 (48 bits), which is slowly being replaced by newer variants, and EM Micro Megamos (96 bits). Since phasing out unsecure technologies takes several years, the immobilizers of the majority of automobiles today rely on secret keys that are considerably shorter than the minimum of 128 bits expected elsewhere.

Being one of the most widely used transponders, Hitag2 has been extensively analyzed by security researchers. Its inner workings were made public in 2007, and 2 years later Courtois, Neil, and Quisquater presented the first attacks against it. Whereas a brute force attack would require 4 years, theirs can find the secret key in 2 days.[87] Two years later, Soos et al. reduced the time needed to less than 7 hours[88] and Stembera and Novotny to less than 2 hours, but only by using specialized hardware equipment.[89] In 2012, Verdult, Garcia, and Balasch presented an even more practical attack and an accompanying device that can identify the secret key and disable the immobilizer of several brands of automobiles in only 6 minutes.[90] In 2013, Verdult, Garcia, and Ege were about to present at a conference a practical attack against the theoretically much more secure Megamos transponder, but were restrained from doing so by an injunction ordered by the High Court of London in the United Kingdom. Automobile manufacturer Volkswagen had argued that it could be used by "a sophisticated criminal gang with the right tools"[91] to break into a wide range of both high-end and low-end automobiles from several manufacturers.

[84]Gutmann, P. and Grigg, I. (2005). Security usability. *Security & Privacy, IEEE*, Volume 3, No. 4, pp. 56–58.

[85]Shannon, C. E. (1949). Communication Theory of Secrecy Systems, *Bell system technical journal*, Volume 28, No. 4, pp. 656–715.

[86]Bono, S., Green, M., Stubblefield, A., Juels, A., Rubin, A., and Szydlo, M. (2005). Security analysis of a cryptographically-enabled RFID device. In *14th USENIX Security Symposium*, Voument 1, pp. 1–15, July 2005.

[87]Courtois, N. T., O'Neil, S., and Quisquater, J. J. (2009). Practical algebraic attacks on the Hitag2 stream cipher. In *Information Security*, pp. 167–176. Springer Berlin Heidelberg.

[88]Soos, M., Nohl, K., and Castelluccia, C. (2009). Extending SAT solvers to cryptographic problems. In *Theory and Applications of Satisfiability Testing-SAT 2009*, pp. 244–257, Springer Berlin Heidelberg.

[89]Stembera, P. and Novotny, M. (2011). Breaking Hitag2 with reconfigurable hardware. In *14th Euromicro Conference on Digital System Design (DSD)*, pp. 558–563, IEEE, August 2011.

[90]Verdult, R., Garcia, F. D., and Balasch, J. (2012, August). Gone in 360 seconds: Hijacking with Hitag2. In *Proceedings of the 21st USENIX conference on Security symposium*, p. 37. USENIX Association.

[91]O'Carroll, L. (2013). Car hacking scientists agree to delay paper that could unlock Porsches, The Guardian, July 30, 2013.

almost all transponders in the automotive industry are relatively weak (see Box 3.5). As such, they cannot provide effective protection against determined attackers.

Taking the concept of the immobilizer a few steps forward, manufacturers have also introduced smart keys offering remote keyless entry.[92] Different manufacturers may use different names and different proprietary protocols, but they usually feature the same functionality, whereby the car owners can keep the smart keys in a pocket or purse when locking, unlocking, or starting their car. The key holder needs to be within 2 meters or so from the car for the doors to unlock, and inside the car (and to push the engine start button) for the engine to start. As with previous generations of car keys, the security of the whole process is protected cryptographically. The physical proximity is estimated based on the strength of a signal induced by the smart key and received by antennas on the car. Short-range (1−2 meters in active mode) Low Frequency (LF) RFID communication determines whether the key holder is inside or just outside the car. Periodically, or when the door handle is operated, the car sends LF signals and waits for a response from the smart key. If the right smart key receives these, it computes the correct cryptographic response and sends it back to the car on a longer-range (10−100 meters) Ultra High Frequency (UHF) channel. The car then verifies the response and unlocks the doors assuming that the owner must be less than 2 meters away. This assumption can be exploited by what is known as a relay attack. The original LF signal from the car is captured, converted, amplified, and retransmitted over a wireless channel controlled by the attacker. A fraudulent device placed near the smart key then receives this signal and relays it to the smart key over LF. Even if it is several meters away from the car (for instance, if the owner is sitting in a café nearby or paying at the parking meter), the smart key assumes that since it got the right message over the LF channel, it must be within 2 meters of the car. So, it initiates the UHF communication for unlocking it (Figure 3.8). Researchers from ETH Zurich[93] tested this attack strategy successfully on cars from eight different manufacturers and a distance of up to 50 meters without line of sight.

The fact that automobiles make extensive use of satellite navigation means that they may be affected by GPS jamming and

[92]Waraksa, T., Fraley, K., Kiefer, R., Douglas, D., and Gilbert, L. (1990). Passive keyless entry system. US patent 4942393.

[93]Francillon, A., Danev, B., and Capkun, S. (2011). Relay Attacks on Passive Keyless Entry and Start Systems in Modern Cars. *In Proceedings of NDSS*, February 2011.

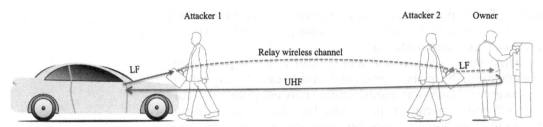

Figure 3.8 A pair of attackers activate the smart key and unlock the car's doors by relaying signals between the car and the smart key in the owner's pocket.

spoofing attacks as discussed for UAVs earlier. In the very near future, when driverless automobiles progress from research prototype[94] to mass production, such attacks and related legal issues[95] may be significant concerns in the industry. Until then, unlike in unmanned vehicles, an automobile's driver is inside the vehicle and sooner or later will notice any significant deviation of the position caused by GPS spoofing, simply by checking the name of the road or whether a road actually exists at the location shown on the satellite navigation device. GPS jamming would cause nothing more than inconvenience, since loss of GPS signal is rather common anyway. To achieve any serious impact, such as leading many drivers toward the same congested route to cause deadlocks or to maximize the number of people affected by an impending physical attack, one would need to employ a GPS software attack[96] that would somehow alter the route suggested by the device rather than the location displayed. Such an attack would be extremely difficult to perform, but there is an alternative way to achieve the same result.

Modern satellite navigation devices alter the recommended route to a destination based on real-time information about accidents, road works, congestion, and so on, and a common technology used for this is Radio Data System-Traffic Message Channel (RDS-TMC).[97] Best known for showing the names of FM channels on the radio display, RDS (or RDBS[98] in the United States) is a

[94]Montemerlo, M. et al. (2008). Junior: The Stanford entry in the urban challenge. *Journal of Field Robotics*, Volume 25, No. 9, pp. 569–597.

[95]Douma, F. and Palodichuk, S. A. (2012). Criminal Liability Issues Created by Autonomous Vehicles. *Santa Clara Law Review*, Volume 52, No. 4, pp. 1157–1169.

[96]Nighswander, T., Ledvina, B., Diamond, J., Brumley, R., and Brumley, D. (2012). GPS software attacks. In *Proceedings of the 2012 ACM conference on Computer and communications security*, ACM, pp. 450–461, October 2012.

[97]Kopitz, D. and Marks, B. (1999). *RDS: the radio data system*. Artech House.

[98]Wright, S. (1998). RBDS versus RDS-What are the differences and how can receivers cope with both systems? *National Radio Systems Committee*, pp. 2–11.

communication protocol used to transmit small amounts of data over FM radio. TMC is the particular technology that uses RDS to transmit traffic and other travel-related information to automobile drivers. In terms of security, it supports a lightweight encryption only for the small part of the message that specifies the location. As explained in the published draft of the encryption standard:[99] "The encryption is only 'light' but was adjudged to be adequate to deter all but the most determined hacker. More secure systems were rejected because of the RDS capacity overhead that was required." Considering the very low capacity of RDS, the decision to pick a lightweight encryption with low overhead was a pragmatic one. However, it was also an invitation for determined hackers to try to overcome it.

In 2007, Barisani and Bianco published detailed schematics and instructions on how to build a custom RDS-TMC receiver and transmitter using only inexpensive electronics.[100] They demonstrated injecting spoofed RDS-TMC messages about congested or closed roads, so that the device avoids these roads when it calculates the recommended route. They also showed how to generate an alert about a fabricated event, such as a terrorist incident on the route to home. Such an alert could affect the behavior of the driver and potentially create panic.[101] In practice, the likelihood of affecting a considerable number of automobiles at the same time and on a particular region or route is low, but the researchers' proof of concept experiments were very interesting nevertheless.

The impact of attacks on the tire pressure sensors, the satellite navigation system, the immobilizer, and the keyless entry can range from mild inconvenience to allowing a thief to steal the vehicle. Still, they are highly unlikely to lead to any truly hazardous situation in the same manner as an attack on the in-vehicle powertrain CAN bus could. The scenario of an adversary accessing a CAN bus through the OBD connector is in most cases unrealistic, but this is not the only way. The key is in the manner modern in-vehicle networks are set up. Critical ECUs may be connected to each other on one bus, while less critical ones on another, as in the simplified case of Figure 3.4. So, in

---

[99]International Standard ISO 14819-6:2006(E): Traffic and Traveller Information (TTI) – TTI messages via traffic message coding. Part 6: Encryption and conditional access for the Radio Data System – Traffic Message Channel ALERT C coding.

[100]Barisani, A. and Bianco, D. (2007). Hijacking RDS-TMC Traffic Information signals, *Phrack*, Volume 64, File 5.

[101]Barisani, A. and Bianco, D. (2007). Unusual car navigation tricks: Injecting RDS-TMC traffic information signals. In *Proceedings of the CanSecWest Conference*, Vancouver, Canada, April 18–20, 2007.

theory, compromising a noncritical function, such as the operation of the media player or the instrument cluster, should not affect a critical function, such as the steering or the braking. However, often ECUs on one bus need to communicate with ECUs on the other, and for this reason there is a small number of ECUs that sit on both networks and can act as network bridges. These are different for each car. For example, in the one used as a cyber-physical security testbed by Koscher et al.,[102] it was the Body Controller Module and the telematics unit (this is not technically a gateway ECU, but practically acts as one). In fact, the latter could be programmed through the low-speed bus. This means that an attacker with access to the network of noncritical functions could upload code to the telematics unit that would make it relay network traffic from the low-speed bus to the high-speed bus, where the safety-critical functions (engine, brakes, etc.) reside.

Making use of this principle, the researchers managed to experimentally demonstrate numerous attacks[103] that previously would have been considered practically impossible, where security breaches of noncritical functions, such as Bluetooth pairing with a malware-containing smartphone or a malicious audio file played on the CD player, would lead to complete control of the car's safety-critical functions. These attacks are extremely important for the automotive industry. They may require a skillset greater than the average cyber criminal's, but they are also truly practical. It is not difficult to see a rogue audio file spreading through Internet peer-to-peer sites and finding its way into multiple cars' media players, or an infected smartphone being within a car's Bluetooth range, and these are only a few of the possible entry points for an attack.

Miller and Valasek have argued that advanced features such as park assist, adaptive cruise control, collision prevention, and lane keep assist can make attacks easier.[104] That is because the existence of one of these features implies also the existence of the corresponding network messages that instruct the appropriate ECUs to perform a safety-critical function (lock up the

---

[102]Koscher et al. (2010). Experimental security analysis of a modern automobile. In the *Symposium on Security and Privacy, IEEE*, pp. 447–462, Oakland, CA, USA, May 16–19, 2010.
[103]Checkoway, S., McCoy, D., Kantor, B., Anderson, D., Shacham, H., Savage, S., Koscher, K., Czeskis, A., Roesner, F., and Kohno, T. (2011). Comprehensive Experimental Analyses of Automotive Attack Surfaces. In *USENIX Security Symposium*, August 2011.
[104]Miller, C. and Valasek, C. (2014). A Survey of Remote Automotive Attack Surfaces, Black Hat 2014, Las Vegas, Nevada, USA.

brakes, turn the steering wheel, etc.). As the automotive industry is taking cyber threats increasingly seriously and such advanced features are maturing, there is a growing emphasis on measures that limit the impact of potential misuse. For example, the lane keep assist network messages may not allow abrupt turning of the steering wheel and park assist may allow turning only at low speed. Still, an attacker with access to the car's network would be able to cause more damage than in another car where such features do not exist and the manufacturer has not defined the corresponding instructions.

Note that we have refrained from discussing the latest automotive communication technologies that allow vehicles to communicate with other vehicles (V2V)[105] or to smart infrastructure (V2I)[106] like smart traffic lights, smart parking spaces, and so on. Instead, we focused on the most popular technologies already in place in most everyday family cars. The following is a brief list summarizing the attacks that could affect the latter:

- Through the OBD port, physically connect a rogue node to the CAN bus network in order to transmit spoofed commands to other nodes, record previous commands, and replay them at a time that they can cause a hazard, or to transmit always at the highest priority to effectively block all other nodes from transmitting.
- Compromise the laptops of a dealership to hijack or manipulate the process of programming ECUs of customers' vehicles.
- Send spoofed activation signals to the tire pressure management sensors, so as to drain their batteries, or to the corresponding ECU, so as to trigger a warning on the dashboard.
- Exploit device-specific vulnerabilities of telematics units, including third party retrofitted ones, or target the smart devices from where the owner can control them.
- Bypass the immobilization system through a brute force or other attack that can identify the secret key.
- Employ a relay attack to bypass the security of the smart key.
- Launch a GPS jamming or GPS spoofing attack against a driverless automobile.
- Transmit spoofed RDS-TMC messages with fake traffic and incident reports along the target vehicle's route, so as to

[105]Eckhoff, D., Sofra, N., and German, R. (2013). A performance study of cooperative awareness in ETSI ITS G5 and IEEE WAVE. In *2013 10th Annual Conference on Wireless On-demand Network Systems and Services*, pp. 196–200, IEEE, March 2013.
[106]Rakha, H. and Kamalanathsharma, R. K. (2011). Eco-driving at signalized intersections using V2I communication. In *14th International IEEE Conference on Intelligent Transportation Systems*, pp. 341–346, IEEE, October 2011.

manipulate the recommended route that is displayed on the vehicle's satellite navigation device.
- Through the low-speed bus, compromise a gateway, which can be used to launch attacks on the high-speed bus and affect safety-critical components.

Summary

On the surface, cyber-physical attacks may appear to be highly complex, requiring very strong technical skills. An understandable misconception is that the more critical or technically complex the target, the more difficult to breach its security, but this is often not the case in practice. Communication systems used in critical functions of implantable medical devices are not too difficult to manipulate and may even be unencrypted. This makes it possible for a cyber attacker to affect a person's health by compromising an insulin pump, a pacemaker, a cardioverter defibrillator or any other implantable device, where life-critical actuation depends on sensor measurements and other wirelessly transmitted information. Of particular interest are attacks that involve capturing and replaying important communication signals, such as those triggering a defibrillator's pulse generator to deliver a shock or an insulin pump to deliver a dose.

The security of a typical automobile's immobilizer depends on cryptographic systems far weaker than those expected for a transaction over the Internet, and even a brute force attack may compromise them. This is only one of several cyber-physical vulnerabilities that have been introduced in the automotive industry over the last two decades, when automobiles moved from being largely mechanical systems to highly computerized systems that are heavily dependent on wired and wireless networks of ECUs and sensors. Of particular interest are attacks that use as entry point a noncritical component, such as the music player, and through a network gateway manage to affect critical functions, including the braking and the steering.

A technology that is seen across different sectors and types of cyber-physical systems is GPS. Yet, despite having become an indispensable part of critical national infrastructures, GPS is relatively easy to render unavailable with inexpensive jamming devices that can be purchased on the Internet. With more sophisticated attacks, such as spoofing of GPS signals, one can even dictate the direction of movement of unmanned vehicles, such as UAVs and robots.

Finally, in many cases, it is not the actual target that is attacked, but the smartphone or laptop controlling it. Remotely installing malware on the ECUs of an automobile may be difficult, but installing a Trojan on the laptops of the mechanics in the dealership is less so. The same holds for UAVs or implantable devices designed to be controlled via smartphones and laptops.

Follow-Up Questions and Exercises

1. Consider an implantable insulin pump and an implantable cardioverter defibrillator. How would a successful jamming attack affect them?
2. Can you fill in the missing text below?
   a. Researchers have managed to dictate the direction of movement of a UAV with a GPS _____ attack.
   b. Military GPS signals are _____, and as such are more difficult to spoof than civilian GPS signals.
   c. A cyber attacker can affect the operation of a satellite by compromising

   _____.

3. The introduction of immobilizers greatly reduced the number of automobile thefts, but an attacker with sufficient technical knowledge can still bypass them. Why is this the case?
   a. The cryptographic protocols used by most immobilizers are open. This makes it easier for attackers to analyze and exploit them.
   b. The automotive industry is unaware of cyber security risks and no measures have been taken to protect immobilizers from cyber attackers.
   c. The secret keys used by many immobilizers are too short.
   d. Immobilizers are based on Bluetooth technology, which has known vulnerabilities.
4. CAN bus uses a priority-based arbitration system so that when two nodes try to transmit messages at the same time and on the same bus the one with the lower priority halts and waits until the other finishes transmission. What do you think is the purpose of this priority system and how can it be exploited?
5. Which of the following statements are correct?
   a. Fuzzing is also known as fuzz testing and is a technique used primarily to detect security flaws in software.
   b. A fuzzing attack can successfully identify messages on class A and B but not on class C automotive networks.

      c. Fuzzing attacks on CAN buses are effective because of the relatively large size of a CAN message.

      d. Fuzzing involves bombarding a system with random data inputs and observing how it behaves.

6. Which of the following statements are correct?

      a. The driver's seat position control is a hard real-time system.

      b. FlexRay cannot be used for hard real-time systems.

      c. A denial of service attack on the FlexRay bus may affect engine control but cannot affect the steering of the automobile.

      d. Being a hard real-time system, ABS typically is controlled through a high-speed CAN or FlexRay bus.

4

CYBER-PHYSICAL ATTACKS ON INDUSTRIAL CONTROL SYSTEMS

Chapter Summary

   Being an area of engineering that the information security community had largely ignored in the past, industrial control systems traditionally have been built with an emphasis on efficiency and safety but not on security. In recent years, scientific experiments, such as the Aurora Generator Test, and high-profile real-world attacks, such as Stuxnet, have contributed both in raising awareness and, indirectly, in generating investment in cyber-physical security research and development. Nevertheless, SCADA and other industrial control systems continue to present a number of challenges that make them particularly difficult to protect against determined attackers. In this chapter, we describe some common security threats to SCADA systems, followed by an overview of Stuxnet and a discussion on its significance, before moving on to the smart grid and the associated security challenges.

Key Terms: Cyber-physical attack; SCADA; RTU; PLC; DNP3; Modbus; Aurora vulnerability; Stuxnet; smart grid; smart meter

Coordinated attacks on small and medium-scale cyber-physical systems, such as medical devices and vehicles, can cause considerable damage to individuals or small groups of people. Attacks on networked industrial control systems, on the other hand, can affect people and geographical areas at a grand scale. For this reason, threats to supervisory control and data acquisition (SCADA), programmable logic controllers (PLCs), and other systems used in critical infrastructures are considered a matter of national security in most of the world. And there are many of these threats.

The goal of this chapter is to familiarize the reader with threats to industrial control systems from three different angles: The most commonly discussed type of such systems and its associated security threats (the first section, SCADA), the most important real-world case study to date (the next section, Stuxnet), and the target that is universally seen as the holy grail of state-sponsored attacks (the final section, The Electric Grid).

SCADA

Systems used for SCADA have existed since long before the 1960s, but it is at about that time that the term SCADA came into use to refer to the computer-based ones. Early SCADA systems featured wired panels with meters and push buttons but essentially had much of the functionality seen in today's systems, including an interface between the human operator and the machine, a mechanism for displaying trends in the data collected, a set of alarms indicating different conditions, and two-way communication with remote terminal units (RTUs). In the past, the processing required for most of these would be carried out centrally on a single master station connected to the RTUs on dedicated lines, in what is known as a monolithic architecture (first generation).[1] Since then, SCADA systems have

---

[1]National Communications System (2004). Supervisory Control and Data Acquisition (SCADA) Systems, Technical Information Bulletin NCS TIB 04-1, Arlington, Virginia.

adopted distributed architectures (second generation) involving multiple servers, each responsible for a different aspect of the system. Initially connected over a single local area network, they are now increasingly networked (third generation), able to operate over large geographical areas and diverse network infrastructures, including wide area networks and the Internet. These transitions in architectures were facilitated by a transition from vendor-specific proprietary protocols to open protocols that allow the use of COTS components. The trend of focusing on interconnectivity and interoperability of diverse technologies continues in the fourth generation of SCADA systems and the advent of the Internet of Things.[2] In the context of industrial control, this is the vision of a fully networked environment of intelligent devices reporting directly through the Internet and without the need for RTUs, and human machine interfaces (HMIs) that are not confined to a central place but are accessible from anywhere via mobile devices.[3] See Figure 4.1 for a visual representation of the evolution of SCADA architectures.

Figure 4.1 (bottom right, third generation) shows an example SCADA architecture, where servers and systems that require communication with RTUs are connected to a control network, separate from the organization's corporate network. (Note that RTUs and PLCs share a lot of functionality and the terms are sometimes used interchangeably in the context of SCADA. For the sake of simplicity, we will refer to RTUs in this section, as representative of all types of field controllers, assuming that they have the capability both to gather data from sensors and to control field devices.) Most operations of the SCADA system are performed at the master station. In small-scale deployments, this can be a single PC, but in larger systems, it can include a data acquisition server, a real-time data server, a data historian, the HMI and its operators' workstations, as well as a number of other servers running various distributed software applications.[4] Data collected from the RTUs are received by the data acquisition server and stored in the databases of the real-time data server, from where they can be made available to other servers, such as the data historian. The latter is the server that preserves data collected over long periods of time, effectively acting as an audit log of a SCADA's activities. It allows

[2]Atzori, L., Iera, A., and Morabito, G. (2010). The internet of things: A survey. *Computer networks*, Volume 54, No. 15, pp. 2787–2805.
[3]Karnouskos, S. and Colombo, A. W. (2011). Architecting the next generation of service-based SCADA/DCS system of systems. In *IECON 2011, 37th Annual Conference on IEEE Industrial Electronics Society*, pp. 359–364, IEEE, November 2011.
[4]Borlase, S. (Ed.). (2012). *Smart grids: infrastructure, technology, and solutions.* CRC Press.

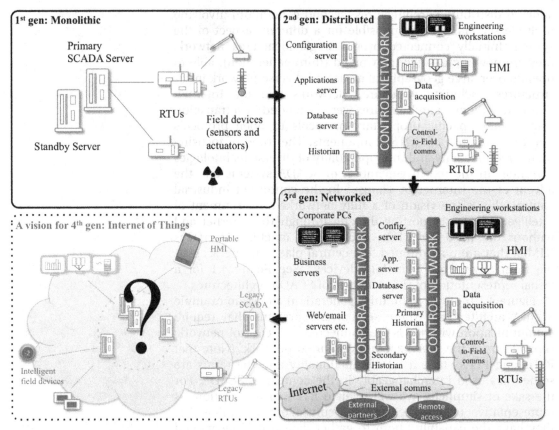

Figure 4.1 The evolution of SCADA from the first generation monolithic and second generation distributed architectures of the past to today's third generation highly networked SCADA. The fourth generation is expected to follow the Internet of Things trends, but there is little consensus regarding architectures yet.

long-term analysis of data, for example to identify problems or optimize processes, but can also be useful for forensic purposes after a security breach.[5] Finally, the HMI allows human operators to remotely request data and issue commands to the RTUs from the control room.

As SCADA architectures, protocols, and technologies can vary considerably, it would be impractical to list the numerous vulnerabilities and threats that may apply to each configuration. Nevertheless, it should be noted that the most commonly

[5]Wu, T., Disso, J. F. P., Jones, K., and Campos, A. (2013). Towards a SCADA Forensics Architecture. In *Proceedings of the 1st International Symposium for ICS & SCADA Cyber Security Research*, British Computing Society, pp. 12–21, Leicester, September 16–17, 2013.

encountered vulnerabilities in SCADA are largely the same as the ones encountered in conventional computer systems. For instance, SCADA systems are as vulnerable to improper input validation as any other computer system that relies on databases. Poor credential management practices are also common (e.g., passwords that are weak, poorly protected, or included in publicly available documentation). A good place to start is the *Guide to Industrial Control Systems Security* by the National Institute of Standards and Technology,[6] which categorizes vulnerabilities into policy and procedure vulnerabilities, platform-specific vulnerabilities, and network vulnerabilities. Our focus here is on the latter, and especially on the weaknesses of communication protocols that were designed specifically for industrial control systems, several years ago, at a time when control networks were thought to be secure by being physically isolated from other networks.

SCADA Network Vulnerabilities

One of the oldest, but still widely used SCADA communication standards is Modbus.[7] It is a master/slave protocol that was designed for simplicity and without particular considerations for security. Modbus has no concept of time, which means that it cannot time stamp events. Its simplicity makes it easier to implement and more lightweight than more advanced protocols, and as a result it is used in several industries and applications, often for communication with individual RTUs and other less powerful systems, where memory and network bandwidth are limited.[8] Modbus does not allow slaves (e.g., RTUs) to transmit unsolicited messages. They can transmit a response or take an action (e.g., open a valve) only when requested to do so by the master. There can be only one master but there is no provision in the protocol to prevent a rogue master from sending messages to the slaves pretending to be the legitimate one. The lack of any particular security measures specified in Modbus means that an attacker that gains access to the communication channel of a SCADA system can cause considerable damage

[6]Stouffer, K., Falco, J., and Scarfone, K. (2011). Guide to industrial control systems (ICS) security. *NIST special publication*, pp. 800–882.
[7]IDA Modbus (2004). Modbus application protocol specification v1. 1a. North Grafton, Massachusetts.
[8]Makhija, J. and Subramanyan, L. R. (2003). Comparison of protocols used in remote monitoring: DNP 3.0, IEC 870-5-101 & Modbus. *Electronics Systems Group, IIT Bombay, India, Tech. Rep.*

rather trivially.[9] Some of the attacks specified by Huitsing et al.[10] include sending fake broadcast messages to slaves (which can easily go undetected since, in Modbus, slaves do not respond to broadcast messages), passively eavesdropping on Modbus communications, recording and replaying older responses, delaying responses until they are out of date,[11] or repeatedly sending fake messages requesting field devices to restart themselves or clear their settings.

The original Modbus was designed to operate over multiple point-to-point connections between the HMI and each RTU, or between one master and multiple slaves forming a chain over a single shared serial cable, but later was extended to operate over a network using the TCP/IP protocol.[12] Modbus TCP[13] allows slaves to communicate concurrently with multiple masters, each master with multiple outstanding connections. As with Modbus serial, again the lack of security measures allows a variety of attacks to be performed after gaining access to the network. For example, one can send a spoofed message requesting to close a specific TCP connection, or perform a traditional denial of service attack by initiating a large number of connections that consume the target's resources and prevent it from accepting any further legitimate connection requests.[14]

The two most common network communication protocols used in currently deployed SCADA are the Distributed Network Protocol v3.0 (DNP3),[15] which is particularly popular in North America, and IEC 60870-5,[16] which has very similar

[9]Byres, E. J., Franz, M., and Miller, D. (2004). The use of attack trees in assessing vulnerabilities in SCADA systems. In *Proceedings of the International Infrastructure Survivability Workshop*, December 2004.

[10]Huitsing, P., Chandia, R., Papa, M., and Shenoi, S. (2008). Attack taxonomies for the Modbus protocols. *International Journal of Critical Infrastructure Protection*, Volume 1, pp. 37–44.

[11]Mo, Y., Kim, T. H., Brancik, K., Dickinson, D., Lee, H., Perrig, A., and Sinopoli, B. (2012). Cyber–physical security of a smart grid infrastructure. *Proceedings of the IEEE*, Volume 100, No. 1, pp. 195–209.

[12]Fall, K. R. and Stevens, W. R. (2011). *TCP/IP illustrated, volume 1: The protocols*. Addison-Wesley.

[13]Swales, A. (1999). Open Modbus/TCP Specification. *Schneider Electric*, March 29, 1999.

[14]Bhatia, S., Kush, N., Djamaludin, C., Akande, A., and Foo, E. (2014). Practical Modbus flooding attack and detection. In *Proceedings of Australasian Information Security Conference (ACSW-AISC 2014)*, Volume 149, Australian Computer Society, Inc.

[15]Clarke, G. R., Reynders, D., and Wright, E. (2004). *Practical modern SCADA protocols: DNP3, 60870.5 and related systems*. Newnes.

[16]Dorronzoro, E., Gomez, I., Medina, A. V., Benjumea, J., Sanchez, G., Martin, S., and Oviedo, D. (2008). Implementing IEC 60870-5 data link layer for an open and flexible remote unit. In *34th Annual Conference of IEEE Industrial Electronics, 2008*, pp. 2471–2476, IEEE, November 2008.

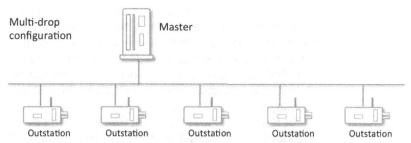

Figure 4.2 A DNP3 network in multidrop configuration.

functionality and is more popular in Europe. For simplicity, in this section we will refer only to DNP3. DNP3 is an open standard developed in the early 1990s to provide interoperability between different SCADA manufacturers' devices. In DNP3 terminology, there is a master, which sends request messages, and outstations (slave devices), which respond with reply messages. In computer science, this is known as polling. The master may poll important outstations multiple times every second and less important ones every few minutes. In the SCADA architectures of Figure 4.1, masters would be the HMI and any servers that require real-time information, while outstations would be the various RTUs. The usual configuration is "multidrop," where all outstations receive all requests but respond only to the ones addressed to them (Figure 4.2).

DNP3 supports modes of reporting that are not available in Modbus, including report by exception, where an outstation is configured to initiate communication over particular events, such as a significant drop in the water level or the failure of a device, without having to wait for a request from the master. It can also provide a timestamp for each event, which helps reconstruct a sequence of events from the DNP3 messages received. In practice, the most common mode of operation involves periodically polling the outstations (at a relatively low frequency) to ensure that they are accessible, and report by exception for the important events, so as not to overburden the network.[17]

DNP3 was originally designed with an emphasis on safety rather than security. As a result, it is not uncommon for DNP3 implementations to lack encryption and authentication, in which cases DNP3 devices effectively trust all messages received.

[17]Torrisi, N. M., Vukovic, O., Dán, G. and Hagdahl, S. (2014). Peekaboo: A Gray Hole Attack on Encrypted SCADA Communication using Traffic Analysis. In *5th IEEE International Conference on Smart Grid Communications*, Venice, Italy.

As a result, an attacker can introduce a rogue DNP3 device in the network to act as man-in-the-middle[18] between master and outstations. This "Rogue Interloper" attack is one of the 28 potential attacks theorized by East et al.,[19] who take the reasonable assumption that an attacker already connected to the network would have the technical means to intercept DNP3 traffic and inject fake DNP3 messages.

In response to an increasing threat of cyber attacks, the DNP3 standard was updated with the introduction of DNP3 Secure Authentication.[20] Its aim is to address a variety of spoofing, unauthorized modification, replay, and eavesdropping attacks by guaranteeing the authenticity and integrity of each message transmitted. To achieve this it specifies the following challenge-response mechanism: When a master wishes to request an action that is deemed critical (e.g., to restart, control, or change the parameters of an outstation), it includes a "critical" code in its message. Upon receiving a message, the outstation inspects it to determine whether it contains a critical code. If it does not, the outstation performs the requested action (and sends back feedback if appropriate). If it does, however, then the outstation challenges the master to prove its identity with a Keyed-Hash Message Authentication Code mechanism.[21] In broad terms, the outstation requests from the master to run a cryptographic hash function[22] with the secret key and a particular message (the challenge) set by the outstation. The outstation then runs the same function with the same challenge. If the hash value (the result of the cryptographic hash function) calculated at the outstation matches the one sent by the master, it is taken as proof that the

[18]Man-in-the-middle involves an attacker connecting independently with two victims (A and B) and making them think that they communicate with each other directly and in private, while in reality it is the attacker that is relaying messages between them. This is achieved by impersonating A when sending messages to B, and impersonating B when sending messages to A.

[19]East, S., Butts, J., Papa, M., and Shenoi, S. (2009). A Taxonomy of Attacks on the DNP3 Protocol. In *Critical Infrastructure Protection III*, pp. 67–81. Springer Berlin Heidelberg.

[20]Gilchrist, G. (2008). Secure authentication for DNP3. In 2008 IEEE Power and Energy Society General Meeting - Conversion and Delivery of Electrical Energy in the 21st Century.

[21]Krawczyk, H., Canetti, R., and Bellare, M. (1997). HMAC: Keyed-hashing for message authentication.

[22]In computer security, hashing is the process of using a special algorithm (e.g., the MD5 message digest algorithm or the Secure Hash Algorithm) to map a string of characters into a usually shorter number of fixed length (the hash value) that represents them. It needs to be extremely unlikely that two different strings of characters could generate the same hash value. One of the many uses of hashes is to prove that one has the right secret key without having to send it.

latter has the correct key and is indeed a legitimate master. The outstation then proceeds with the requested action. If they do not match, then the master's request is ignored. For added security, the session keys change regularly (15 minutes by default[23]). Also, the challenge-response mechanism is bidirectional, which means that not only the outstation can challenge a command coming from the master, but also the master can challenge data coming from an outstation.

DNP3 Secure authentication has been received with enthusiasm in the industry, because it addresses effectively and efficiently a large number of attacks. However, it cannot be seen on its own as a guarantee of security. Errors in implementation that leave security holes are not uncommon. Also, rather importantly, the standard does not specify encryption for the confidentiality of information transmitted. It is limited to authentication and integrity, which are generally seen as more important than confidentiality in the context of industrial control systems. This is largely true. However, an eavesdropper finding out that a device is transmitting a large number of unsolicited responses will know that this is an indication of a severe event. A denial of service attack against the particular device would cause a network disruption at that critical moment and would further aggravate the situation. Other information that can be inferred from unencrypted DNP3 traffic is the range of a device's operational values that are considered acceptable and would not trigger an alert.[24] A stealthy attacker would use this information to reduce the chances of being detected. Information on what sensor values are realistic would also be useful. For instance, a tampered message reporting an unrealistically high voltage measurement would be automatically discarded as a communication channel error or would generate suspicions of an ongoing data integrity attack.[25] Thus, a reconnaissance attack breaching confidentiality might not pose an immediate threat to an industrial control system by itself, but it can facilitate future data integrity or availability attacks, maximize their impact, and help prevent their detection. In fact, through theoretical analysis of the protocol, researchers were able to identify a potential approach (albeit a

[23]Benoit, J. (2011). An Introduction to Cryptography as Applied to the Smart Grid. *Cooper Power Systems.*
[24]Mander, T., Cheung, R., and Nabhani, F. (2010). Power system DNP3 data object security using data sets. *Computers & Security,* Elsevier, Volume 29, No. 4, pp. 487–500.
[25]Sridhar, S. and Manimaran, G. (2010). Data integrity attacks and their impacts on SCADA control system. In *Power and Energy Society General Meeting,* pp. 1–6. IEEE, July 2010.

rather complex one) for directly affecting both the integrity and availability of DNP3 communication by exploiting a weakness in the handling of unexpected messages.[26]

Other attacks target specifically hierarchical SCADA configurations, where there may be one or more submasters, which act as masters in one part of the network and as outstations in another. An example would be a high-level RTU that acts as master for the other RTUs but as an outstation for the master station. RTUs may transmit data, such as temperature readings, periodically or in response to requests by the submaster. The latter aggregates the data received from all RTUs and transmits them to the master when requested. Jin, Nicol, and Yan[27] have demonstrated an attack that exploits the very existence of data aggregating submasters. The attacker starts either by introducing a rogue DNP3 outstation device (e.g., a rogue RTU) in the network or by compromising an existing one. (Outstation security is often limited to a single password, and poor password practices, such as using default passwords,[28] dictionary words, or the same password for multiple devices and for long periods of time, traditionally have been common in the industry.) All data received from outstations are stored in a "sequence of event" buffer at the submaster at least until the master requests them. If the compromised outstation floods the network with many fake updates (unsolicited responses) that exceed the buffer's capacity, any subsequent legitimate updates from other outstations will be dropped because there will be no space to store them (Figure 4.3). In this manner, the attacker could prevent critical alerts from reaching the SCADA operators.

Communication between RTUs and the master station is often based on wireless radio, especially when data need to be transmitted over long distances and a wired network infrastructure would be impractical. Usually, there is a single master radio and one or more slave radios. When Reaves and Morris[29] experimented with

---

[26]Amoah, R., Suriadi, S., Camtepe, S. A., and Foo, E. (2014). Security analysis of the non-aggressive challenge response of the DNP3 Protocol using a CPN Model, In *IEEE International Conference on Communications*, June 10–14, 2014, Sydney, Australia.
[27]Jin, D., Nicol, D. M., and Yan, G. (2011). An event buffer flooding attack in DNP3 controlled SCADA systems. In *Proceedings of the Winter Simulation Conference*, pp. 2619–2631, December 2011.
[28]Hahn, A., Kregel, B., Govindarasu, M., Fitzpatrick, J., Adnan, R., Sridhar, S., and Higdon, M. (2010). Development of the PowerCyber SCADA security testbed. In *Proceedings of the Sixth Annual Workshop on Cyber Security and Information Intelligence Research*, No. 21, ACM, April 2010.
[29]Reaves, B. and Morris, T. (2009). Discovery, infiltration, and denial of service in a process control system wireless network. In *eCrime Researchers Summit. eCRIME'09*, pp. 1–9, IEEE, September 2009.

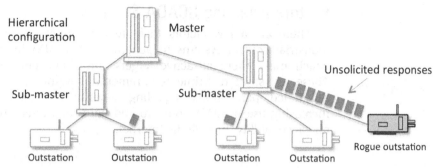

Figure 4.3 A rogue outstation flooding a submaster with unsolicited responses.

a modern commercial radio system used widely in SCADA, they were able to perform successfully a number of attacks, including connecting to the control network without authorization, eavesdropping on network traffic, injecting their own data into the network, and preventing RTUs from communicating with the master station. In the particular model of radio system (which, sensibly, the researchers did not reveal), access is controlled through a list of the serial numbers of radio devices that are meant to belong to a network and a 12-bit number that identifies the particular network. Slave devices need to know the data rate at which they can transmit, and there are also a few other parameters that determine the schedule of the frequency-hopping[30] scheme used. However, there is no mechanism for preventing someone from exhaustively checking all possible configurations. The researchers simply went through all 539,400 possible combinations of parameters (network identifiers, data rates, frequency hopping parameters, etc.) until they found the correct one and were able to join the network as a rogue slave radio device. From then on, it would be trivial to perform an attack, such as to flood the network with fake data so as to prevent legitimate devices from communicating with the master.

Note that adversaries may target not only the command and control communication, which is the communication between the master station and the RTUs, but also the communication between the RTUs and the field devices[31] (intelligent electronic devices for sensing and actuation, such as motors, circuit breakers, valves, console lights, etc.).

---

[30]Frequency hopping is a technique that changes the radio frequencies at which two parties are communicating. Both parties need to know the list and sequence of frequencies to be used, the time to be spent on each frequency, etc.
[31]Some examples of field communication protocols are the Foundation Field Bus, Interbus, Profibus, the Factory Instrumentation Protocol, and Modbus.

Factors Affecting SCADA Security

There are a few factors that are commonly encountered in industrial control systems in general, and SCADA in particular, which make them attractive targets and challenging to secure. These are strict real-time requirements, continuous availability, misguided perceptions regarding security in legacy systems, increasing use of COTS software and hardware, interconnectivity, and accessibility through the Internet.

Strict Real-Time Requirements

SCADA systems are hard real-time systems, where every operation needs to be completed before its deadline. SCADA is not merely used for convenience or as an auxiliary system, but as the primary safety system in an industrial environment. A slowed-down SCADA can cause a disaster or impede response to one by delaying its detection.[32]

Zhu and Sastry[33] have observed that when evaluating the time-criticality requirement of SCADA one needs to take into account both the responsiveness of the system and the freshness of the data. The former is about ensuring that a command to an actuator is received and executed without delay, while the latter is about the extent to which data collected by sensors are still valid when they reach their intended recipient. In the case of the Bellingham pipeline incident (Chapter 2: E2), it was the responsiveness of the system that was affected. The pipeline's operators would have taken actions to alleviate the pressure build up and the catastrophe would have been prevented had the SCADA system been responsive. Rather significantly, it is its unresponsiveness that has been determined to be the proximate cause of the rupture.[34] In the case of the San Bruno pipeline incident (Chapter 2: E9), erroneous low pressure readings caused the pressure control valves to open fully and increase the pressure to dangerously high levels.[35] Both cases

---

[32]Dondossola, G., Garrone, F., Szanto, J., and Gennaro, F. (2008). A laboratory testbed for the evaluation of cyber attacks to interacting ICT infrastructures of power grid operators. In *SmartGrids for Distribution, IET-CIRED. CIRED Seminar*, pp. 1–4, IET, June 2008.

[33]Zhu, B. and Sastry, S. (2010). SCADA-specific intrusion detection/prevention systems: a survey and taxonomy. In *Proceedings of the 1st Workshop on Secure Control Systems (SCS)*, April 2010.

[34]Abrams, M. and Weiss, J. (2007). *Bellingham, Washington, Control System Cyber Security Case Study*. NIST.

[35]Parformak, P. W. (2012). *Pipeline Cybersecurity: Federal Policy*. Congressional Research Service Report for Congress, August 16, 2012.

were accidents but there are several types of network security attacks that would have had the same effect. For instance, a denial of service attack on the network would impede the delivery of commands and data through it, as in the case of the disabled safety display at the Davis-Besse nuclear power plant (Chapter 2: E3). Chabukswar et al.[36] have evaluated the effects of such a denial of service attack in the simulated SCADA environment of a chemical plant. Their results confirmed that even a limited attack against particular sections of the network can delay communication to such extent that controllers are rendered blind to sensors or take decisions based on old measurements.

Of course, the real-time nature of industrial control systems is important not only for the victim but also for the perpetrator of the attack. A denial of service attack aiming to disrupt communication with a flood of illegitimate commands will probably benefit from an already slow network with high packet losses. However, if the aim is to force a process to exceed its operational limits by carefully timing fake Modbus or DNP3 messages sent to the RTUs, then the real-time state of the network[37] (average delay, rate of lost packets, background network traffic, etc.), its segmentation in virtual local area networks (VLANs),[38] as well as physical characteristics of the targets, such as the time that it takes a valve to open or close,[39] can affect the success of the attack.

Continuous Availability

Responsiveness of a SCADA system is closely related to its availability. The latter can be measured as the fraction of time that a system is available over its lifetime, or as the maximum time that it takes to repair it when unavailable. In the context of critical infrastructures, it is common to expect availability of "five nines," which means that a system should be available at

[36]Chabukswar, R., Sinópoli, B., Karsai, G., Giani, A., Neema, H., and Davis, A. (2010). Simulation of network attacks on SCADA systems. In *First Workshop on Secure Control Systems*, April 2010.

[37]Genge, B. and Siaterlis, C. (2012). Cyber-physical attacks: The role of network parameters. 6th Edition of the Inderdisciplinarity in Engineering International Conference "Petru Maior", University of Tigru Mures, Romania.

[38]Genge, B. and Siaterlis, C. (2012). An experimental study on the impact of network segmentation to the resilience of physical processes. In *Networking 2012*, pp. 121–134. Springer Berlin Heidelberg.

[39]Genge, B., Siaterlis, C. and Hohenadel, M. (2012). Impact of network infrastructure parameters to the effectiveness of cyber attacks against industrial control systems. *International Journal of Computers, Communications & Control*, Volume 7, No. 4, pp. 673–686.

least 99.999% of the time (or unavailable for less than 5.26 minutes in a whole year).[40]

In normal circumstances (when there is no attack in progress), availability issues can be a matter of hardware failure, network failure, or (commonly) software failure.[41] From the perspective of security, unavailability can be seen as an extreme case of unresponsiveness. A low-intensity denial of service attack, one that involves the transmission of attack traffic at a rate that is low relative to the capacity of the network, may affect only the time that information takes to transfer and be acted upon, while a high-intensity one can render the network completely unavailable. Hence, the discussion on responsiveness is applicable here too.

A second matter that arises from the requirement of continuous availability is that SCADA field devices may run for years without rebooting. In the process, they accumulate fragmentation, which makes them particularly vulnerable to buffer overflow.[42] Buffers are regions in computer memory used to temporarily hold data before they are used by a program. An overflow occurs when a program continues writing data to a buffer beyond the latter's boundaries, and consequently starts overwriting adjacent regions in the memory. By writing where it is not meant to, the attacker aims to point a program to execute an undesired function or run malicious code. The survey of attacks and defenses from back in 2000, where Cowan et al. characterized buffer overflow as the "vulnerability of the decade,"[43] is still a good read today. Yet, even though software developers are aware of its significance and know how to prevent it, buffer overflow is still very common. It can affect field devices that are embedded systems running real-time operating systems (RTOS),[44] as well as the SCADA workstations and servers that are standard computer systems running variants of Microsoft Windows and other general-purpose operating systems.

---

[40]The usual formula is: Availability $= \frac{MTBF}{MTBF + MTTR} \cdot 100\%$, where MTBF is the mean time between failures and MTTR is the mean time to repair.

[41]Jensen, M., Sel, C., Franke, U., Holm, H., and Nordstrom, L. (2010). Availability of a SCADA/OMS/DMS system — a case study. In *Innovative Smart Grid Technologies Conference Europe (ISGT Europe), IEEE PES*, pp. 1–8. IEEE, October 2010.

[42]Zhu, B. (2014). Resilient Control and Intrusion Detection for SCADA Systems. PhD Thesis, Technical Report No. UCB/EECS-2014-34, University of California, Berkeley, USA.

[43]Cowan, C., Wagle, P., Pu, C., Beattie, S., and Walpole, J. (2000). Buffer overflows: Attacks and defenses for the vulnerability of the decade. In Proceedings of *DARPA Information Survivability Conference and Exposition*, Vol. 2, pp. 119–129, IEEE.

[44]Shao, Z., Zhuge, Q., He, Y., and Sha, E. M. (2003). Defending embedded systems against buffer overflow via hardware/software. In *Proceedings of the 19th Annual Computer Security Applications Conference. Proceedings*, pp. 352–361, IEEE, December 2003.

Between 2010 and 2014, ICS-CERT issued alerts for buffer overflow affecting software from nine high-profile SCADA vendors.[45] In January 2014, a prolific zero-day vulnerability discoverer publicly disclosed a buffer overflow vulnerability of well-known SCADA software without having first informed the company that developed it.[46] For the one day that passed between disclosure and fixing of the vulnerability, attackers could have exploited it to disable the web-based HMI of industrial facilities in 38 countries across the world.

Misguided Security Perceptions

Until a few years ago, SCADA security was thought to benefit from the relative obscurity of the proprietary technologies used. The logic was that the less known a technology, especially a proprietary one, the less likely it would be for an attacker to know how it works and to discover security flaws. While obscurity can have its benefits,[47] the logic of relying on it for security is considered deeply flawed, especially for industrial control systems that are particularly attractive to attackers.[48] A determined attacker will always discover flaws, and obscure proprietary technologies are unlikely to have been independently assessed in terms of robustness as thoroughly as well-known open-standard ones. When carrying out a risk analysis of a SCADA system, one needs to assume that the attacker has precise and detailed knowledge of the hardware, the architecture, the network protocols, the software, and the security measures in place. Documentation on every related system, including legacy and obscure ones, is nearly always available on the Internet. More than anything, "security by obscurity" creates a false sense of security, which is dangerous by itself.

Commercial-off-the-Shelf Hardware and Software

In the past, SCADA systems were built on special-purpose hardware and software; now they are based increasingly on

---

[45]ICS-CERT. Alerts by Vendor. http://ics-cert.us-cert.gov/alerts-by-vendor.

[46]Higgins, K. J. (2014). SCADA Researcher Drops Zero-Day, ICS-CERT Issues Advisory. Dark Reading, January 15, 2014.

[47]During war, an efficient approach for secret communication is to use an obscure language that the enemy is unlikely to understand. The most famous example is the use of Navajo "code talkers" by the United States Marine Corps in World War II. Encryption and decryption is nearly instant for one who speaks Navajo, but difficult for everyone else.

[48]Mercuri, R. T. and Neumann, P. G. (2003). Security by obscurity. *Communications of the ACM*, Volume 46, No. 11, p. 160.

commercial-off-the-shelf computer servers running general-purpose operating systems, such as Microsoft Windows. This can reduce both cost and time to design a SCADA network. However, it also means that malware designed for general-purpose computer systems may well infect a SCADA server if it finds its way into one. Interconnectivity and accessibility over the Internet further aggravate the problem.

Interconnectivity

In the past, security in SCADA systems would benefit from a relative isolation of their networks. An employee would have to show a badge to a security guard before entering a facility from where the control network would be accessible. Reports on the operation of the system would be printed and physically taken to the organization's headquarters. There would be no network connection between the corporate network and the control network and no means to reach the latter remotely. Assuming that only authorized employees had access to the facility, there was little need to ensure security of communication with the RTUs, and the design of an industrial control system's architecture would generally be based on trust. This is no longer the case. Even legacy SCADA systems are commonly retrofitted with wired and wireless networking capabilities. In theory, all connections between the corporate and SCADA networks should go through firewalls that block unauthorized traffic. However, whether because the firewalls are not always configured correctly or because they are simply not put in place, the results of US-CERT's Project Shine in 2012 showed that over 7,200 industrial control systems in the United States were directly accessible via the Internet.[49]

The practice of ensuring that one network (e.g., the control network of a plant) is physically isolated from other networks (e.g., the plant's corporate network and the Internet) is called air gapping. Air gaps can certainly make an attacker's job difficult, but they are not completely secure. Even if there is no network connection between a system and the outside world, it is still possible to infect it via other means[50] like an engineer's laptop or a USB stick (see the discussion on Stuxnet[51] in the next section), or to breach its confidentiality via a Tempest/Emsec attack (see Chapter 7).

[49]ICS-CERT. Situational Awareness. *ICS-CERT Monitor*, October – December 2012.
[50]Byres, E. (2013). The air gap: SCADA's enduring security myth. *Communications of the ACM*, Volume 56, No. 8, pp. 29–31.
[51]Farwell, J. P. and Rohozinski, R. (2011). Stuxnet and the future of cyber war. *Survival*, Volume 53, No. 1, pp. 23–40.

Here, we can also include security challenges caused by sharing networks with external trusted partners, such as sister utilities, suppliers, consultants, and so forth. A security breach in a partner's network can affect a SCADA operator's network and vice versa.

Internet Accessibility

Allowing access to a SCADA system's HMI and databases through the Internet can have several benefits, such as the ability to remotely monitor the system's state from anywhere in the world. However, it also introduces web-based vulnerabilities. For example, it has been repeatedly reported[52] that Structure Query Language (SQL) databases used in SCADA systems can be vulnerable to various forms of SQL injection.[53] This is a technique that exploits poor coding practices in web-enabled databases. Unless the software developer has taken specific precautions to validate what can be submitted through a web form's input box, a user can gain unauthorized access by inputting carefully crafted SQL code where the database would normally expect a name or a number. From then on, any change in the historical data stored in a database can cause operational and even regulatory problems.

In summary, an attacker could attempt the following:
- Compromise a computer on the corporate network by infecting with malware and exploit interactions between corporate and control network to affect or gain access to the latter. The initial infection is usually the result of social engineering, such as a phishing e-mail (see Chapter 5).
- Through physical access (e.g., through a USB stick), compromise a RTU and gain access to the control network.
- Having gained access to the control network, exploit known security weaknesses of the communication protocol used (Modbus, DNP3, etc.) to modify messages from sensors or messages to actuators, flood the network with fake updates that exceed the "sequence of event" buffer at a submaster, and so on.
- Exploit web-based or database vulnerabilities related to the web accessibility of the system's HMI or databases.

---

[52]ICS-CERT (2011). Advisory (ICSA-11-082-01), Ecava Integrator SQL, April 30, 2013.
[53]Clarke, J. (Ed.). (2012). *SQL injection attacks and defense*. Elsevier.

Stuxnet: A Milestone in Industrial Control System Security

Stuxnet has been heralded as the first cyber-physical weapon. At the time it was discovered, it certainly was the most impressive malware seen outside a laboratory, as well as a catalyst for the acceptance of the significance of cyber-physical attacks in military circles. Stuxnet's targets were all industrial facilities in Iran, including a uranium enrichment facility in Natanz.

The Background

The Iranian nuclear program dates back to the 1950s and an American program called "Atoms for Peace,"[54] which aimed to share nuclear expertise and equipment with allies, including Iran.[55] Iranian nuclear collaboration with the United States, as well as with several European nuclear powers, continued until the 1979 revolution, which overthrew the Shah and abruptly changed the country's political alignments. Since then, the west has watched the Iranian nuclear program with the suspicion that it aims to change the geopolitical balances of the Middle East by developing atomic weapons,[56] since U-235, the type of uranium used to fuel nuclear power plants, is the same type that is used to make nuclear bombs.

In nature, U-235 is found mixed with U-238, which is much less useful for nuclear purposes. Natural uranium contains only 0.72% U-235,[57] the rest being U-238. To enrich uranium, which means to increase the percentage[58] of U-235 by concentrating it and separating it from U-238, centrifuges are required. A centrifuge is equipment that spins uranium at such high speed that, due to differences in weight, U-238 particles concentrate on the walls, while U-235 particles concentrate near the center. The process is repeated again and again in cascades of centrifuges

---

[54]Fuhrmann, M. (2012). *Atomic assistance: How "Atoms for Peace" programs cause nuclear insecurity.* Cornell University Press.
[55]The Soviet Union followed suit by sharing nuclear technology with Libya, Bulgaria, and North Korea.
[56]Cordesman, A. H. (2000). Iran and Nuclear Weapons. *Background Paper for the Senate Foreign Relations Committee*, Center for Strategic and International Studies, Washington, DC.
[57]Wilson, P. D. (Ed.). (1996). *The nuclear fuel cycle: From ore to wastes.* Oxford University Press.
[58]For comparison, most civilian nuclear power plants require 3–5% U-235, while the requirements of research reactors go up to about 20% and nuclear warheads exceed 90%.

that are chained together, and the greater the number of centrifuges and the greater their speed of rotation, the more the enriched uranium they produce. For as long as they were allies with western nuclear powers, the Iranians were sourcing enriched uranium primarily from them, but after the revolution they needed to produce their own.

In the late 1980s, Dr. A. Q. Khan, one of Pakistan's senior nuclear scientists, made a secret visit to provide Iran with designs and key components for such centrifuges.[59] It is believed that the centrifuges used at the time of the Stuxnet attack were of the relatively old design that Khan provided. They were particularly unreliable, failing constantly and underperforming. Without access to a better technology, Iran's approach was to master their production, so as to produce them at a rate that was higher than the rate of failure, and to limit the impact of the continuous failures with the use of two protection systems. The first one used shut-off valves to isolate problematic centrifuges when sensors detected excessive vibration. However, too many centrifuges being shut off would lead to a buildup of pressure in the enrichment stage. This is what the second protection system purportedly was for.[60] When sensors detected excessive pressure, overpressure relief valves would be activated and would release it into a dump system. (Note that there is some disagreement regarding the precise nature of the second set of valves. Symantec's analysts have suggested that they were auxiliary valves blocking whole cascades of centrifuges when needed.)[61] These two protection systems were anything but elegant. In his excellent technical analysis of Stuxnet, *To Kill a Centrifuge*,[62] Ralph Langner refers to them as workarounds. Nevertheless, they were useful workarounds, because despite the reliability issues of the centrifuges, they could continue to enrich uranium. It can be argued that centrifuge failures were so common that the two protection systems were not merely useful but vital for the continuation of the program. This made them an attractive target for an attack.

[59]Linzer, D. (2005). Iran was offered nuclear parts. Washington Post, February 27, 2005.
[60]Langner, R. (2013). To Kill a Centrifuge: A technical analysis of what Stuxnet's creators tried to achieve. The Langner Group, November 2013.
[61]McDonald, G., Murchu, L. O., Doherty, S., and Chien, E. (2013). Stuxnet 0.5: The Missing Link. *Symantec Security Response*.
[62]Langner, R. (2013). To Kill a Centrifuge: A technical analysis of what Stuxnet's creators tried to achieve. The Langner Group, November 2013.

In the past, an attack against a nuclear facility would have involved either a targeted air strike[63] or a secret agent infiltrating it and carrying out some form of sabotage. Stuxnet proved that there is another way; a cyber-physical one.

The Payload and the Attack

A centrifuge can be damaged by excessive pressure or a rotation speed that would cause vibrations. To achieve either, a cyber attack would need to target the PLC controllers of the centrifuges' rotors, valves, and sensors. In the case of the specific centrifuges at Natanz, the buildup of excessive pressure would not be a problem on its own, as it was a common occurrence anyway. Knowing the precise setup of the centrifuges and the reliance on the two protection systems, the challenge would be to prevent the shut-off valves and the overpressure relief valves from activating when needed. Since their activation would be triggered by reports from vibration sensors and pressure sensors, an attack would need to somehow interfere with the operation of the controllers of both the sensors and the valves. The particular model of PLC used in Natanz was the Siemens S7-417.

An early variant of Stuxnet, referred to as Stuxnet 0.5 by Symantec's analysts,[64] focused precisely on these valves. Stuxnet 0.5 replaces parts of the original programs running on these S7-417 PLCs. It first checks whether the PLC that it has landed on is its intended target. If its configuration matches a specific configuration (presumably, the one found in Natanz), then it activates. In a manner akin to traditional man-in-the-middle attacks, the malicious code of Stuxnet 0.5 sits between the PLC and the valves and sensors to which the particular PLC is connected. The attack involves recording the sensor measurements gathered during normal operation of the centrifuges and then replaying them, so that the system and the human operators continue thinking that everything is normal (somewhat similar to a security guard looking at fake footage or a photo placed in front of the security camera, while a thief moves in undetected). Stuxnet 0.5 proceeds by closing the shut-off valves of some of the centrifuges, waiting 2 hours for the pressure to build up and then closing the overpressure relief valves too.

[63]Iran's two nuclear reactors in Bushehr were repeatedly targeted by Iraqis airstrikes between 1984 and 1988. More recently in 2007, an Israeli air strike destroyed Syria's Al-Kibar nuclear reactor.
[64]McDonald, G., Murchu, L. O., Doherty, S., and Chien, E. (2013). Stuxnet 0.5: The Missing Link. *Symantec Security Response*.

Symantec has estimated that development for Stuxnet 0.5 must have started as early as 2005. In 2007, an unidentified person submitted it to VirusTotal, a free online malware scanning service, where, unsurprisingly, it did not raise any alarms.[65] Its code would not have matched any of the signatures of malware code stored in antivirus databases at the time, and it would have been impossible to recognize its purpose. This early variant had been designed to stop operating after a particular date in 2009, presumably to reduce the chances of getting noticed and alarming the engineers at Natanz, while a new variant was being developed.

It is unclear how effective Stuxnet 0.5 was. The variant that most certainly had an impact, and is known simply as Stuxnet, included only an incomplete part of unused code relating to the Siemens S7-417 controllers. Instead, it had a new target: the Siemens S7-315 controllers, which were responsible for the rotors' drives and ultimately the speeds of the centrifuges.[66] Stuxnet's aim was to manipulate the operation of these controllers and damage the centrifuges by temporarily running them at speeds that would be too low, too high, or such that would cause resonant vibrations.[67] Low-speed sessions would drop the centrifuges to a mere two revolutions per second (120 rpm) for 50 minutes, while high-speed ones would reach 1,410 revolutions per second (84,600 rpm) for 15 minutes. During this time, the legitimate program running on the PLCs would be suspended and replaced by Stuxnet's attack code. Attacks would be separated by weeks between them, so that Stuxnet would go unnoticed for a long period of time.

The Delivery

Clearly, for security reasons, a nuclear facility's PLCs would not be connected to the Internet. That would have made them a constant target for cyber attacks. So, how does one infect a

---

[65]Zetter, K. (2013). Stuxnet missing link found, resolves some mysteries around the cyberweapon, Wired, February 26, 2013.

[66]To be more specific, the PLCs control the frequency converters, which in turn regulate the power supplied to the centrifuges, effectively controlling their speed. The normal speed of the particular type of centrifuges is estimated to be around 1,050 revolutions per second (63,000 rpm).

[67]Every object has resonant frequencies, which are frequencies at which it vibrates more easily. That is why troops marching in step can force a bridge to collapse, and an opera singer hitting a high note may break a glass (when the frequency of the note is a resonant frequency of the glass). A centrifuge slowly increasing or reducing its speed (frequency of revolution) is likely to momentarily rotate at a resonant frequency. This would cause excessive vibration and possibly permanent damage.

machine remotely if there is no network connection to it? To answer this question, we need to remember that the infection does not have to happen in real time, so there is no need to perform it through a computer network. Instead, Stuxnet 0.5 would propagate through infected USB sticks, with someone having to manually plug one in an authorized Natanz employee's or contractor's computer. If this computer were later connected to a PLC (e.g., to reconfigure it) and run the standard application[68] for programming it, it would then infect the PLC too. Stuxnet 0.5 could also replicate via infected files of this application if engineers shared them between them, for instance via e-mail. This was a rather covert approach that would require a fair amount of secret agent type of work to physically infect (presumably) an engineer's portable computer and then wait for Stuxnet to replicate in this manner. It was probably not as effective as Stuxnet's developers intended; otherwise, there would have been little need to change it.

The delivery strategy for the later version of Stuxnet was much more aggressive. The target PLCs were connected to an internal control network so as to be able to receive commands remotely from the human operators and the facility's SCADA systems; therefore Stuxnet was now given self-replication functionality. If one machine was infected, for example again via a USB stick, then Stuxnet would propagate to any other machines running Microsoft Windows on the same network. Kaspersky Lab researchers have identified five Iranian organizations in the industrial control systems industry[69] as the first to have been infected by Stuxnet.[70] To ensure that security software would miss it and it could install itself on the machines, Stuxnet used stolen digital certificates from Realtek Semiconductor Corp. and JMicron Technology Corp. to make it look like an authentic product from a trusted company. It would then check whether the host machine had the configuration of the particular Siemens industrial control systems used in Iran. If that were the case, it would attempt to connect to the Internet to download its own latest version, and would then try to compromise the target PLC's programming logic. For all this to be possible, Stuxnet used four zero-day vulnerabilities: one helping it to spread via USB stick, one to spread in networks

---

[68]Stuxnet targeted the project files of SIMATIC STEP 7, which is the standard software for programming the particular Siemens PLCs.

[69]Three are vendors of equipment for industrial control systems, one is a supplier of components, and one is a developer of centrifuges.

[70]Zetter, K. (2014). *Countdown to Zero Day: Stuxnet and the Launch of the World's First Digital Weapon*. Random House LLC.

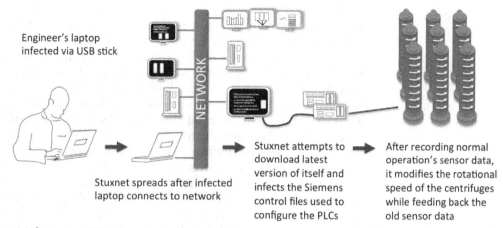

Engineer's laptop
infected via USB stick

NETWORK

Stuxnet spreads after infected
laptop connects to network

Stuxnet attempts to
download latest
version of itself and
infects the Siemens
control files used to
configure the PLCs

After recording normal
operation's sensor data,
it modifies the rotational
speed of the centrifuges
while feeding back the
old sensor data

Figure 4.4 Stuxnet exploited four zero-day vulnerabilities to manage to reach the PLCs controlling the centrifuges.

with shared printers, and two to gain system-level privileges on the target computers (Figure 4.4). To put this into perspective, the total number of zero-day vulnerabilities discovered globally and documented by Symantec in 2009 was only 12.[71]

The Impact and the Aftermath

Although it is rather certain that Stuxnet had very specific targets, 4 months after its discovery it was found to have already infected another 100,000 systems,[72] 40% of which were outside Iran (Chevron's computer network being a notable example in the United States.)[73] It is unclear to what extent this was allowed by its designers or was unintentional. There have been some unconfirmed reports of Stuxnet affecting nuclear facilities outside Iran,[74] but the fact remains that for the vast majority of computers carrying it worldwide Stuxnet had no effect at all. It was designed to manipulate PLCs with a very particular configuration, unlikely to be found in many places other than the centrifuge control systems at Natanz, and carried a built-in expiration date of June 24, 2012.

[71]Fossi, M., Turner, D., Johnson, E., Mack, T., Adams, T., Blackbird, J., Entwisle, S., Graveland, B., McKinney, D., Mulcahy, J., and Wueest, C. (2010). Symantec global Internet security threat report – Trends for 2009. *Symantec Enterprise Security,* Volume XV.

[72]Espiner, T. (2010). Siemens: Stuxnet infected 14 industrial plants. ZDNet, September 16, 2010.

[73]Ashford, W. (2012). Stuxnet hit Chevron's systems, the energy giant admits. ComputerWeekly.com, November 9, 2012.

[74]Vincent, J. (2013). Russian nuclear power plant infected by Stuxnet malware says cyber-security expert. The Independent, November 12, 2013.

Since its discovery and technical analysis, Stuxnet has been added to most antivirus products' databases of known malware, making it a low-risk threat—easy to contain and easy to remove. The zero-day vulnerabilities it exploited have been patched and Siemens has issued updates for the software of the PLCs that were affected. It is now yet another threat of the past, unlikely to cause any major concern today or in the future. Regarding its intended target, it is believed that Stuxnet's impact was of the order of 1,000 damaged centrifuges (possibly more),[75] which is significant but not crippling for a nuclear program that had already learned to live with faulty centrifuges and had the capacity to quickly replace them with new ones. In fact, enrichment data from that period have shown that despite a noticeable reduction of available centrifuges, the total enrichment capacity slightly increased.[76] (Perhaps engineers at Natanz were introducing some performance improvements at around the time that Stuxnet struck.) Nevertheless, even if Stuxnet had limited effect then and is operationally irrelevant now, its impact on strategic thinking has been anything but irrelevant. It has been described as a "paradigm shift"[77] and a "game changer."[78] From a technical perspective, elements of Stuxnet have served as blueprints for cyber criminals seeking new and more effective attack strategies. For example, the number of malware using stolen digital certificates has increased dramatically since 2010.[79] Researchers have also started working on innovative ways of attacking[80] and defending[81] PLCs, an area of security that was largely ignored previously. From a geopolitical perspective, Stuxnet accelerated the inevitable weaponization of the cyber domain. Suppose that a government's cyber security department

[75]Barzashka, I. (2013). Are Cyber-Weapons Effective? Assessing Stuxnet's Impact on the Iranian Enrichment Programme. RUSI Journal, Volume 158, No. 2, pp. 48–56, Taylor & Francis, April 2013.
[76]Barzashka, I. (2011). Using enrichment capacity to estimate Iran's breakout potential. Federation of American Scientists Issue Brief, January 21, 2011.
[77]European Network and Information Security Agency (2010). EU Agency Analysis of "Stuxnet": A paradigm shift in threats and critical information infrastructure protection. Press Release, October 7, 2010.
[78]Benson, P. (2010). Computer virus Stuxnet a "game changer", DHS official tells senate. CNN, November 18, 2010.
[79]Ashford, W. (2013). McAfee Focus 2013: Digitally signed malware a fast-growing threat, say researchers. ComputerWeekly.com, October 4, 2013.
[80]Basnight, Z., Butts, J., Lopez Jr, J., and Dube, T. (2013). Firmware modification attacks on programmable logic controllers. *International Journal of Critical Infrastructure Protection*, Volume 6, No. 2, pp. 76–84.
[81]McLaughlin, S., Zonouz, S., Pohly, D., and McDaniel, P. (2014). A Trusted Safety Verifier for Process Controller Code. In *Proc. ISOC Network and Distributed Systems Security Symposium (NDSS)*, February 2014.

identifies a zero-day vulnerability in commercial software used widely around the world. What would that government do? Inform the software provider so that the problem is fixed, or keep it secret in case it can be utilized in a future cyber attack against an enemy? It would be naïve to think that governments are not currently stockpiling with zero-day vulnerabilities that they have discovered themselves or purchased.[82] Stuxnet needed four and this was only the beginning. In fact, it can be argued that Stuxnet acted as a catalyst for an already flourishing "digital arms trade"[83] where firms source vulnerabilities from their networks of trusted hackers and sell them to governments and companies.

Looking at these developments from the perspective of ethics, Dorothy Denning and Bradley Strawser have suggested that not only a Stuxnet-like cyber-physical attack with no human casualties is "morally better," [84] but under specific conditions, "states are morally obliged to use cyber weapons instead of kinetic weapons when they can be deployed for a purpose already deemed just under the law of armed conflict and without any significant loss of capability."[85] Of course, this is an idealistic view where a highly effective cyber-physical attack is somehow also guaranteed to not harm people. Even if the premise is uncertain, it shows one more reason why we can expect political and military cyber-physical attacks to become increasingly common over the next few years.

The Electric Grid

Almost every aspect of life in a modern society relies on the availability of electricity, which is generated, transmitted, distributed, and eventually consumed through electric grids. In its simplest form, an electric grid is the infrastructure required to provide electricity from a power generator to a neighborhood. In practice, the national electrical infrastructures of most countries have evolved into single or small numbers of very large electric grids. For example, there are currently three electric grids covering the whole of the continental United States. They include power generators, substations, transformers, and large networks of high-voltage transmission lines and distribution

[82]Perlroth, N. and Sanger, D. E. (2013). Nations Buying as Hackers Sell Flaws in Computer Code, New York Times, July 13, 2013.
[83]The Economist (2013). The digital arms trade. March 30, 2013.
[84]Denning, D. E. (2012). Stuxnet: what has changed? *Future Internet*, Volume 4, No. 3, pp. 672–687.
[85]Denning, D. E. and Strawser, B. J. (2014). Moral Cyber Weapons. In *The Ethics of Information Warfare*. Springer International Publishing, pp. 85–103.

lines, delivering electricity to homes, businesses, and industrial plants. Its scale is such that the electric grid has been characterized as the "world's largest engineered system."[86]

Power Generators

At around the same time that Stuxnet was in development, the general public became aware of a staged cyber-physical attack that had some similar characteristics. We have already referred to this in Chapter 2 (E4) as the Aurora Generator test, and the vulnerability that it exploited as the Aurora vulnerability. Since the Aurora Generator test, the North American Electric Reliability Corporation (NERC) has issued Aurora guidance documents focusing on cyber and physical access control. Although footage of the experiment was broadcast on CNN and parts of the disabled generator were exhibited in the International Spy Museum in Washington, DC, the precise details of the experimental setup, especially the configuration of the power generator's protection systems and the attack approach, were kept secret until 2014. At that point, a lot of previously classified information was disclosed in response to a Freedom of Information Act request. Rather comically, the request was actually for the completely unrelated Operation Aurora[87] and not for the Aurora Generator Test.

The Aurora vulnerability is not really a cyber vulnerability, but a physical vulnerability. However, it can be exploited through cyberspace, assuming that an adversary has gained control of a communication link between a control room and a generation or transmission relay.[88] Power generators are protected by large relays and circuit breakers that interrupt the flow of current when they sense any abnormal condition such as short circuits, overloads, and other electrical faults. When a fault is detected, the breaker opens to interrupt the current flow, waits for the fault to clear, and then closes again, allowing the current flow to restart. To connect a generator to the grid, for example after protective relays and breakers have temporarily removed it, key electrical parameters (e.g., the frequency) of the generator and the grid must be matched. For this to be

---

[86]Mo, Y., Kim, T. H., Brancik, K., Dickinson, D., Lee, H., Perrig, A., and Sinopoli, B. (2012). Cyber–physical security of a smart grid infrastructure. *Proceedings of the IEEE*, Volume 100, No. 1, pp. 195–209.

[87]Operation Aurora was a vast cyber espionage campaign of Chinese origin carried out against high tech, security, and defense companies in 2010.

[88]Srivastava, A., Morris, T. H., Ernster, T., Vellaithurai, C., Pan, S., and Adhikari, U. (2013). Modeling Cyber-Physical Vulnerability of the Smart Grid With Incomplete Information. *IEEE Trans. Smart Grid*, Volume 4, No. 1, pp. 235–244.

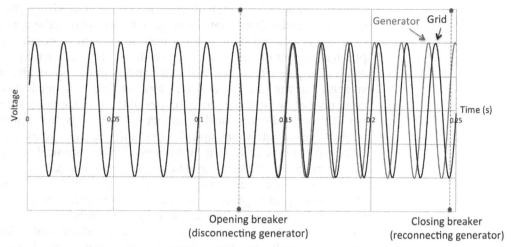

Figure 4.5 Disconnecting and very rapidly reconnecting a power generator to the electric grid before physical protection mechanisms detect that it is out of synchronism.

achieved, there is a system that continuously checks whether their key parameters are sufficiently close within a short period of time and denies connection when they are not. The attack works by intentionally and repeatedly attempting to disconnect the generator, wait for it to slip out of synchronization, and rapidly reconnect it (see Figure 4.5). This causes mechanical and electrical stress that may eventually damage the rotating equipment. Although it continuously monitors for differences, a protective relay does not immediately trigger a protection action when it senses a synchronization fault. It needs to make sure that this is the case. So, it first collects and analyzes a few measurements in succession (perhaps averaging them out) before determining that there is indeed a fault. This delay of a few hundredths or a few tenths of a second is the window of opportunity that an Aurora-like attack needs.[89]

In practice, there are multiple cyber security and safety measures that one needs to circumvent before reaching the stage of being able to remotely control protective relays. Unless an insider, the attacker would need to know which relay to target and how to compromise the network connection to be able to communicate with the relay, and then to identify the password for controlling or programming it (assuming that it has not been left with the

---

[89]Salmon, D., Zeller, M., Guzman, A., Mynam, V., and Donolo, M. (2007). Mitigating the aurora vulnerability with existing technology. *Schweitzer Engineering Laboratories, Inc.*

default password[90]). Even if all these are compromised, any physical safety mechanisms that are in place for protecting the generator from accidental damage may well be enough to counter the physical impact of the attack. As a result, Aurora is generally seen as a cyber-physical attack that can happen under some circumstances, but the likelihood is very low, and like Stuxnet it would certainly not be within the capabilities of the average cyber criminal. Although the practical relevance of Aurora is still unclear, NERC's Aurora advisories and the dramatic footage broadcast by CNN were useful in raising awareness of cyber-physical security threats in the energy sector and industrial control in general.

Sridhar, Hahn, and Govindasaru[91] have identified three elements of power generation that can be targeted by a cyber-physical attack: the automatic voltage generator, which maintains a constant voltage level; the governor control, which maintains a constant speed; and the automatic generation control, which adjusts the frequency over an area of the grid. The first two do not involve communication with any external entity, and as such would be vulnerable only to someone physically connecting to the local area network of the substation and infecting it with malware, perhaps through a USB stick. The third one, though, involves remote communication of optimal operating positions to multiple generating stations in an area. An attacker that would compromise this communication would be able to manipulate the values reported to the stations and consequently the values at which they would operate. Sridhar and Manimaran have provided a mathematical model[92] that estimates what data values an integrity attack should choose in order to evade detection and maximize impact.

The Smart Grid

As one would expect, a system that is as large and complex as the electric grid cannot be particularly flexible. One of its important challenges is to generate enough power to cover demand, but predicting demand is a great challenge by itself. Yet we are all used to instant delivery of electricity whenever we need it, even during times of peak demand. To achieve this and

---

[90]Zeller, M. (2011). Myth or reality – Does the Aurora vulnerability pose a risk to my generator? In the *64th Annual Conference for Protective Relay Engineers, IEEE,* pp. 130–136, April 2011.
[91]Sridhar, S., Hahn, A., and Govindarasu, M. (2012). Cyber–physical system security for the electric power grid. *Proceedings of the IEEE,* Volume 100, No. 1, pp. 210–224.
[92]Sridhar, S. and Manimaran, G. (2010). Data integrity attacks and their impacts on SCADA control system. In *Power and Energy Society General Meeting, IEEE,* pp. 1–6, July 2010.

ensure that there is always enough power, the grid needs to overgenerate it, which is costly both financially and in terms of carbon emissions. Another challenge is that it is difficult to detect outages, and even when these are detected, it is difficult to identify what caused them and, crucially, where. This is where the concept of the smart grid comes in. Gellings has defined it as "the use of sensors, communications, computational ability and control in some form to enhance the overall functionality of the electric power delivery system."[93] The aim is to provide situational awareness so that operators can better respond to changing demands and outages, and more effectively incorporate sources of renewable energy. Wind power, solar power, and most other renewable energy sources generate energy rather intermittently. In this context, the smart grid helps forecast how environmental conditions, such as less wind or more clouds, will affect power generation, and can switch between different sources when needed.[94]

Because the smart grid is a concept rather than a specific standard system, its configuration may differ depending on local needs and regulations. Figure 4.6 shows a fairly representative example configuration, where power is generated from both fossil fuel and renewable sources, and is then transmitted to a substation, from where it is distributed to households, businesses, charging bays for electric vehicles, and so on. In fact, the smart grid allows entities that traditionally have been consumers of electricity to also become generators of electricity. For instance, electric vehicles that are enabled with "vehicle-to-grid" technology may provide their excess rechargeable battery capacity to the grid,[95] when they are parked and connected to it.

Phasor measurement units (PMUs)[96] continuously measure the voltage, current, and frequency at specific locations in the transmission system, to help the operators assess the grid's condition in real time and detect parts that are getting out of synchronization with the rest. The requirement to monitor and control different aspects of the grid remotely and efficiently has

[93]Gellings, C. W. (2009). *The smart grid: enabling energy efficiency and demand response*. The Fairmont Press, Inc.

[94]Kempener, R., Komor, P., and Hoke, A. (2013). Smart Grids and renewables: A guide for effective deployment, IRENA, November 2013.

[95]Fang, X., Misra, S., Xue, G., and Yang, D. (2012). Smart grid – The new and improved power grid: A survey. *Communications Surveys & Tutorials, IEEE*, Volume 14, No. 4, pp. 944–980.

[96]Hart, D. G., Uy, D., Gharpure, V., Novosel, D., Karlsson, D., and Kaba, M. (2001). PMUs – a new approach to power network monitoring. *ABB Review*, Volume 1, pp. 58–61.

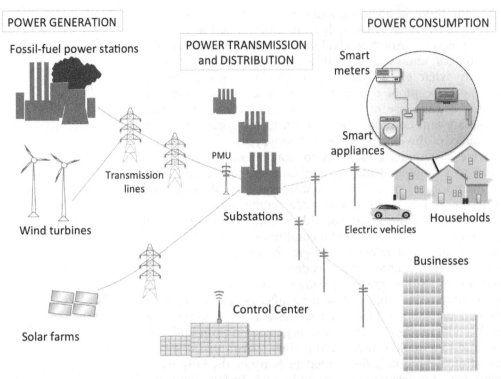

Figure 4.6 Example smart grid architecture with multiple sources of energy, a power transmission and distribution network, and multiple types of electricity consumers. Data collected from across the grid are sent to the system operator's control center (usually not directly, but from collection points where each neighborhood's smart grid data are aggregated). The operator analyzes the data and accordingly adapts the grid's configuration.

made the extensive use of SCADA technologies a key element of the smart grid. So, although we will not repeat them here, the SCADA-related security issues discussed earlier are applicable in the smart grid too.[97]

An integral and arguably defining aspect of the smart grid is the wide adoption of smart meters. These are devices that use sensors to measure a household's energy consumption at near real time and report it to the utility. In doing so, they ensure that the customer is charged for the correct amount of electricity used rather than an estimation, and contribute to a better balance between energy supply and demand. They typically offer bidirectional communication, which means that they are able to both send and receive data. They do so through a variety of communication technologies, such as ZigBee, Z-Wave, power-line

[97]Metke, A. R. and Ekl, R. L. (2010). Security technology for smart grid networks. *Smart Grid, IEEE Transactions on*, Volume 1, No. 1, pp. 99–107.

communication, the Internet, and cellular technologies, each with their own strengths and security vulnerabilities.[98] Smart meters are currently being introduced in massive numbers across many parts of the world with the frontrunner being Italy, where an early type has already been deployed to most customers since 2005. In the United Kingdom and France, the intention is to have smart meters in all homes by the end of 2020. The United States, China, and the rest of the European Union have all set similarly ambitious goals.[99]

One of the widely discussed privacy implications of smart meters reporting fine-grained energy data is that based on them one can infer detailed information about household activities. Molina-Markham et al.[100] have presented such an experiment, where they successfully identified the number of people in a household, as well as their eating and sleeping routines, based only on statistical analysis of energy consumption data collected by smart meters. Taking the concept to rather extreme lengths, Greveler et al.[101] then showed that it is technically possible to even tell what TV channel the occupants are watching, if there are no other appliances consuming significant energy at the same time. This is interesting at a theoretical level only, as the sampling rate required is an unrealistically high one measurement per two seconds; smart meters usually record consumption every 30 minutes. Nevertheless, attacks where fine-grained profiling of the power consumed by a system helps infer confidential information have always been possible[102] (see Chapter 7) and the widespread use of smart meters is gradually making them more likely to occur. It is not difficult to see in the future a technically sophisticated gang of burglars employing them to systematically identify empty properties.

Another class of potential smart meter exploitations that has been discussed widely is false data injection. It involves an

---

[98]Gungor, V. C., Sahin, D., Kocak, T., Ergut, S., Buccella, C., Cecati, C., and Hancke, G. P. (2011). Smart grid technologies: communication technologies and standards. *IEEE transactions on Industrial informatics*, Volume 7, No. 4, pp. 529–539.

[99]Tweed, K. (2014). China pushes past U.S. in Smart Grid spending. *IEEE Spectrum*, February 21, 2014.

[100]Molina-Markham, A., Shenoy, P., Fu, K., Cecchet, E., and Irwin, D. (2010). Private memoirs of a smart meter. In *Proceedings of the 2nd ACM workshop on embedded sensing systems for energy-efficiency in building*, ACM, pp. 61–66, November 2010.

[101]Greveler, U., Justus, B., and Loehr, D. (2012). Multimedia content identification through smart meter power usage profiles. *Computers, Privacy and Data Protection (CDPD)*, Brussels, Belgium, January 25, 2012.

[102]Laughman, C., Lee, K., Cox, R., Shaw, S., Leeb, S., Norford, L., and Armstrong, P. (2003). Power signature analysis. *Power and Energy Magazine*, Volume 1, No. 2, pp. 56–63, IEEE.

attacker gaining control of a number of smart meters and making them report false measurements to the utility's control center. An obvious reason for this would be to reduce the attacker's own energy charges by underreporting energy consumption. A less obvious one would be to financially harm competing businesses by intentionally increasing their electricity bills.

From the perspective of cyber-physical attacks, another sinister reason would be to manipulate the state of the grid. As the smart grid adapts itself based on its knowledge of its own state, which partly depends on the meters' reported data, a large-scale manipulation would potentially knock it off balance. For example, consider the extreme case of all smart meters in a large geographical area reporting energy consumption that is considerably lower than the real one. In response to this, the smart grid would ask power generators to reduce the energy production, but since the real consumption is not reduced, this could lead to a power outage. This is an extreme case, but Liu, Ning, and Reiter have reported[103] that a sophisticated attacker with knowledge of a grid's configuration can launch a coordinated injection of false data that would bypass commonly used bad data detection techniques (techniques deployed by grid operators to detect wrong measurements that are caused by natural errors rather than by malicious attacks) and would change the state of the grid. This attack has generated a lot of interest and has been analyzed and extended by several other research groups. Most notably, Kosut et al.[104] have developed a mathematical model that estimates the number of meters that would have to be compromised for the smart grid to fail to detect the bad data. Surprisingly, this number is relatively low and the degree of coordination required is also modest.[105]

For a grid to be stable it needs all its sections to be synchronized at the same frequency; otherwise it can lead to a blackout. The optimal grid frequency is 60 Hz in the Americas and Asia, and 50 Hz in Europe and most of the rest of the world. When generators or transmission lines fail and there is more demand (power load) than supply (power generation), frequency

[103]Liu, Y., Ning, P., and Reiter, M. K. (2011). False data injection attacks against state estimation in electric power grids. *ACM Transactions on Information and System Security (TISSEC)*, Volume 14, No. 1, p. 13.
[104]Kosut, O., Jia, L., Thomas, R. J., and Tong, L. (2011). Malicious data attacks on the smart grid. *IEEE Transactions on Smart Grid*, Volume 2, No. 4, pp. 645–658.
[105]Giani, A., Bitar, E., Garcia, M., McQueen, M., Khargonekar, P., and Poolla, K. (2011). Smart grid data integrity attacks: characterizations and countermeasures. In *IEEE International Conference on Smart Grid Communications (SmartGridComm)*, IEEE, pp. 232–237.

declines. When supply is more than demand, frequency rises. Slight variations are normal and there are a number of mechanisms in place to ensure that frequency does not deviate too much, but sometimes disturbances are unavoidable. Assuming that it is possible to somehow compromise a number of smart meters across a large geographical area, Costache et al.[106] have suggested that an attacker may order many compromised smart meters to simultaneously turn off their load, wait for the utility to reduce the power, and then turn them all on again at the same time. The result will be a sudden variation in the grid's frequency that may be sufficiently large to cause a blackout.

Nevertheless, it is important to note that large-scale false data injection attacks are anything but straightforward. On the Internet one can find various techniques, devices, and software for bypassing the security of their own smart meters to fraudulently lower their energy bills,[107] for example through optical snooping. Smart meters have optical ports that are used by technicians to connect to them and diagnose problems, but can also be used by attackers to alter their settings. Also, Carpenter et al. have described a methodology for extracting the password and any secret keys by physically tampering with the smart meter[108] and McLaughlin et al. have demonstrated meter spoofing,[109] whereby a laptop computer impersonates a meter and transmits false information to the utility. However, there is no known approach for remotely compromising several of them. Also, for a coordinated data injection attack to have a meaningful physical impact on a target grid, it would require considerable insider information on its configuration. Such information is not publicly available and would require a large, possibly state-sponsored probing campaign, perhaps such as the one alleged to have been conducted by Russian and Chinese cyberspies on the US grid.[110]

Crucially, a smart meter allows two-way communication. Not only does it transmit data, but it also receives data, such as

---

[106]Costache, M., Tudor, V., Almgren, M., Papatriantafilou, M., and Saunders, C. (2011). Remote control of smart meters: friend or foe? In *Seventh European Conference on Computer Network Defense (EC2ND)*, IEEE, pp. 49–56, September 2011.

[107]Krebs, B. (2012). FBI: Smart meter hacks likely to spread. krebsonsecurity.com, April 9, 2012.

[108]Carpenter, M., Goodspeed, T., Singletary, B., Skoudis, E., and Wright, J. (2009). Advanced metering infrastructure attack methodology. *InGuardians white paper*.

[109]McLaughlin, S., Podkuiko, D., and McDaniel, P. (2010). Energy theft in the advanced metering infrastructure. In *Critical Information Infrastructures Security*, Springer Berlin Heidelberg, pp. 176–187.

[110]Gorman, S. (2009). *Electricity Grid in U.S. penetrated by spies*. Wall Street Journal, April 4, 2009.

current energy prices, from the utility as part of what is called demand response.[111] This involves altering a customer's energy usage in response to changing supply conditions. In essence, demand response aims to help the grid cope with demand during peak times,[112] for example by offering financial incentives to customers who voluntarily cut down their consumption, in what is known as demand bidding or buyback program.[113] Demand response can be as low-tech as calling plant managers one by one to ask them to turn down factory lines, but the aim is to make it fully automated, for example with the Open Automated Demand Response (OpenADR) standard[114] being adopted in North America. The intention is for the utility's systems to be able to communicate with the end users' building or industrial control systems and automatically cut off electrical supply based on prior agreements. However, the more automated the process, the more vulnerable it is to malicious attacks. As each nation state and often each utility may implement demand response differently, it is still difficult for security experts to authoritatively analyze related threats and detail how they can be realized in practice. A scenario that is commonly discussed is that an insider or a sophisticated adversary, such as an enemy state or terrorist organization, may attempt to compromise the control centers that receive information from smart meters and enforce targeted power cuts. This is not to say that utilities or departments of energy are unaware of security risks and are not investing in security measures. Indeed, there has been considerable progress over the last few years.[115] However, even the most secure organizations have been shown to be vulnerable to social engineering attacks, malware infections, and zero-day attacks. This is significant because an adversary managing to compromise a center that controls demand response would be able to cut off electrical supply on a grand scale.[116] In

[111]U.S. Department of Energy (2010). Communications Requirements of Smart Grid technologies.
[112]Conejo, A. J., Morales, J. M., and Baringo, L. (2010). Real-time demand response model. *IEEE Transactions on Smart Grid*, Volume 1, No. 3, pp. 236–242.
[113]Albadi, M. H. and El-Saadany, E. F. (2007). Demand response in electricity markets: An overview. In *IEEE Power Engineering Society General Meeting*, Volume 2007, pp. 1–5.
[114]Holmberg, D. G., Ghatikar, G., Koch, E. L., and Boch, J. (2012). OpenADR Advances. *ASHRAE Journal*, Volume 54, No. 11.
[115]Government Accountability Office (2011). *Electricity Grid Modernization – Progress being made on cybersecurity guidelines, but key challenges remain to be addressed (GAO-11-117)*. Washington, DC, USA.
[116]Anderson, R. and Fuloria, S. (2010). Who controls the off switch? In *First IEEE International Conference on Smart Grid Communications (SmartGridComm)*, IEEE, pp. 96–101, October 2010.

the past, this would have been possible only via a physical attack, such as the sniper attack that in April 2013 methodically knocked out 17 transformers providing electricity to Silicon Valley.[117] Automated demand response has made a cyber-physical attack a possibility too. It might require deep knowledge of the target grid's configuration, a number of zero-day vulnerabilities, possibly social engineering, and a combination of innovative malware techniques, but, after Stuxnet, this possibility no longer seems far-fetched. It is difficult to exaggerate the impact that switching off a nation's electricity would have.

While smart meters collect measurements from the side of consumption, PMUs collect measurements from the side of transmission, which they report wirelessly to phasor data concentrators (PDCs) found in substations. The PDCs are computers that aggregate data from PMUs, check their quality, and forward them to control centers where they can be analyzed by advanced software. As PMUs and PDCs provide vital information on the health of the grid, the security of their communications is considered particularly important.[118] A jamming or other availability attack[119] that would congest the communication network would deny the grid from this information or delay its delivery enough to lead to decisions taken based on information that is out of date.[120] Such an attack would be particularly damaging if it coincided with a natural physical event leading to overloading of the grid. This is not only because the human operators would be unaware of the event and would delay taking action to avert a blackout. Network delays can directly affect the stability of a power system. This theme has been explored by a number of researchers and for several different elements of the electric grid. As an example, let us consider the static VAR compensator (SVC), effectively a cyber-physical system for regulating transmission voltage. A SVC controller receives voltage measurements from a

[117]Smith, R. (2014). Assault on California Power Station Raises Alarm on Potential for Terrorism. The Wall Street Journal, February 5, 2014.
[118]Stewart, J., Maufer, T., Smith, R., Anderson, C., and Ersonmez, E. (2010). Synchrophasor Security Practices. Schweitzer Engineering Laboratories, Pullman, Washington.
[119]Morris, T., Pan, S., Lewis, J., Moorhead, J., Reaves, B., Younan, N., King, R., Freund, M., and Madani, V. (2011). Cybersecurity testing of substation phasor measurement units and phasor data concentrators. In *The 7th Annual ACM Cyber Security and Information Intelligence Research Workshop (CSIIRW)*, October 2011.
[120]Qiu, M., Su, H., Chen, M., Ming, Z., and Yang, L. T. (2012). Balance of security strength and energy for a PMU monitoring system in smart grid. *Communications Magazine*, IEEE, Volume 50, No. 5, pp. 142–149.

network of distributed sensors and instructs actuators (thyristor controlled reactors, thyristor switched capacitors, etc.) to alter the voltage. Chen et al.[121] have shown that when a denial of service or man-in-the-middle attack adding a fixed delay on the network packets from the sensors to the SVC controllers coincides with a large-scale physical disturbance, it is considerably more difficult for the power system to regain a stable state of operation.

In general, communication delay is more important in the smart grid than in most other industrial control system environments,[122] and for this reason the Institute of Electrical and Electronics Engineers (IEEE) has specified strict requirements for its upper bound.[123] Messages relating to protection actions, such as opening a circuit breaker to prevent damage from high voltage, need to be received in less than 4 ms if received internally within a substation, or 12 ms if received from outside the substation. The International Electrotechnical Commission (IEC) has also published similar requirements.[124]

In order to ensure that measurements of the state of the grid (e.g., voltage and frequency) taken at different locations can be comparable, all PMUs and any other grid devices collecting measurements are synchronized based on GPS (see Box 3.1 in Chapter 3). In practice, GPS allows timestamping each measurement transmitted through the grid's communication network with the precise date and time that it was taken.[125] However, this reliance on GPS introduces GPS-related threats to the smart grid, with the primary concern being the possibility of a GPS spoofing attack. Researchers from the University of Texas and Northrop Grumman Information Systems have demonstrated such an attack using their own custom-made Civil GPS spoofer device to remotely change the time reference used by a

---

[121]Chen, B., Butler-Purry, K. L., Nuthalapati, S., and Kundur, D. (2014). Network delay caused by cyber attacks on SVC and its impact on transient stability of smart grids. In *PES General Meeting, Conference and Exposition*, IEEE, July 2014.

[122]Wang, W., Xu, Y., and Khanna, M. (2011). A survey on the communication architectures in smart grid. *Computer Networks*, Volume 55, No. 15, pp. 3604–3629.

[123]IEEE (2005). IEEE Std. 1646-2004. IEEE Standard Communication Delivery Time Performance Requirements for Electric Power Substation Automation, pp. 1–24.

[124]IEC (2003). IEC 61850-5. Communication networks and systems in substations – Part 5: Communication requirements for functions and device models.

[125]Martin, K. E., Benmouyal, G., Adamiak, M. G., Begovic, M., Burnett Jr, R. O., Carr, K. R., Cobb, A., Kusters, J. A., Horowitz, S. H., Jensen, G. R., Michel, G. L., Murphy, R. J., Phadke, A. G., Sachdev, M. S., and Thorp, J. S. (1998). IEEE standard for synchrophasors for power systems. *IEEE Transactions on Power Delivery*, Volume 13, No. 1, pp. 73–77.

real PMU[126] (the same team had used a slightly different GPS spoofer to take control of a small UAV, as discussed in Chapter 3). The impact of such an attack can be severe if the smart grid includes some form of automated remedial action based on PMU measurements. For example, measurements that would indicate that supply needs to be reduced could trigger the automated disconnection of a generator from the grid. If the measurements were inaccurate due to wrong timing information, then the resulting (but unneeded) remedial action could knock the grid off balance by putting it in a state of lower supply (fewer generators working) than demand. Akkaya et al.[127] and Zhang et al.[128] have also shown that GPS spoofing can lead to missed or delayed detection of disturbances in the grid and can deteriorate its ability to identify the physical locations of faults, since these are also estimated based on the time they occurred.

In summary, an attacker could attempt the following:
- Attempt to exploit the Aurora vulnerability and damage a generator, potentially causing cascading overload effects in the grid.
- Infer information about occupants and activities in a household by analyzing the power consumption data collected by smart meters.
- Inject false data on a large number of smart meters, so as to affect the operation of the smart grid and potentially the generation of electricity.
- Manipulate demand response to cut off electrical supply to consumers.
- Carry out a jamming or availability attack on the communication network so as to disrupt the sharing of PMU measurements.
- Introduce network delays during a time of large-scale physical disturbance, so as to impede the power system's ability to regain stability.
- Carry out a GPS spoofing or meaconing attack to affect the synchronization of PMU measurements and reduce the grid's ability to detect and respond to faults.

[126]Shepard, D. P., Humphreys, T. E., and Fansler, A. A. (2012). Evaluation of the vulnerability of phasor measurement units to GPS spoofing attacks. *International Journal of Critical Infrastructure Protection*, Elsevier, Volume 5, No. 3, pp. 146–153.
[127]Akkaya, I., Lee, E. A., and Derler, P. (2013). Model-based evaluation of GPS spoofing attacks on power grid sensors. In *Workshop on Modeling and Simulation of Cyber-Physical Energy Systems (MSCPES)*, IEEE, pp. 1–6, May 2013.
[128]Zhang, Z., Gong, S., Dimitrovski, A. D., and Li, H. (2013). Time synchronization attack in smart grid: Impact and analysis. *IEEE Transactions on Smart Grid*, Volume 4, No. 1, pp. 87–98.

Summary

Although computer-based SCADA systems have been used widely for the remote monitoring and control of equipment since the 1960s, it is only in recent years that their cyber threats have attracted considerable attention. Researchers tend to focus on the particular vulnerabilities introduced by Modbus, DNP3, and other industrial control communication protocols, most of which were originally designed for simplicity and efficiency rather than security. Yet, in practice, the vulnerabilities that are most commonly exploited have little to do with the particular protocols and are largely the same as in conventional computer systems, ranging from software flaws to poor password practices. The difference is in the impact of exploiting them, because a security breach can directly affect public safety. Also, securing a SCADA system can be very challenging due to its strict real-time nature, the requirement for continuous availability, a misguided perception that legacy SCADA technologies are inherently secure merely by being obscure, increasing use of COTS components, and interconnectivity with other networks, such as corporate networks and even the Internet.

The most significant of real-world incidents involving industrial control systems was the Stuxnet attack against a uranium enrichment facility in Natanz, Iran. An example of exceptionally advanced malware aiming primarily at causing physical damage, Stuxnet targeted particular types of PLCs controlling different aspects of the uranium enrichment process. An early variant of Stuxnet, designed to stop operating in 2009, targeted safety valves; the variant that is the best known aimed to damage centrifuges by manipulating the speed of rotation. Stuxnet used stolen digital certificates, four zero-day vulnerabilities, and a variety of innovative techniques to manage to find its way into the facility's air-gapped network of PLCs. The scale of the impact of the attack is unclear, but the impact on strategic thinking, attack trends, and people's awareness of the potential of cyber-physical attacks has been profound.

With almost every aspect of life in a modern society depending on the generation, transmission, and distribution of electrical energy, the electric grid is the area of application of industrial control systems where cyber attacks are feared the most. An early example of a staged attack in this area was the Aurora Generator Test, where a generator was damaged by repeatedly disconnecting it and reconnecting it out of synchronization. Moreover, the advent of the smart grid is bringing with it several new threats. The fine-grained data on individual households' energy utilization collected by smart meters can help infer number of occupants, sleeping patterns, and so on. Beyond confidentiality concerns, integrity and availability are also very important. The automated nature of the smart grid, where supply is influenced by the energy consumption data reported by smart meters in near real time, makes false data injection attacks particularly harmful. Availability attacks disrupting communications and increasing delays, as well as GPS attacks affecting time synchronization have also been shown to be able to impede the grid's ability to detect and cope with physical disturbances.

Follow-Up Questions and Exercises

1. Originally designed for the electric utility industry, DNP3 is now also used widely in the water, transportation, oil, and gas industries. Which of the following statements is correct?
    a. In DNP3 terminology, a RTU can be a submaster or an outstation depending on the configuration of the system.
    b. Unlike the older Modbus protocol, DNP3 was designed with an emphasis on security from the beginning.
    c. DNP3 Secure Authentication was introduced to guarantee the confidentiality and availability of control operations.
2. Provide a brief description of the challenge-response mechanism specified in DNP3 Secure Authentication.
3. In most cases, relying on security by obscurity is considered a mistake. Provide two reasons why this is the case for SCADA systems.
4. Which of the following statements are correct?
    a. As a highly targeted piece of malware, Stuxnet propagated only to machines connected to the network of a nuclear facility at Natanz, Iran.
    b. Stuxnet made use of four zero-day vulnerabilities. This was an indication that it could not have been the product of the average cyber criminal.
    c. Stuxnet had a predecessor, often referred to as Stuxnet 0.5, that was less covert, which is why it was abandoned by its developers.
    d. Although Stuxnet aimed to cause excessive vibration by changing the speed of rotation, Stuxnet 0.5 aimed to cause excessive pressure by manipulating related valves.
5. Utility meters are far from new; they have existed since the commercial exploitation of electricity took off in the late nineteenth century. Bypassing and manipulation of energy

meters to avoid paying for electricity has also been going on since at least the 1930s.[129] Why are the newest types of meters characterized as smart meters and why are they seen as particularly attractive targets for misuse, especially from cyber attackers?

6. In what manner could a GPS spoofing, meaconing, or jamming attack affect the operation of the electric grid?

---

[129]Mitchell, E. A. (1938). *Electricity theft prevention device*, U.S. Patent No. 2,117,565, U.S. Patent and Trademark Office, Washington, DC.

5

CYBER-PHYSICAL ATTACK STEPS

Chapter Summary

Successfully performing a meaningful cyber-physical attack requires research, reconnaissance, and an ability to discover exploitable vulnerabilities and appropriate entry points, in the process ensuring to hide one's traces and evade detection. In this chapter, we provide examples for each stage of the attack process, with a particular emphasis on the identification of entry points for different cyber-physical systems, as well as a glossary of common attack techniques.

Key Terms: Research; reconnaissance; vulnerability discovery; intrusion; attack delivery; antiforensics; cyber-physical attack entry points

Cyber-physical security threats exhibit similarities even across very different platforms. In all, the attacker aims to identify entry points from where it is possible to directly communicate with actuators and sensors or indirectly affect their operation by manipulating their control and communication infrastructure. In most cases, the discovery and exploitation of relevant vulnerabilities requires considerable research and planning. Here, we discuss the general steps followed by an adversary, including an abstract representation of the potential entry points of cyber-physical attacks. Where appropriate, we match each attack mechanism with the corresponding countermeasures discussed in Chapter 6.

Preliminary Research and Reconnaissance

A preliminary step where the adversary selects a target and tries to learn useful information about it. This may include IP addresses, the topology of its network infrastructure, types and versions of software and hardware used, and so on. It usually starts with an Internet search for any information on the target that is publicly available.

Internet Research

Often underestimated, it is surprising how much intelligence one can gather about a target through a mere Google search.

Equipment used in an organization's cyber-physical systems can be identified on the web site of one of the likely suppliers (as a business success of the latter). Job adverts can reveal the software, hardware, and network technologies used by listing the desired skills and experience expected of applicants. Also useful to an attacker is the fact that most manufacturers publish installation instructions on their web site. It is common for such material to include default usernames and passwords, which often remain unchanged by operators. This is particularly true for home automation devices.

For large-scale cyber-physical systems, such as those used in critical infrastructures, anyone can identify his or her precise geographical location using Google Maps, Google Earth, Yahoo! Maps, and many other free satellite imagery programs and search engines. This can help choose a target that can maximize the knock-on effects on the environment and nearby communities.

The Internet can also be used to locate and purchase an example of a particular cyber-physical system, so as to experiment with it and identify ways to breach its security. Mowery et al. have argued that it would not have been possible for them to devise effective cyber-physical attacks against a particular type of full-body scanner if they had not purchased and reverse-engineered one found on eBay.[1] Experimentation with the particular device was necessary to fine-tune the details of their attacks. In their words, "keeping the machine out of the hands of would-be attackers may well be an effective strategy for preventing reliable exploitation, even if the details of the machine's operation were disclosed."[2]

Social Engineering

Primary target: Any cyber-physical system operated by human users or connected to a corporate network

Description: Social engineering is a prevalent mechanism for reconnaissance of cyber-physical systems and especially industrial control systems. In fact, it can be assumed that prior to a high-impact cyber-physical attack, a determined adversary has at least attempted first a social engineering attack. That is because even the strongest technical security protections can be bypassed if a system's legitimate user is manipulated into

[1]At the time of writing (December 2014), two government surplus full-body scanners of the same model could be found on eBay at $7,995 each.
[2]Mowery, K., Wustrow, E., Wypych, T., Singleton, C., Comfort, C., Rescorla, E., Checkoway, S., Halderman, J. A., and Shacham, H. (2014). Security analysis of a full-body scanner. In *23rd USENIX Security Symposium*, August 20–22, 2014, San Diego, CA.

divulging a password or clicking a link to malicious web site. As Kevin Mitnick, possibly the world's best-known hacker, has pointed out, "the human side of computer security is easily exploited and constantly overlooked. Companies spend millions of dollars on firewalls, encryption and secure access devices, and it's money wasted, because none of these measures address the weakest link in the security chain."[3]

Social engineering can be nontechnical. It can start with "dumpster diving,"[4] a fake ID, or a simple phone call, impersonating a colleague, an authority figure, or a representative from a software supplier's support department.[5] In recent years, it has become increasingly technical (sometimes referred to as semantic attack[6]) and usually involves exploiting a human-computer interface. The adversary may first try to find information about a SCADA system's engineer[7] through her social network profile and then send her an e-mail. The e-mail may be crafted to look like it comes from the finance department and may contain an attachment whose file name and extension resemble that of a legitimate financial spreadsheet, but it is in fact malware. It may be programmed to log the engineer's keystrokes or perhaps allow unauthorized remote access to the SCADA system. This type of attack is known as **phishing** when it has no specific target, **spear-phishing** when it does, and **whaling** when the targeted individual is a senior executive of an organization. Spear-phishing has proven exceptionally effective against even the most security-aware individuals. Famously, the personal computer of Professor Jean-Jacques Quisquater, a superstar in the area of cryptography with several computer security patents in his name, is believed to have been infected with an advanced

---

[3]Poulsen, K. (2000). Mitnick to lawmakers: People, phones and weakest links. *SecurityFocus*, March 2000.

[4]Dumpster diving is the act of rummaging through an organization's or individual's trash looking for bank statements, USB sticks, project proposal drafts, letters, and other material that can reveal sensitive information. An extreme form of dumpster diving is to purchase an organization's discarded photocopiers so as to get hold of their internal hard drives. These are often not wiped by their owners even though they contain years' worth of scanned documents.

[5]ICS-CERT (2012). *ICS-CERT Monitor*, March 2012.

[6]Schneier, B. (2000). Inside risks: semantic network attacks. *Communications of the ACM*, Volume 43, No. 12.

[7]Names and e-mails of an organization's employees can be found in newsletters, listings of awards, related trade magazine articles, etc. Their age, address, hobbies, professional background, and other more specific details can be found on people finder web sites and social networks.

piece of malware (probably Regin[8]) after clicking a spoofed LinkedIn invitation from a nonexistent employee of the European Patent Office.

Cyber impact: Unauthorized acquisition of critical information, including login/password credentials, as well as delivery of malware that will facilitate next steps

Physical impact: No immediate impact

Complexity: Low to moderate

Defense: Antimalware, as well as awareness training can help but may not be sufficient.

Watering Hole

Primary target: Any cyber-physical system operated by human users or connected to a corporate network

Description: In spirit similar to spear-phishing, a watering hole is an attack strategy where the attacker observes or guesses what web site a particular target (an individual or group) visits frequently and then implants malware on that web site. Since 2012 when it was first discovered, the watering hole attack has emerged as a considerable threat to critical national infrastructure, and especially the energy sector.[9]

Cyber impact: Unauthorized acquisition of critical information, including login/password credentials, as well as delivery of malware that will facilitate next steps

Physical impact: No immediate impact

Complexity: Moderate

Defense: Antimalware, as well as awareness training can help but may not be sufficient.

Vulnerability Discovery

After gaining some preliminary information about the target, the adversary tries to expand on this information by scanning for specific vulnerabilities. Three of the most popular tools for network scanning are Nmap,[10] Nessus,[11] and Wireshark.[12] Collectively, they can determine the operating system running

---

[8]Kaspersky Lab (2014). The Regin platform: Nation-state ownage of GSM networks. Kaspersky Lab report, November 24, 2014.

[9]Wueest, C. (2014). Targeted attacks against the energy sector. *Symantec Security Response*, Mountain View, CA.

[10]http://nmap.org

[11]http://www.tenable.com/products/nessus

[12]http://www.wireshark.org

on the target, eavesdrop on network traffic, and scan for open network ports, misconfigurations, default passwords, and the like. Note though that many of these automated tools are easy to detect due to the suspicious network traffic that they generate when probing a system. We have also already mentioned Shodan[13] (Chapter 2), which is a tool that has proven particularly useful in attacks against Internet-connected cyber-physical systems. It provides the results of port scanning that it has previously conducted at a global scale. It does so in the same manner as a conventional search engine, but its emphasis is on devices that are connected to the Internet, including cameras, smart appliances, industrial control systems, and more.

In fact, even conventional search engines can be employed to identify vulnerable devices by using their advanced search operators, such as Google's 'inurl:' and 'intitle:'. Known as Google hacking,[14] this approach is not particularly useful against specific or well-protected targets, but can be surprisingly effective at identifying targets of opportunity on the Internet, such as vulnerable IP cameras. It is all too common to read in the news about web sites aggregating live feeds from thousands of private webcams, security cameras, and baby monitor devices that their owners have left to their default passwords.[15]

Intrusion

In several cases, it is relatively easy for an unauthorized user to gain access to a system or network. An ex-employee may be using an old password for a wireless router or a remote maintenance login account that was never disabled by the administrators. Through research and reconnaissance, an attacker may get hold of authentication credentials, such as the default password found in a device's documentation or employee's password for example. A successful spear-phishing or watering hole campaign may lead to backdoor malware finding its way into an employee's computer.

Through vulnerability scanning, the attacker may have become aware of potential vulnerabilities of the targeted system. Unlike conventional computer systems, where published vulnerabilities are addressed with regular updates, vulnerabilities in industrial control systems and embedded systems may remain

[13]http://www.shodanhq.com
[14]Long, J. (2011). *Google hacking for penetration testers: 2*, Syngress.
[15]Kelion, L. (2014). Breached webcam and baby monitor site flagged by watchdogs. BBC News, November 21, 2014.

unpatched for long periods of time. How often would one update the software of their IP camera, fridge, or car? The same holds for traffic lights, RTUs, and other systems used in critical infrastructures. Basic Internet research is often enough to identify walkthrough guides and YouTube videos describing how to exploit a particular vulnerability and gain unauthorized access to a system or network. In some cases, the process can be simplified with user-friendly tools, such as Gleg SCADA+ and the open-source Metasploit Framework.[16]

In order to identify what to protect, it is helpful to have an understanding of an adversary's potential entry points. For this, one can construct a diagram showing the interactions and connections between control, communication, sensing, and actuation elements. See Figure 5.1 for the abstract and generic cyber-physical system architecture that we will use in our examples. The six potential cyberspace entry points in this

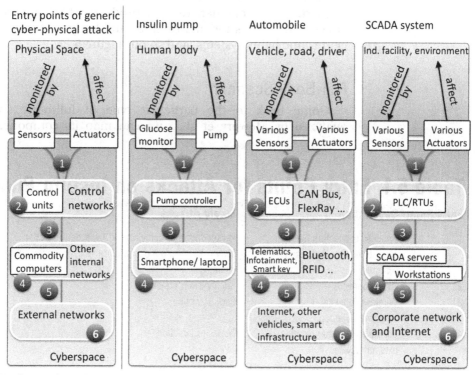

Figure 5.1 Entry points of a generic cyber-physical attack, including examples for an insulin pump, an automobile, and a SCADA system.

[16]www.metasploit.com

architecture are (1) the communication channels for collection of sensor data and control of actuators; (2) the control network, including the individual control units such as ECUs, PLCs, RTUs, and such; (3) the communication channel or gateway between the control network and any secondary internal network included in the cyber-physical system; (4) secondary internal networks and their nodes (usually general-purpose computers); (5) the communication channel between internal and external networks; and (6) external networks, including the Internet and other cyber-physical systems.

In Chapters 3 and 4, we discussed the potential attacks for insulin pumps, automobiles, and SCADA systems in detail. In Tables 5.1–5.3 we can try to map these attacks to the abstract diagram for the generic cyber-physical attack of Figure 5.1, omitting components that cannot be realistically exploited and attacks that are highly impractical or not meaningful. Attacks that are common across multiple domains are listed here only by name and are described in more detail later.

In the same manner, we can produce tables for potential attack entry points for smart homes, full-body scanners, intelligent traffic lights systems, and so on (Figure 5.2).

Full-Body Scanner

Going back to the particular type of full-body scanner analyzed by Mowery et al.,[17] we can map its components as

Table 5.1 Entry Points for Attacks on Insulin Pumps

Entry Point	Description	Likely Attacks
1	Wireless connection between glucose monitor and pump controller	Packet sniffing, replay attack, false data injection, command injection, denial of service, communication jamming
2	Pump controller	Supply chain attack
3	Wireless connection to smartphone/laptop	Packet sniffing
4	Smartphone/laptop or other external device	Malware infection

[17]Mowery, K., Wustrow, E., Wypych, T., Singleton, C., Comfort, C., Rescorla, E., Checkoway, S., Halderman, J. A., and Shacham, H. (2014). Security analysis of a full-body scanner. In *23rd USENIX Security Symposium*, August 20–22, 2014, San Diego, CA.

Table 5.2 Entry Points for Attacks on Automobiles

Entry Point	Description	Likely Attacks
1	Wireless connection between sensors and ECUs (example: TPMS)	False data injection, packet sniffing
2	The in-vehicle network of ECUs (CAN Bus, FlexRay, etc.)	Command injection, false data injection, fuzzing, supply chain attack, firmware modification, replay attack, denial of service, rogue node
3	Communication between in-vehicle network of ECUs and other internal networks for telematics, infotainment, smart key, etc.	Relay attack, command injection, false data injection
4	Telematics, infotainment, smart key, and other add-on technologies	Malware infection (e.g., malicious MP3 file), supply chain attack
5	External communications (RDS-TMC, GPRS, 3G, 4G LTE, V2V, V2I)	False data injection, packet sniffing, communication jamming
6	Internet, smart infrastructure, and other vehicles	Web-based attacks (malware, SQL injection, etc.) affecting web-based immobilization

Table 5.3 Entry Points for Attacks on SCADA Systems

Entry Point	Description	Likely Attacks
1	Radio communication between RTUs/PLCs and sensors/actuators	Communication jamming, command injection, false data injection, communication jamming
2	RTUs/PLCs and communication with SCADA servers	Code injection/firmware modification, malware infection, denial of service, jamming, replay attack, command injection, false data injection, black hole/gray hole, network isolation, rogue node
3	Control network, including SCADA servers and engineers' workstations	Malware infection, denial of service, man-in-the-middle
4	Communication gateway/link between control and corporate network (e.g., connection between primary and secondary historian)	Denial of service, false data injection (database-based)
5	Corporate network	Malware infection, social engineering
6	Internet and networks of partners	Web-based attacks (malware, SQL injection, etc.), social engineering

Full-body scanner

Body, environment

X-Ray backscatter detectors | X-Ray Tube

System Control Board ②

③

User Console

④

Cyberspace

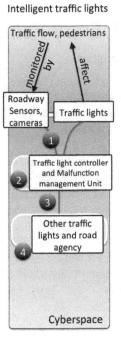

Intelligent traffic lights

Traffic flow, pedestrians

Roadway Sensors, cameras | Traffic lights

①

Traffic light controller and Malfunction management Unit ②

③

Other traffic lights and road agency

④

Cyberspace

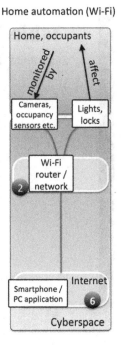

Home automation (Wi-Fi)

Home, occupants

Cameras, occupancy sensors etc. | Lights, locks

Wi-Fi router / network ②

Smartphone / PC application | Internet ⑥

Cyberspace

Figure 5.2 Entry points of potential cyber-physical attacks in the case of a full-body scanner, an intelligent traffic light system, and a smart home.

Table 5.4 Entry Points for Attacks on Full-Body Scanner

Entry Point	Description	Likely Attacks
1	System control board	Physically swap chip with a maliciously modified one
2	Serial cable	Command injection, code injection
3	User console	Malware infection

follows (Table 5.4). We can consider the X-ray tube and the mobile platform on which it is mounted as the actuation subsystem, since this is what generates the X-rays. The sensing subsystem is a set of sensors of different types that collectively allow the scanner to produce an image based on the backscatter radiation. Scanning is controlled by the system control board, an embedded computer that receives simple commands (scan up, scan down, etc.) from a user console through a serial RS-232 cable. The user console is a conventional PC running the MS-DOS operating system, including a keyboard and a screen.

From the perspective of a cyber-physical adversary, this is the most accessible entry point, since an insider or a person who temporarily gains access to the PC can infect it with malware. Mowery et al. demonstrated this with a malicious clone of the legitimate software that could save and help exfiltrate scanned images (affecting physical privacy) or replace real scans with a fake image.

A second entry point is the communication between the user console and the system control board. Without any security mechanism in place, an adversary can inject commands through the serial cable. The researchers tried to inject code so as to modify the system control board's firmware remotely, but they did not find any error to exploit in the particular scanner's code. They were able to introduce modified firmware only by physically replacing the chip with one already modified by them (third entry point). A potential modification allowed by the firmware would be to deliver an elevated radiation dosage at a specific spot on the body.

Intelligent Traffic Lights

Here, we will refer to the particular network traffic signal system analyzed by Ghena et al. of the University of Michigan in 2014 (Chapter 2, T7).[18] The two sensors of the system are an induction loop buried in the roadway and a wireless camera. The former is used only to detect cars, while the latter can be used both to detect cars and to transmit live images to the road agency. Actuation relates to the actual operation of the lights for cars or pedestrians (green, orange, red). Control of sensing and actuation is performed by an embedded traffic light controller, and there is also a malfunction management unit that ensures that no invalid state can occur (e.g., green lights in all directions). All traffic lights are connected over a single private network using two proprietary wireless communication protocols, a high-speed one at 5.8 GHz and a low-speed one at 900 MHz, where there is no line-of-sight connection. For both, connections are unencrypted and use the default usernames and passwords. In practice, the only protection against a command injection attack from a rogue wireless device is that the particular model is normally not sold to the public.

---

[18]Ghena, B., Beyer, W., Hillaker, A., Pevarnek, J., and Halderman, J. A. (2014). Green Lights Forever: Analyzing the Security of Traffic Infrastructure. In Proceedings of *the 8th USENIX Workshop on Offensive Technologies*, August 2014.

The traffic light controller is based on a well-known real-time operating system (VxWorks). The researchers found two ways for accessing it: A network port left open for debugging, through which they were able to inject code, stop processes, and reboot the controller, and a remote control functionality that was designed for operators to remotely configure the controller but did not feature any authentication measure, encryption, or protection against replay attacks. Table 5.5 contains the main attacks that are possible by exploiting these vulnerabilities. There is also the possibility of infecting with malware (perhaps through spear-phishing) the corporate network of the road agency, so as to breach physical privacy or affect the operation of the traffic lights remotely from there.

Home Automation

By home automation, we refer to the practice of adding network capabilities to home appliances, lights, thermostats, plugs, garage doors, security cameras, and other devices, so as to be able to control them remotely. Communication can be based on network protocols developed specifically for home and building automation, such as X-10, ZigBee, Z-Wave, and KNX, or on technologies already existing in a home environment, such as Bluetooth and Wi-Fi. For the sake of simplicity, let us pick the latter for this example and consider Wi-Fi-enabled light bulbs, smart locks, and a camera that are connected to the home's existing Wi-Fi router (Table 5.6).

For reasons of convenience, it is common for home automation devices to be accessible over the Internet, typically using a

Table 5.5 Entry Points for Attacks on Intelligent Traffic Lights

Entry Point	Description	Likely Attacks
1	Network connection between sensors and traffic light controller	False data injection, command injection
2	Traffic light controller and malfunction management unit	Code injection/firmware modification, command injection
3	Traffic light private network	Fuzzing, command injection, code injection, replay attack, communication jamming
4	Road agency corporate network	Malware infection

password-protected web interface or smartphone app. However, a poor password or a particular vulnerability in the authentication process can allow intruders to access any information collected by sensors and, if the web interface or app allows, also control its actuators. Note that actuation features can also be found on devices that are primarily used for sensing and vice versa. For instance, a baby monitor device may feature two-way communication, allowing not only the reception of a live image and audio from inside a nursery room, but also the ability to swivel the camera and talk to a baby through an onboard speaker.[19] A smart TV not only displays an image, but also records information through a microphone and a front-mounted camera. A maliciously modified smart TV can be instructed to record audio and image from one's living room and forward it to an adversary, even when the TV appears to be switched off.[20]

The central point of failure of a Wi-Fi-based home automation setup is the Wi-Fi router. This is significant because a wireless router is by nature accessible remotely, and it is not particularly complex for an adversary in the vicinity to crack its password using automated tools like Aircrack-ng. In the past, the usual motivation was to get free Internet access from neighbors, and less frequently to eavesdrop on their communications. With so many physical devices now relying on secure Wi-Fi, the motivation may easily be to take control of them and adversely affect physical space. For instance, if already on the Wi-Fi network, an adversary can launch a denial of service attack to stop network traffic coming from a security camera, effectively freezing the image that the owner sees.

Table 5.6 Entry Points for Attacks on a Smart Home

Entry Point	Description	Likely Attacks
2	Wi-Fi network and Wi-Fi router	Password cracking for Wi-Fi router, packet sniffing, denial of service, rogue node, communication jamming
6	Smartphone or PC application for Internet-based control	Password cracking for smartphone or PC application, malware on smartphone or PC

[19]Abramson, A. (2013). Baby monitor hacking alarms Houston parents. ABC News, August 13, 2013.
[20]Lee, S. and Kim, S. (2013). Hacking, Surveilling, and Deceiving Victims on Smart TV. Black Hat, July 2013.

Attack Delivery

After intrusion comes attack delivery. The following are some of the methods commonly employed in cyber-physical attacks. They are presented in alphabetical order so that this section can also be used as a reference.

Black Hole/Gray Hole

Primary target: The smart grid

Description: Rather than flooding the network with large volumes of traffic, an adversary can affect data availability by compromising a network node and simply dropping any network packets travelling through it. If the attack drops all packets, it is known as black hole attack. In many cases, it may be preferable to drop packets selectively rather than all of them, perhaps to evade detection. This is known as gray hole attack. For example, consider a SCADA network running the DNP3 protocol. As discussed in Chapter 4, DNP3 communication can include periodic polling or report by exception messages. As the latter are unsolicited messages that the master does not anticipate at specific times, a gray hole attack dropping only them would be difficult to detect.[21]

Cyber impact: Breach of network system integrity at compromised nodes and loss of network availability.

Physical impact: Similar to denial of service attack. Delayed or altogether prevented actuation due to disrupted communication of instructions to actuators or of data collected from sensors. Again, delays in the communication with sensors can also indirectly cause incorrect actuation, because it will be based on old sensor data.

Complexity: Moderate

Defense: Authentication mechanisms, intrusion detection systems, network redundancy with diversity

Code Injection

Primary target: Cyber-physical systems that rely on general-purpose computers and databases, as well as embedded systems running poorly designed software

---

[21]Torrisi, N. M., Vukovic, O., Dán, G. and Hagdahl, S. (2014). Peekaboo: A Gray Hole Attack on Encrypted SCADA Communication using Traffic Analysis. In *5th IEEE International Conference on Smart Grid Communications*, Venice, Italy.

Description: The adversary extends the intended operation of a computer program by introducing additional instructions to its code with malicious intent. The best-known code injection attack is SQL injection,[22] which exploits common design flaws in database-driven web sites to allow unrestricted access to a database. Because industrial control networks rely extensively on databases and often feature Internet accessibility, protection against SQL injection is of high importance.

Cyber impact: Breach of confidentiality and integrity

Physical impact: Impact can range from unauthorized control to transmitting information to an adversary, rendering the target system unavailable or causing it to physically damage itself or another system. In practice, all five types of impact specified in Chapter 1 are possible.

Complexity: Low to high, depending on public availability of exploits and attack guidelines. SQL injection can be performed even by attackers with low skill, but code-injection attacks on embedded systems, such as ECUs, require high skill (see firmware modification).

Defense: Integrity verification and intrusion detection. For well-known code injection attacks, the most effective defense is to eliminate the vulnerabilities by fixing the corresponding design flaws.

Command Injection

Primary target: Any device controlling an actuator directly or indirectly

Description: An adversary with access to a target control unit or network executes a command with malicious intent. Command injection differs from code injection in that the code executed is not the adversary's, but is already defined in the target system. For instance, an adversary may use command injection attacks to reset or alter the settings of a RTU,[23] and a rogue ECU can inject commands on the CAN bus network to force a vehicle to brake, unlock a door, and so on. Command injection can benefit from fuzzing and packet sniffing, where the adversary attempts to identify which network packet or sequence of bits corresponds to which command. Note that the vast majority of cyber-physical attacks exploit existing functionality of

---

[22]Halfond, W. G., Viegas, J., and Orso, A. (2006). A classification of SQL-injection attacks and countermeasures. In *Proceedings of the IEEE International Symposium on Secure Software Engineering*, March 2006.

[23]Gao, W., Morris, T., Reaves, B., and Richey, D. (2010). On SCADA control system command and response injection and intrusion detection. In *eCrime Researchers Summit*, IEEE, October 2010.

their target. An adversary would not be able to send a "brake" command if this command had not already been defined by the automobile's manufacturer.

Cyber impact: Breach of the integrity of the target system's operation

Physical impact: Primarily unauthorized actuation, incorrect actuation, delayed actuation, or prevented actuation. If the command is to activate a sensor or transmit sensor data, then breach of physical privacy is possible too.

Complexity: High

Defense: Encryption, strong authentication

Communication Jamming

Primary target: Any cyber-physical system that relies on wireless communication

Description: Communication jamming is the intentional generation of interference that impedes the reception of a signal. In its simplest form, where a user A communicates with a user B over a wireless channel, the adversary needs to be in the vicinity of either A or B and to transmit a sufficiently strong wireless signal in the same frequency range.[24] Wireless signal jammers are inexpensive and relatively easy to use. Jamming can be proactive, in which case the adversary jams the wireless channel continuously, or reactive, in which case the adversary eavesdrops on the wireless channel and jams it only when legitimate communication is detected. This simple form of jamming is not strictly a cyber-physical attack, since it originates in physical space. Its first order impact in cyberspace is the disruption of communications, which may in turn affect a physical process.

Cyber impact: Loss of network availability

Physical impact: Typically, delayed or prevented actuation with regard to physical processes that require wireless communication. Depending on the design of a system, incorrect/unauthorized actuation is also possible. For instance, loss of wireless communication with a control center may trigger an automated action, such as a UAV entering a "return to base" mode.

Complexity: Low

Defense: Jamming detection techniques typically monitor the strength of a signal, the level of noise, the time it takes a wireless channel to become available for transmission, and the ratio

[24]Xu, W., Wood, T., Trappe, W., and Zhang, Y. (2004). Channel surfing and spatial retreats: defenses against wireless denial of service. In *Proceedings of the 3rd ACM workshop on Wireless security*, pp. 80–89, ACM, October 2004.

of packets delivered to packets sent.[25] Conventional antijamming response measures usually involve evasion of the attack, for example by switching to different transmission frequencies or physically moving to different locations.

Denial of Service

Primary target: Cyber-physical systems that are connected to the Internet or rely on networks that are potentially accessible by external users

Description: In a sense the cyber equivalent of jamming, denial of service is a cyber attack that aims to impede network availability by bombarding a network device or system with large volumes of meaningless network traffic.[26] If the target is connected to the Internet, it can be found through specialized search engines, such as Shodan. The adversary may then rent on the black market a large number of compromised computers (bots) and instruct them to simultaneously send network traffic, such as connection requests, to the same target. Having to receive and process the network packets that are arriving at a very high rate, the targeted system may be overwhelmed and rendered unable to respond to any legitimate connection requests received at the same time. Of course, what very high rate means is different from system to system and has increased remarkably over the years. For example, none of the denial of service attacks that collectively crippled the network infrastructure of Estonia in 2007 exceeded 100 Mbps,[27] when globally the largest attack at the time was around 24 Gbps. By 2013, the largest attack had already reached 400 Gbps.[28]

To hide their identity and impede defense, attackers typically spoof their source address by stating a fake address in the headers of the attack network packets. It is generally very difficult for the recipient to establish the true source of a spoofed network packet. This becomes even more difficult in a reflection attack, where the bots do not send traffic directly to their target. Instead, they send connection requests to legitimate computers

[25]Sufyan, N., Saqib, N. A., and Zia, M. (2013). Detection of jamming attacks in 802.11 b wireless networks. *EURASIP Journal on Wireless Communications and Networking*, Volume 2013, No. 1, pp. 1–18.
[26]Loukas, G. and Öke, G. (2010). Protection against denial of service attacks: a survey. *The Computer Journal*, Oxford University Press, Volume 53, No. 7, pp. 1020–1037.
[27]Lesk, M. (2007). The new front line: Estonia under cyberassault. *IEEE Security & Privacy*, 5(4), 0076-79.
[28]Prince, M. (2013). The DDoS that almost broke the internet. *CloudFlare blog*, March 27, 2013.

across the world stating as source address the IP address of their target. When the legitimate computers try to respond to these requests, they all unknowingly respond to the attack's target. In general, flood-based (also known as volumetric) distributed denial of service attacks exploit the fact that every computing system or component has an upper limit of what it can handle before getting overwhelmed. More subtle denial of service attacks using low network traffic rates are also possible but are far more challenging and far less common; they require a relevant vulnerability to be found for the particular network protocol that is used. (See the low-rate TCP attack by Kuzmanovic and Knightly[29] as an example.)

If the targeted cyber-physical system is not connected to the Internet, the nature of a denial of service attack is usually different. That is because the adversary needs to first gain access to the network the target belongs to and then send network traffic at a rate that can affect it. Without being able to utilize bots, as in the Internet, the attacker needs to consider different strategies. For instance, in the case of the automobile's network discussed in Chapter 3, a rogue ECU achieves denial of service by constantly transmitting messages of artificially high priority over the CAN bus, effectively blocking every other ECU's messages.

In the context of cyber-physical attacks, denial of service may also be used to increase the power consumption of a mobile device, remote sensor, or vehicle and ultimately exhaust its battery. That is because a flood of incoming network packets or connection requests can increase the load on the processor, which in turn affects the power consumption.[30]

Cyber impact: Increase in network/processing load, loss of network availability

Physical impact: Similar to the impact of a jamming attack. Typically, it delays or altogether prevents actuation by disrupting the communication of instructions to actuators or of data collected from sensors. Delays in the communication with sensors can also indirectly cause incorrect actuation, because it will be based on old sensor data. It has been shown repeatedly

[29]Kuzmanovic, A. and Knightly, E. W. (2003). Low-rate TCP-targeted denial of service attacks: the shrew vs. the mice and elephants. In *Proceedings of the 2003 conference on Applications, technologies, architectures, and protocols for computer communications*, pp. 75–86, ACM, August 2003.

[30]Nash, D. C., Martin, T. L., Ha, D. S., and Hsiao, M. S. (2005). Towards an intrusion detection system for battery exhaustion attacks on mobile computing devices. In *Third IEEE International Conference on Pervasive Computing and Communications Workshops*, pp. 141–145. IEEE, March 2005.

that a well-timed denial of service attack can lead a control system to an unsafe state.[31] Prevention of actuation can also be the result of increased power consumption due to a flood-based denial of service attack.

Complexity: Low to moderate

Defense: Authentication mechanisms, intrusion detection systems, firewalls, and redundancy measures can strengthen defense and survivability to denial of service attacks. None of these measures is enough in isolation, and even defense-in-depth measures can fail if the attack rate is just too high.

False Data Injection: Communication-Based

Primary target: The smart grid, and in general, any cyber-physical system that relies on sensor data received through a vulnerable communication channel

Description: The adversary compromises the communication channel used to report sensor measurements, blocks the legitimate ones, and transmits false data instead. If communication is carried out over a network, the adversary can achieve this by hijacking an intermediary node used to relay the data to the control center.

Cyber impact: Breach of data integrity

Physical impact: Incorrect actuation caused by incorrect data

Complexity: Moderate

Defense: Bad data detection[32] approaches designed to address naturally occurring errors in sensor measurements are commonly proposed for maliciously injected false data too. For example, if statistical analysis detects an abrupt and unexpected change in the sensor data, this can indicate an attack but may also indicate a naturally occurring error. A sophisticated adversary with insider knowledge can overcome these techniques by injecting data that look statistically correct. In these cases, protecting the confidentiality of the sensor data (e.g., using encryption) can help, as the adversary cannot estimate which data will look correct without having access to the real-time measurements that are reported. In addition, network defense techniques, such as message authentication, network intrusion

---

[31]Krotofil, M., Cárdenas, A. A., Manning, B., and Larsen, J. (2014). CPS: driving cyber-physical systems to unsafe operating conditions by timing DoS attacks on sensor signals. In *Proceedings of the 30th Annual Computer Security Applications Conference*, pp. 146–155, ACM, December 2014.

[32]Van Cutsem, T. and Ribbens-Pavella, M. (1985). Bad data identification methods in power system estimation – A Comparative study. *IEEE Transactions on Power Apparatus and Systems*, Volume 104, No. 11.

detection systems, the use of a separate and secure communication channel for sensor data, as well as replication can help detect and prevent false data injection.

False Data Injection: Database-Based

Primary target: SCADA and other industrial control systems that rely on databases

Description: Exploiting database vulnerabilities, the adversary compromises a database[33] such as a SCADA system's data historian to add erroneous records of sensor measurements and delete legitimate ones. SQL injection (see code injection) is a common threat.

Cyber impact: Breach of data integrity

Physical impact: Incorrect actuation caused by incorrect data

Complexity: Moderate

Defense: Database access control and replication of the data over different locations can prevent and detect such attacks.

False Data Injection: Sensor-Based

Primary target: The smart grid and, in general, any cyber-physical system with sensors that are physically exposed or controlled by computers that can be hijacked

Description: The adversary compromises a computer controlling a sensor (e.g., a RTU) and reports false data rather than the actual measurements collected by the sensor. For example, a large number of compromised smart meters that report false data can affect not only billing but also the grid's ability to estimate its own state and prevent disturbances and blackouts. False data injection against the smart grid's state estimation is an area of intense scientific research.[34]

Another approach, discussed in more detail in Chapter 7, is to deceive a sensor by physically manipulating the environment that it monitors (e.g., common window glass deceives infrared sensors, anechoic surfaces deceive ultrasonic sensors, etc.). This is particularly relevant for driverless vehicles that use sensors to constantly map the terrain and avoid obstacles.

Cyber impact: Breach of data integrity

[33]Giampapa, J. A., Hug-Glanzmann, G., and Kar, S. (2014). SCADA Resilience via Autonomous Cyber-Physical Agents. Carnegie Mellon University.
[34]Liu, Y., Ning, P., and Reiter, M. K. (2011). False data injection attacks against state estimation in electric power grids. *ACM Transactions on Information and System Security*, Volume 14, No. 1.

Physical impact: Incorrect actuation caused by incorrect sensor data

Complexity: Moderate

Defense: Again, bad data detection approaches can be applicable. With regard to sensor deception through physical means, sensor redundancy and diversity can limit the impact of the attack. Different types of sensors have different weaknesses and are unlikely to be deceived in the same manner.

Firmware Modification

Primary target: Embedded systems, such as PLCs, Internet of Things devices, and network hardware

Description: To maximize control over an embedded system and allow a wide range of physical impacts, an adversary may attempt to modify the embedded system's firmware. This has been demonstrated repeatedly in hacking conferences[35] and academic publications. Firmware modification can be seen as a particular class of code injection that is specific to embedded systems. A representative approach described by Basnight et al.[36] starts with acquiring samples of a device's firmware from the official firmware updates available on the manufacturer's web site, and then analyzing them, disassembling them, and attempting to infer the method used by the device to validate the integrity of any update it receives. Following a lot of trial and error, the aim is to identify sections of the code where modifications would not be flagged as invalid by the update validation method. The whole process is very complex, time-consuming, and potentially expensive, as the adversary needs to possess one or more devices of the same type, so as to test firmware modifications, and always runs the risk of "bricking" them (rendering them permanently unable to function) by loading invalid firmware on them.

Note that the adversary does not always need to modify the firmware of its ultimate target device to affect it (say the PLC). It may be easier to modify the firmware of a less critical device, such as a network router, an engineer's workstation, or the printer[37] that is intended to be used in the same network.

[35]Cui, A., Costello, M., Kataria, J., and Stolfo, S. J. (2013). Stepping P3wns: Adventures in Full-spectrum Embedded Exploitation and Defense. BlackHat USA.
[36]Basnight, Z., Butts, J., Lopez Jr, J., and Dube, T. (2013). Firmware modification attacks on programmable logic controllers. *International Journal of Critical Infrastructure Protection*, Volume 6, No. 2, pp. 76–84.
[37]Cui, A., Costello, M., and Stolfo, S. J. (2013). When Firmware Modifications Attack: A Case Study of Embedded Exploitation. In *20th Annual Network and Distributed System Security Symposium*, Internet Society, February 2013.

Cyber impact: Breach of the integrity of the target's firmware

Physical impact: Impact can range from unauthorized control to transmitting information to an adversary, rendering the target system unavailable or causing it to physically damage itself or another system. In practice, all five types of impact specified in Chapter 1 are possible.

Complexity: High

Defense: Integrity verification and behavior-specification intrusion detection[38]

Fuzzing

Primary target: Any cyber-physical system, as long as the adversary has the time and access required

Description: After having gained access to a network, the adversary bombards it with random messages and observes which ones have a physical effect. Although very simple, it is an effective technique for systems that feature no or weak authentication and the number of possible messages that one can send is not immensely high. It has been used most impressively by Koscher et al.[39] to reveal a particular car's CAN bus messages that disable its engine, lock individual brakes, prevent braking, and so on.

Cyber impact: Probing to disclose network messages that lead to actuation. It can help command injection.

Physical impact: Preparatory stage for the identification of attacks that can lead to unauthorized, incorrect, delayed, or prevented actuation

Complexity: Moderate

Defense: Strong authentication measures can prevent fuzzing because it requires access to the network with enough privileges to be able to transmit messages.

GPS Jamming

Primary target: Ships, aircraft, land vehicles, the smart grid, and any other cyber-physical system that relies heavily on GPS availability for positioning, navigation, or timing synchronization.

[38]Zimmer, C., Bhat, B., Mueller, F., and Mohan, S. (2010). Time-based intrusion detection in cyber-physical systems. In *Proceedings of the 1st ACM/IEEE International Conference on Cyber-Physical Systems*, pp. 109–118, ACM, April 2010.

[39]Koscher, K., Czeskis, A., Roesner, F., Patel, S., Kohno, T., Checkoway, S., McCoy, D., Kantor, B., Anderson, D., Shacham, H., and Savage, S. (2010). Experimental security analysis of a modern automobile. In the *Symposium on Security and Privacy, IEEE*, pp. 447–462, Oakland, CA, USA, May 16–19, 2010.

Description: Similarly to communication jamming, the adversary transmits high-power signals to impede reception of legitimate GPS signals. Considering the already very low strength of the latter, this is not a difficult feat.

Cyber impact: Loss of GPS availability

Physical impact: Disruption of the target's ability to establish its position, navigate autonomously, or benefit from GPS-based synchronization. For instance, a UAV would be unable to return to base, and the power grid would be unable to detect faults and respond to changing conditions accurately.

Complexity: Low

Defense: GPS antijamming devices and jamming-resilient GPS receivers[40]

GPS Spoofing/Meaconing

Primary target: Ships, aircraft, land vehicles, the smart grid, and any other cyber-physical system that relies heavily on GPS availability for positioning, navigation, or timing synchronization.

Description: In GPS spoofing, the adversary synthesizes and transmits a false GPS signal so as to deceive a GPS receiver regarding its location. Researchers from the University of Texas have demonstrated experimental devices that can spoof a GPS signal in such a manner that they can effectively steer a UAV in flight[41] (Figure 5.3) or change the time reference used by PMUs in the smart grid. Less sophisticated GPS spoofing can be performed with commercial GPS simulators designed for testing GPS receivers. A bit less complex than GPS spoofing is GPS meaconing, where the attacker captures a legitimate GPS signal

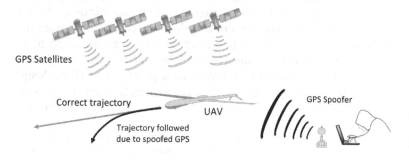

Figure 5.3 A GPS spoofing attack changing the trajectory of a UAV.

[40]Zhang, Y. D., and Amin, M. G. (2012). Anti-jamming GPS receiver with reduced phase distortions. *Signal Processing Letters*, IEEE, Volume 19, No. 10, pp. 635–638.
[41]Shepard, D. P., Bhatti, J. A., Humphreys, T. E., and Fansler, A. A. (2012). Evaluation of smart grid and civilian UAV vulnerability to GPS spoofing attacks. In *Proceedings of the ION GNSS Meeting*.

and rebroadcasts it with a slight delay. The delay affects the receiver's estimation of distance from the satellite, and, consequently, of its own location.

Cyber impact: Breach of GPS data integrity

Physical impact: Typically causes incorrect actuation, by disrupting a system's ability to establish its position and navigate autonomously. In an extreme case, it can also allow unauthorized control of the target's movement if the latter is fully autonomous and depends solely on GPS.

Complexity: Moderate (GPS meaconing); High (GPS spoofing)

Defense: Thanks to encryption, military GPS is more resilient to spoofing and meaconing than civilian GPS. Also, GPS spoofing and meaconing can be detected by monitoring the GPS signal's power levels or more complex statistical characteristics.[42]

Malware Infection

Primary target: Cyber-physical systems that are connected to corporate networks, conventional PCs, and smartphones

Description: A portmanteau of the words "malicious" and "software," the term "malware" is used collectively to denote viruses, logic bombs, worms, Trojan horses, backdoors, rootkits, bots, key loggers, and any other "software that fulfills the deliberately harmful intent of an attacker"[43] such as unauthorized access, damage or disruption of a system, and data exfiltration. In practice, the majority of cyber-physical attacks discussed in this book have been launched or facilitated by some sort of malware. The following are the main types available.

The media and sometimes even specialists refer to most malware as viruses, although the latter are less common nowadays if we follow their strict definition: **Viruses** are parasitic programs that infect other programs with malicious code and are activated only when users run these infected host programs. They also spread only with human action (e.g., attached to an e-mail, shared over a network, carried in a USB stick, etc.). Nilsson and Larson have referred to a program of their design that launched a simulated attack on a vehicle when it detected a door lock message on its CAN bus as a vehicle virus.[44]

---

[42]Psiaki, M. L., O'Hanlon, B. W., Bhatti, J. A., Shepard, D. P., and Humphreys, T. E. (2011). Civilian GPS spoofing detection based on dual-receiver correlation of military signals. *Proceedings of the Institute of Navigation GNSS.*

[43]Moser, A., Kruegel, C., and Kirda, E. (2007). Exploring multiple execution paths for malware analysis. In *Symposium on Security and Privacy*, pp. 231–245, IEEE, May 2007.

[44]Nilsson, D. K. and Larson, U. E. (2008). Simulated attacks on CAN buses: vehicle virus. In *IASTED International Conference on Communication Systems and Networks (AsiaCSN)*, pp. 66–72, April 2008.

It can probably be described more accurately as a **logic bomb**, which is a type of malware that lays dormant until a certain time or until some predefined conditions are met.

Worms are very similar to viruses but can also self-replicate without human action and can infect other computers in the same network in an automated manner. They can do so by e-mailing a copy of themselves to everyone on the contact list of the infected computer, remotely by subverting a legitimate network service, shared on removable media, and so on. Whether intentionally and in a targeted manner like Stuxnet (Chapter 4) or not, worms often cause severe disruption in physical space. Examples include Slammer infecting the Davis-Besse nuclear plant (Chapter 2, E3), Conficker infecting medical equipment worldwide (Chapter 2, H6), and Sobig.F affecting the dispatching and signaling systems of the US railway CSX (Chapter 2, T3).

Backdoors allow unauthorized access to the systems in which they are installed. In fact, there have been several reports and widespread speculation about vendors deliberately implanting backdoors into their electronic chips and telecommunication equipment, especially those supplied to large corporations, foreign governments, and military organizations.[45]

Bots are installed on compromised computers to launch (often simultaneously) flooding (distributed denial of service, spam e-mail, etc.) or other attacks when activated. An example is the denial of service attack that affected the Port of Houston in 2001 (Chapter 2, T2). The compromised machines are also called bots, and a group of them controlled by an adversary is called a **botnet**. Usually, although not always, the larger the botnet, the greater the potential disruption it can cause. Interestingly, the user of a botnet is not necessarily its owner. It is common for hackers to compromise large numbers of computers to form a botnet that they can then lease to other cyber criminals. A botnet of around 10,000 bots, which is enough to disrupt a major web site with a denial of service attack, may be rented for as little as $200 per day. Interestingly, prices can vary depending on the geographical location of the bots, with US-based ones being usually the most expensive.[46]

Rootkits are sets of software tools that aim mainly to conceal the presence of an adversary who has already broken into a

[45]Rostami, M., Koushanfar, F., and Karri, R. (2014). A Primer on Hardware Security: Models, Methods, and Metrics. *Proceedings of the IEEE*, Volume 102, No. 8, pp. 1283−1295.

[46]Danchev, D. (2013). How much does it cost to buy 10,000 U.S.-based malware-infected hosts? Webroot Threat Blog, February 28, 2013.

system. In addition to being the first worm specifically designed to target a SCADA network, Stuxnet is also believed to have carried the first rootkit specifically designed for PLCs. **Key loggers** record keystrokes on the computers in which they are installed, as in the case of the infected machines of UAV operators in 2011 (Chapter 2, D3).

A **Trojan horse** is software that appears to be useful and may indeed have a useful function, but also has a hidden malicious function, such as a rootkit or a key logger. Researchers from the University of Washington and the University of California San Diego have demonstrated an experimental Trojan horse application for smartphones that was designed to search for nearby cars with telematics units and upload malicious code on them via Bluetooth (Chapter 2, T9).

Cyber impact: Breach of system integrity followed by a potential breach of all other properties depending on the type of malware

Physical impact: All five types of physical impact are possible.

Complexity: Low to moderate, depending on access and type of cyber-physical system

Defense: Antimalware countermeasures, intrusion detection

Man-in-the-Middle

Primary target: Cyber-physical systems that rely on a communication channel potentially accessible by adversaries

Description: An adversary connects independently with two computers with the purpose to relay any messages sent between them. The two computers believe that they communicate directly and privately, but in reality the adversary can both actively eavesdrop on their communication and inject or manipulate messages (Figure 5.4).

The usual approach is to first compromise an existing node or connect a rogue one on the targeted computers' network (see Rogue node), and then exploit weaknesses of the communication mechanism that is used. The simplest and one of the most effective techniques is address resolution protocol (ARP) spoofing, where the adversary broadcasts fake replies to ARP requests for the physical address of a legitimate node, leading other nodes on the network to believe that it has the address of the rogue node.

Cyber impact: Breach of confidentiality, authenticity, and integrity. Effectively, an unauthorized user masquerades as an authorized one. Breach of availability is also possible if the adversary selectively drops messages exchanged between the two computers (see Black hole/Gray hole attack).

Physical impact: All forms of physical impact are possible.

Complexity: Moderate

Defense: Strong authentication and data integrity measures. The communication protocol needs to ensure the identity of both ends of a communication channel.

Network Isolation

Primary target: Large-scale cyber-physical systems, such as the smart grid and traffic light management systems

Description: Shin et al.[47] have used the term to refer to attacks that aim to isolate a particular physical geographical area from a network. No particular approach is dictated, but one way to achieve it is by compromising the network nodes that enclose the targeted area, selectively dropping or delaying network packets from and to them. In practice, it is a coordinated black hole attack, where the targets are chosen based on the physical geographical area they serve. The adversary needs to have a detailed knowledge of the geographical coverage of a

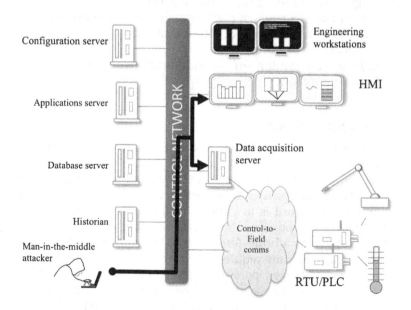

Figure 5.4 A man-in-the-middle attack targeting the communication between the HMI and the data acquisition server in a SCADA network.

[47]Shin, D. H., Koo, J., Yang, L., Lin, X., Bagchi, S., and Zhang, J. (2013). Low-complexity secure protocols to defend cyber-physical systems against network isolation attacks. In *Conference on Communications and Network Security (CNS)*, pp. 91–99, IEEE, October 2013.

network and to coordinate attacks against a large number of network nodes. It is a potential threat in the smart grid, since the high impact could justify an adversary's investment in the detailed network reconnaissance and identification of exploits that may be required.

Cyber impact: Breach of network system integrity at compromised nodes and loss of network availability

Physical impact: The same as black hole attack, but focused on a specific geographical area's sensors and actuators

Complexity: High

Defense: Strong authentication measures, as well as redundancy with diversity can reduce the likelihood of the same vulnerability affecting several network nodes.

Packet Sniffing

Primary target: Any cyber-physical system that relies on wireless networks or generally networks that are potentially accessible by external users

Description: After having gained access to a network, the adversary uses packet-sniffing software to eavesdrop on the messages transmitted through the network.

Cyber impact: Breach of confidentiality of communications

Physical impact: Breach of physical privacy

Complexity: Low to moderate

Defense: Encryption of communications restricts packet sniffing significantly.

Password Cracking

Primary target: Any password-protected cyber-physical system

Description: Most cyber-physical systems have at least some elements that are password protected. The simplest method for cracking a password is to guess it or find it in documentation, and if this is not possible then try all possible combinations, in what is known as a brute-force attack. The number of trials and consequently the time required is reduced dramatically by using dictionaries of known passwords and variations of them. Note that password authentication mechanisms work by comparing not the actual plaintext passwords (the one typed in against the one expected for a particular user), but their hashes.[48]

[48]If actual passwords were stored, they would be disclosed if the file where they were stored was stolen. That is why hashes are stored instead.

Instead of computing the hash for every password in real time, password cracking applications use tables with precomputed hashes for all passwords in known dictionaries. An advanced form of this approach is the rainbow table, which achieves better performance for tough passwords through intelligent manipulation of the hashes.

Cyber impact: Breach of authenticity, leading primarily to breach of confidentiality and integrity

Physical impact: It depends on the functionality of the system whose password has been cracked.

Complexity: Low to moderate

Defense: Two-factor authentication, strong password policies, and use of large salt value, which is a random input to the hashing process that aims to defeat precomputed hash tables

Relay Attack

Primary target: Automobiles' keyless entry systems, high-security building access control, and other location-sensitive authentication systems

Description: In token-based authentication, the physical range constraints of a communication link, such as the short range of LF RFID, are often used as implicit proof of the proximity of a token (e.g., a smart key) to its legitimate token reader (e.g., the corresponding car). However, adversaries can capture a signal transmitted from one and relay it to the other through an additional longer-range communication link that is in their control (see Chapter 3, Figure 3.8). This can trick the token reader into thinking it is in the proximity of the token.

Cyber impact: Breach of authenticity

Physical impact: Unauthorized actuation, such as the unlocking of an automobile's or security building's door

Complexity: High

Defense: Common countermeasures include setting a time constraint (as a relayed signal takes longer to arrive than an authentic one that really is in proximity), estimating actual distance based on time (distance bounding), and using an additional factor of authentication, such as a PIN or a password. None of these is considered completely satisfactory.[49]

---

[49]Hancke, G. P., Mayes, K. E., and Markantonakis, K. (2009). Confidence in smart token proximity: Relay attacks revisited. *Computers and Security*, Volume 28, No. 7, pp. 615–627.

Replay Attack

Primary target: Any cyber-physical system. In general, any system where sensor and control data are transmitted remotely and need to be up to date.

Description: The adversary observes and records a communication sequence in order to replay it later. If replaying communication that carries sensor measurements, it is a deception attack that affects the freshness of the data upon which the cyber-physical system depends. Stuxnet famously employed such an attack to prevent the nuclear facility's controllers from noticing the abnormal state of the system. If replaying communication that carries control commands, such as "close the valve," "deliver insulin," "unlock the door," a replay attack effectively allows control of a cyber-physical system's actuators without having to fully understand how each network packet and each command is structured. Indeed, this is its great strength. It does not require detailed knowledge of the internal workings of the targeted system; only the observation that a particular communication sequence is followed by a particular action. Its shortcoming is that it cannot produce a sensor measurement or a control command that has not been transmitted and captured before.

Cyber impact: Breach of authenticity and integrity. Effectively, an unauthorized user masquerades as an authorized one.

Physical impact: Primarily unauthorized actuation when replaying an actuation command, and incorrect actuation when replaying old sensor data measurements. It can also prevent (and possibly delay) actuation if that is the purpose of the command it replays.

Complexity: Moderate

Defense: Replay attacks are typically countered by using for each communication session a randomly generated identifier that expires after a short period of time. An attacker replaying communication after that time would be using an expired identifier. Another approach is to try to detect discrepancies between the time claimed by the sender (the timestamp included in the message) and the time estimated by the recipient. Several more advanced techniques have been proposed at an experimental level but they usually require a substantial redesign of the control system that is to be protected.[50]

---

[50]Mo, Y. and Sinopoli, B. (2009). Secure control against replay attacks. In *47th Annual Allerton Conference on Communication, Control, and Computing*, pp. 911–918, IEEE.

Rogue Node

Primary target: Smart grid, in-vehicle networks, home automation, and other networks of controllers or sensors

Description: Using compatible wired or wireless equipment,
the adversary introduces a rogue device in a network posing as
a legitimate node. In the case of an automobile, this can be
done by physically connecting to the OBD port. A rogue node
can read all communications on the network and generate its
own messages, including commands to actuators.

Cyber impact: Breach of system integrity. Introducing a rogue
node is a preliminary step that facilitates other attacks, such as
denial of service, man-in-the-middle, command injection,
packet sniffing, and so on.

Physical impact: No direct impact. The physical impact
depends on the attack that will be launched from the rogue
node.

Complexity: Low to high, depending on network's authentication measures and physical configuration

Defense: Strong authentication and encryption

Sleep Deprivation

Primary target: Vehicles, robots, remote sensors, and other
networked devices and systems that are battery-powered

Description: The autonomy of sensors and actuators that are
difficult to reach is limited by their batteries. For this reason,
they are usually configured to perform their tasks in an energy-
efficient manner (i.e., periodically and only if needed). An adversary can rapidly exhaust their batteries by forcing them to never
sleep and to constantly perform an action, or to receive, process,
or transmit data. Sleep deprivation has been researched primarily in the context of wireless sensor networks,[51] but is applicable
in several other contexts. In Chapter 3, we mentioned a plausible
attack, where the adversary continuously transmits connection
requests to an implantable medical device with the purpose to
exhaust its battery.

Cyber impact: Increased or constant activity in cyberspace

Physical impact: Increased rate of battery exhaustion, eventually leading to prevention of actuation

Complexity: Low to moderate

---

[51]Pirretti, M., Zhu, S., Vijaykrishnan, N., McDaniel, P., Kandemir, M., and Brooks, R.
(2006). The sleep deprivation attack in sensor networks: Analysis and methods of
defense. *International Journal of Distributed Sensor Networks*, Volume 2, No. 3,
pp. 267–287.

Defense: Behavior-based and especially behavior-specification based intrusion detection can be helpful, for example by monitoring the time that a device is awake and the rate at which a nearby wireless transmitter requires communication.

Supply Chain Attack

Primary target: Critical national infrastructure and military equipment

Description: The adversary gains access to suppliers' computer systems and networks and modifies the firmware and pre-installs backdoors (software that provides the adversary with unauthorized access to the system) and other malware into the devices they produce before they ship them out. In this case, the end users' security measures are largely ineffective, as the integrity of the devices has already been affected. Managing the cyber security risks stemming from supply chains is an extremely challenging problem, which requires governmental controls to be in place both domestically and internationally.

From our perspective, we can consider as equivalent to a supply chain attack any malicious modification of software or hardware that occurs before the legitimate user purchases or starts using it. For instance, the embedded controller of an implantable medical device cannot be physically accessed after it is implanted in a patient's body. Any physical manipulation that has occurred prior to this is, for our purposes, equivalent to a supply chain attack.

Cyber impact: Breach of integrity of the software/firmware installed in the system

Physical impact: Unauthorized, incorrect, delayed, or prevented actuation, or breach of physical privacy through exfiltration of sensor data to unauthorized parties, as dictated by the rogue software.

Complexity: Moderate

Defense: Software integrity verification, as well as security compliance certifications for suppliers, such as the Cyber Essentials certification[52] introduced in the United Kingdom in 2014.

Antiforensics

Attacks always leave traces in cyberspace. The process of eliminating these traces and covering one's tracks is called

[52]Cabinet Office (2014). Use of Cyber Essentials Scheme certification. Procurement policy Note, Action Note 09/14, September 25, 2014.

antiforensics. It may involve deleting files created during the attack, hiding data in seemingly innocuous files (steganography), temporarily disabling logs, removing lines from logs, or changing them so as to cause confusion.[53] An even simpler method is to just wait for a few days before initiating the next step of an attack, so as to make it difficult to establish a connection between two security incidents. For example, one of the measures taken by Stuxnet 0.5 was to wait for 20 days before forcing a reboot (by generating a "blue screen of death") on an infected machine.[54] At the network level, deletion of network logs and the use of source address spoofing, bots, proxy servers,[55] and encryption can also be considered as forms of antiforensics.[56]

The careful use of antiforensic techniques is an integral characteristic of advanced persistent threats (see Box 5.1). It suggests that the attacker is at least somewhat if not very capable. On the other hand, countermeasures to antiforensics are still in their infancy. They usually revolve around protecting log files (e.g., by keeping remote replicas) and generally improving the intelligence of the current tools used by network forensic investigators.[57]

Summary

Breaching the cyber security of a system with the primary purpose of affecting physical space is not easy. One needs to have an understanding of the relevant cyber-physical dependencies and the knowledge and opportunity to affect the right element in cyberspace. This requires considerable planning and research. Largely mirroring the usual stages of an intentional and organized cyber attack, we can consider as the first stage any preliminary research that is based on information available on the Internet. It is surprising how much one can find out about suppliers of equipment, network technologies and

[53]Harris, R. (2006). Arriving at an anti-forensics consensus: Examining how to define and control the anti-forensics problem. *Digital investigation*, Volume 3, pp. 44–49.
[54]McDonald, G., Murchu, L. O., Doherty, S., and Chien, E. (2013). Stuxnet 0.5: The missing link. *Symantec Report*.
[55]A computer requesting a service from a remote server can do so via an intermediary to conceal its real identity. The intermediary is called a proxy server, and can be an application or a computer.
[56]Chandran, R. and Yan, W. Q. (2013). A Comprehensive Survey of Antiforensics for Network Security. *Managing Trust in Cyberspace*, pp. 419–447.
[57]Garfinkel, S. (2007). Anti-forensics: Techniques, detection and countermeasures. In *2nd International Conference on i-Warfare and Security*, pp. 77–84, March 2007.

Box 5.1 Advanced Persistent Threat (APT)

The term typically refers to professional adversaries, often acting on behalf of nation states and employing a wide range of advanced intelligence gathering techniques against a particular individual or organization.[58] APTs are stealthy and well coordinated. They can remain undetected for very long periods of time, thanks to considerable effort invested in preparatory stages, from intelligence gathering via social engineering to the design of often innovative malware,[59] and systematic use of advanced antiforensic techniques.

software used, geographical locations, names of key people, addresses, phone numbers, design diagrams, and, on occasion, even default usernames and passwords. Social engineering can be used both in this stage for collecting information and in later stages for helping deliver an attack.

Next, the attacker may attempt to actively look for specific vulnerabilities on the targeted system. Internet research can help here too, but there are also several automated scanning tools available. Having discovered a likely vulnerability, the attacker attempts to exploit it. Again, there is the possibility of using automated tools that help exploit many of the existing and well-known vulnerabilities. Often the vulnerability is not technical at all. It is not uncommon for devices used in industrial control, health, and many other safety-critical environments to be left to their default usernames and passwords.

Having exploited a vulnerability and gained access to a network or control unit of a cyber-physical system, there are usually many ways in which an attacker can affect physical space. For example, packet sniffing or malware that redirects network traffic received from sensors to a device controlled by an adversary can be used to breach physical privacy. Replaying of commands, injection of new commands or code, and especially modification of a device's firmware can lead to unauthorized, incorrect, delayed, or prevented actuation. Throughout this process, capable attackers use advanced antiforensic techniques to evade detection during the attack and to prevent future investigations from identifying the perpetrator.

[58]Chen, P., Desmet, L., and Huygens, C. (2014). A Study on Advanced Persistent Threats. In *Communications and Multimedia Security*, pp. 63−72, Springer Berlin Heidelberg.
[59]Kovacs, E. (2014). Attackers Using USB Malware to Steal Data From Air-Gapped Networks, SecurityWeek, November 11, 2014.

Follow-Up Questions and Exercises

1. Based on the information in Chapter 3, draw a diagram with the main entry points of potential cyber-physical attacks targeting an implantable cartioverter defibrillator.
2. Based on the information in Chapter 3, draw a diagram with the main entry points of potential cyber-physical attacks targeting a civilian UAV.
3. Which of the following attacks can be sufficient in leading a cyber-physical system to incorrect actuation? Explain your reasoning with examples.
   a. Packet sniffing
   b. Denial of service
   c. Command injection
   d. GPS spoofing
4. Which of the following statements are correct?
   a. A botnet is a piece of malware that compromises a machine in order to launch a denial of service attack against another machine.
   b. Denial of service can affect a cyber-physical system's power consumption.
   c. Denial of service can be achieved only by overwhelming the target with very high rates of data traffic.
   d. Denial of service can introduce delays that can affect the integrity of a cyber-physical system's actuation.
5. A smartphone application that allows a patient to monitor her blood glucose levels remotely, but unknowingly to the patient also transmits the same information to her insurance company could be characterized as what type of malware?
   a. Worm
   b. Trojan horse
   c. Logic bomb
   d. Rootkit
6. Which of the following statements are correct?
   a. Capable adversaries use antiforensic techniques to evade detection and ensure that they cannot be identified as the perpetrators behind a security incident.
   b. Social engineering can be used both to collect intelligence about a target and to deliver malware.
   c. Google hacking can be used to attack any type of cyber-physical system, whether it is connected to the Internet or not.
   d. Shodan can be used for port scanning. Its disadvantage is that it is easy for a target's defense systems to detect and identify Shodan users.

6

PROTECTION MECHANISMS AND SECURE DESIGN PRINCIPLES

Chapter Summary

The traditional families of protection mechanisms used in cyberspace are largely applicable on cyber-physical systems but not always in the same manner or with the same effectiveness as on conventional computer systems. For example, whitelisting approaches tend to be more effective than blacklisting ones, protection of integrity and availability may have higher priority than protection of confidentiality, and intrusion detection may rely not only on cyberspace metrics but also on information collected by sensors in physical space. The aim of this chapter is to describe the protection mechanisms that have been deployed on cyber-physical systems, in real-world or laboratory environments, as well as the age-old secure design principles that have stood the test of time for conventional computer systems and are proving highly applicable in this context as well.

Key Terms: Authentication; access control; intrusion detection; firewall; antimalware; whitelisting; cryptography; integrity verification; survivability; secure design principles

As cyber-physical attacks are initiated in cyberspace, several of the cyber security protection mechanisms and principles developed for conventional computer systems over the last decades are applicable. Others are less mature but have been developed specifically for these attacks, for example to protect SCADA systems, modern vehicles, or medical devices. Our aim in this chapter is to go through both old and new defense approaches that have been shown to be effective against cyber-physical attacks, in real-world or laboratory-based deployments. We will discuss them primarily in terms of their applicability to cyber-physical systems, which are the most representative targets of cyber-physical attacks.

Protection Mechanisms

Authentication

Password-based authentication is often the first line of defense for computer systems, and this is also the case in many types of cyber-physical systems that involve control by human users. Despite being in use in computing for over half a century, how people choose passwords and what constitutes a strong password are not very well understood. Massive lists of passwords leaked online after a barrage of security breaches involving popular web sites in the early 2010s has been enormously helpful both to hackers and to researchers trying to understand real usage trends.[1] However, we are still some way from determining optimal policies for choosing passwords that are

---

[1]Veras, R., Collins, C., and Thorpe, J. (2014). On the semantic patterns of passwords and their security impact. In *Network and Distributed System Security Symposium*, February 2014.

sufficiently secure yet not terribly difficult for a user to remember (or type). Instead, we are quite good at assigning blame to users (see *Users Are Not the Enemy* by Adams and Sasse[2] for an excellent discussion on this matter) and condemning cringe-worthy practices encountered in safety-critical systems. For the latter, there is some justification, since reports of traffic light systems,[3] medical devices, SCADA systems,[4] and other safety-critical systems protected by three-character passwords or left with factory default passwords abound. In 2013, researchers Rios and McCorkle reported to have identified hard-coded passwords in over 300 medical devices from 40 different vendors.[5] These were used to gain privileged access in surgical and anesthesia devices, ventilators, drug infusion pumps, external defibrillators, patient monitors, and laboratory and analysis equipment.

Passwords, along with passphrases and secret questions, authenticate through "what you know," but there are two important problems with this. What one knows or values enough to choose to type multiple times every day often has some sort of significance in their life, and consequently can be guessed through their social network profiles or just by knowing them personally. The second problem is that cyber-physical systems are highly dependent on network communications and authentication may need to be done remotely. Even a relatively strong password can become worthless if captured by an adversary while in transit through the network, especially if it is sent in plaintext, which is not uncommon for things like smart appliances and medical devices.[6]

Instead or in addition to "what you know," authentication can also be based on "what you have," "what you are," and increasingly on "where you are" (as well as on "who you know"[7] but that approach is not as mature or as relevant for protecting

---

[2]Adams, A. and Sasse, M. A. (1999). Users are not the enemy. *Communications of the ACM*, Volume 42, No. 12, pp. 40—46.

[3]Ghena, B., Beyer, W., Hillaker, A., Pevarnek, J., and Halderman, J. A. (2014). Green Lights Forever: Analyzing the Security of Traffic Infrastructure. In Proceedings of *the 8th USENIX Workshop on Offensive Technologies* (WOOT), August 2014.

[4]Marks, P. (2011). Reaching critical point. *New Scientist*, Volume 212, No. 2841.

[5]Sun, L. H. and Dennis, B. (2013). FDA, facing cybersecurity threats, tightens medical-device standards. The Washington Post, June 13, 2013.

[6]Hanna, S., Rolles, R., Molina-Markham, A., Poosankam, P., Fu, K., and Song, D. (2011). Take two software updates and see me in the morning: The case for software security evaluations of medical devices. In *Proceedings of the 2nd USENIX Workshop on Health Security and Privacy*, August 2011.

[7]Brainard, J., Juels, A., Rivest, R. L., Szydlo, M., and Yung, M. (2006). Fourth-factor authentication: somebody you know. In *ACM conference on computer and communications security*, pp. 168—178, October 2006.

against cyber-physical attacks). The "what you have" is referred to as a security token and can be a USB stick, a key fob, a smart card, or any other physical device used to electronically identify and authenticate a user.[8] Smart cards are pocket-sized plastic cards that carry an embedded microprocessor chip and are commonly used to enable some form of secure service to their owners, such as ticketing in public transit, mobile phones (in the form of SIM cards), banking cards, and building access control. They do so by performing cryptographic operations on their chip, and the more high end the smart card, the more complex the cryptographic functions that it supports.

Contact smart cards need to be inserted in a smart card reader device to work, both to communicate with the reader and to power the smart card's chip through the reader's electrical contacts. Contactless smart cards, such as the ones used in electronic passports, are powered again by the reader but using a tiny embedded antenna instead. The reader creates an electromagnetic field around it and when the smart card enters this field, the antenna gathers energy from it and powers the chip. In SCADA systems, smart cards can be used as part of a two-factor authentication process in conjunction with the normal login/password process. In implantable medical devices they are typically used on their own. The patient is issued with a smart card that is configured with a secret key, and when the doctor needs to access the secure communication link to the device, she gets the smart card from the patient and inserts it into a reader, which checks the credentials and authorizes the communication.[9]

An interesting alternative approach proposed by Denning, Fu, and Kohno[10] is to use a cloaker device in the form of a smart bracelet that shares a secret key with the implant and can communicate wirelessly with it. While the bracelet is worn, the implant is configured to reject any communication by other devices. When the doctor wishes to access the implant, the patient takes the bracelet off and thus reenables communication with external devices. The advantage of a cloaker-based authentication system is that it does not compromise safety in case of an emergency. An emergency caregiver would not need

[8]Sauter, T. and Schwaiger, C. (2002). Achievement of secure Internet access to fieldbus systems. *Microprocessors and Microsystems*, Volume 26, No. 7, pp. 331–339.
[9]Bergamasco, S., Bon, M., and Inchingolo, P. (2001). Medical data protection with a new generation of hardware authentication tokens. In *Mediterranean Conference on Medical and Biological Engineering and Computing*.
[10]Denning, T., Fu, K., and Kohno, T. (2008). Absence Makes the Heart Grow Fonder: New Directions for Implantable Medical Device Security. In *Proceedings of the 3rd conference on Hot topics in security*, No. 5, July 2008.

to find the security token but only to remove the bracelet from the patient's wrist. Shen et al.[11] have explored a similar concept, whereby the communication channel is continuously jammed until an authorized person needs to configure the implant. However, jamming can disrupt the communications of other nearby devices too, and may violate radio interference laws.

The third type of authentication ("what you are") is the use of biometric recognition, which is the family of technologies that attempts to identify individuals based on physiological and behavioral characteristics of theirs. Biometric characteristics need to be quantitatively measurable, universal (everyone must have them), distinctive (different for any two persons), and permanent for a period of time.[12] The most commonly used characteristics are the fingerprint, face, iris, and retina, and less commonly the ear, gait, voice, keystroke pattern, and hand geometry, among others.[13] Biometric recognition can be used as an authentication mechanism in SCADA systems,[14] door locks,[15] automobiles, and so on. Especially with regard to automobiles, fingerprint recognition typically is used to prevent the disarming of the car's immobilizer. The particular approach received a lot of bad press in 2005 when a gang of car thieves in Malaysia cut off a Mercedes S-class owner's finger when they realized that they could not start up the engine without it.[16] As Bruce Schneier had remarked in his *Beyond Fear* book,[17] illthought car security measures can cause "the weakest link to move from the ignition switch to the driver." Today, most fingerprint scanners feature liveness detection[18] technologies, which

[11]Shen, W., Ning, P., He, X., and Dai, H. (2013). Ally friendly jamming: How to jam your enemy and maintain your own wireless connectivity at the same time. In *IEEE Symposium on Security and Privacy*, pp. 174–188, IEEE, May 2013.

[12]Jain, A. K., Ross, A., and Prabhakar, S. (2004). An introduction to biometric recognition. *IEEE Transactions on Circuits and Systems for Video Technology*, Volume 14, No. 1, pp. 4–20.

[13]Jain, A. K., Ross, A. A., and Nandakumar, K. (2011). *Introduction to biometrics*. Springer.

[14]Wiles, J., Claypoole, T., Drake, P., Henry, P. A., Johnson Jr, L. J., Lowther, S., Miles, G., Tobias, M. W., and Windle, J. H. (2008). Biometric Authentication for SCADA Security. *Techno Security's Guide to Securing SCADA: A Comprehensive Handbook On Protecting The Critical Infrastructure*. Syngress.

[15]Keogh, C. R. and Keogh, K. D. (2003). Fingerprint biometric lock, *U.S. Patent No. 20,030,141,959*. Washington, DC: U.S. Patent and Trademark Office.

[16]Shaikh, S. A. and Dimitriadis, C. K. (2008). My fingers are all mine: Five reasons why using biometrics may not be a good idea. In *International Symposium on Biometrics and Security Technologies*, IEEE, April 2008.

[17]Schneier, B. Beyond Fear: Thinking Sensibly About Security in an Uncertain World. 2003.

[18]Schuckers, S. A. (2009). Liveness Detection: Fingerprint. In *Encyclopedia of Biometrics*, pp. 924–931, Springer US.

can tell whether a fingerprint comes from a live finger and not from a silicone replica (or a severed one). Hopefully, this is known to car thieves too. In the automotive industry, the use of biometrics is expected to increase anyway for the purpose of enhancing driver safety. In addition to current techniques that detect drowsiness by monitoring the driver's input and the car's position on the road, biometric measurements of eye movement, heart rate, and skin conductance can detect stress and distraction more accurately.[19] If the biometric systems for measuring these characteristics are available in the car's cabin, it makes sense to also use them to authenticate the driver.

The fourth type of authentication ("where you are") can relate to a system's proximity from a person or object, or to its precise location.[20] Proximity-based authentication may be useful in reducing the likelihood of a remote attack against an implantable medical device, an automobile's keyless entry system, or any other system where a device's legitimate operator needs to be close to it. Normally, the fact that a device is equipped only with close-range communication capabilities, such as low frequency RFID, implies that anyone connected to it must be in close proximity, and this is enough to authorize access (to allow the doctor to configure an implant, the owner of a car to unlock it, etc.). However, by relaying the legitimate authentication messages over a rogue communication link, it is possible for an attacker to extend the effective distance from where a device can be operated (see Figure 3.8 in Chapter 3 for an example of a relay attack against a car's keyless entry system). As a countermeasure, one may choose to verify physical proximity using distance bounding, which is a technique that estimates the actual distance between two devices based on the time it takes to exchange radio[21] or ultrasonic[22] messages between them.

The concept of location-based authentication is particularly suitable for mobile devices and vehicles. It has not yet seen wide use, but most proposals involve using the physical

[19]Coughlin, J. F., Reimer, B., and Mehler, B. (2009). Driver wellness, safety and the development of an AwareCar. *AgeLab, Mass Inst. Technol., Cambridge, MA.*
[20]Denning, D. E. and MacDoran, P. F. (1996). Location-based authentication: Grounding cyberspace for better security. *Computer Fraud & Security*, Volume 1996, No. 2, pp. 12–16.
[21]Rasmussen, K. B. and Capkun, S. (2010). Realization of RF Distance Bounding. In *USENIX Security Symposium*, pp. 389–402, August 2010.
[22]Rasmussen, K. B., Castelluccia, C., Heydt-Benjamin, T. S., and Capkun, S. (2009). Proximity-based access control for implantable medical devices. In *Proceedings of the 16th ACM conference on Computer and communications security*, pp. 410–419, ACM, November 2009.

location of a device as one of multiple factors of authentication (e.g., you need to have the right secret key, produce the right biometric readings, and be physically located at the right place[23]) or as the criterion that determines the type of authentication to be used. For example, an Apple Inc. patent[24] published in July 2014 specifies that if a smartphone is located at home (as shown by the GPS module or simply by being within range of the home Wi-Fi network), then it can be unlocked with only a four-digit passcode, but if it is located in a public place, such as a shopping mall, then it may require two-factor authentication. Another idea would be to use one's smartphone as a biometric authentication system that unlocks a door at a facility if the location of the smartphone matches the location of the specific facility, and the user's biometric characteristics, as measured by the smartphone's sensors and software, match those of an authorized user.[25]

Two-factor authentication has always combined cyber and physical elements, such as "what you know" with "where you are." In cyber-physical systems, such two-factor cyber-physical authentication is naturally suitable and can address a number of security problems that may be encountered in the near future. For instance, consider the application of electric vehicles being charged in the smart grid. A desirable property of the smart grid would be to prevent an unauthorized vehicle, such as one that has been stolen, to be charged on it. This means that there is a need for authenticating electric vehicles remotely against some database at a central authentication server. For reasons of practicality, it also means that the authentication process should be conducted wirelessly. In the case of a legitimate vehicle, the vehicle wirelessly proves that it has the correct secret key and unlocks the charging bay. However, a car thief can overcome this by placing an authorized vehicle next to a stolen one to pass the wireless authentication challenge, while plugging in the stolen one to the charging bay.[26] So, how does

[23]Zhang, F., Kondoro, A., and Muftic, S. (2012). Location-based authentication and authorization using smart phones. In *11th International Conference on Trust, Security and Privacy in Computing and Communications*, pp. 1285–1292, IEEE, June 2012.

[24]Reitter, A., Amm, D., Missig, J., and Walsh, R. (2012). Location-sensitive security levels and setting profiles based on detected location. *U.S. Patent Application 13/731,893.*

[25]Fahmi, A. P. N, Kodirov, E., Ardiansyah, Deokjai, C., and Lee, G. (2013). Hey Home, Open Your Door, I'm Back! Authentication System using Ear Biometrics for Smart Home. *International Journal of Smart Home*, Volume 7, No. 1, pp. 173–182.

[26]Chia, M. W., Krishnan, S., and Zhou, J. (2012). Challenges and Opportunities in Infrastructure Support for Electric Vehicles and Smart Grid in a dense urban environment-Singapore. In *International Electric Vehicle Conference (IEVC)*, IEEE, March 2012.

one address this problem? The challenge is proving that the car being charged is the same as the car being authenticated. One way to do this is by using the actual cable used for charging to also deliver part of the authentication challenge. An example prototype system has been implemented by Chan and Zhou,[27] which ensures that a vehicle cannot be authenticated if it is not the vehicle that is physically plugged in to the particular charging bay.[28]

Access Control

While authentication is concerned with determining whether a subject (a user, an application, a process, or a device) should be granted access at all, access control aims to constrain what an authenticated subject can do.[29] Historically, this has been based on assigning specific permissions to individual subjects (by defining access control lists[30]) or to the specific roles that subjects can be assigned to (role-based access control[31]). The more general, more flexible, but also more resource-intensive approach is attribute-based access control,[32] where access is granted based on attributes of the subject (e.g., affiliation, qualifications, and priorities), attributes of the resource that is to be accessed (e.g., criticality, availability, or location), and attributes of the environment (e.g., the current date and time). The flexibility of this approach is particularly useful in highly dynamic cyber-physical systems, where the priorities of a process and the availability of its requested resource may be changing rapidly.[33]

[27]Chan, A. F. and Zhou, J. (2014). Cyber-Physical Device Authentication for Smart Grid Electric Vehicle Ecosystem. *IEEE Journal on Selected Areas in Communications*, Volume 32, No. 7, IEEE, pp. 1509–1517.
[28]The North American standard charging cable, JAE J1772, has a control pilot pin that allows communication between the vehicle and the charging bay, to detect that there is a vehicle connected, indicate readiness to supply energy, etc. The researchers used this pin to also transmit an authentication challenge.
[29]Sandhu, R. S. and Samarati, P. (1994). Access control: principle and practice. *Communications Magazine, IEEE*, Volume 32, No. 9, pp. 40–48.
[30]Cankaya, H. C. (2011). Access Control Lists. In *Encyclopedia of Cryptography and Security*, pp. 9–12. Springer US.
[31]Ferraiolo, D., Cugini, J., and Kuhn, D. R. (1995). Role-based access control (RBAC): Features and motivations. In *Proceedings of the 11th annual computer security application conference*, pp. 241–248, December 1995.
[32]Wang, L., Wijesekera, D., and Jajodia, S. (2004). A logic-based framework for attribute based access control. In *Proceedings of the ACM workshop on Formal methods in security engineering*, pp. 45–55. ACM, October 2004.
[33]Burmester, M., Magkos, E., and Chrissikopoulos, V. (2013). T-ABAC: An attribute-based access control model for real-time availability in highly dynamic systems. In *IEEE Symposium on Computers and Communications*, pp. 143–148, IEEE, July 2013.

Of particular interest are location-based access control mechanisms,[34] where a subject's attributes might include its precise location, its mobility dynamics (speed, acceleration, direction), and interactions with other subjects (proximity to a system, number of subjects in an area, etc.). A simple example is the location-based disarming of the speed limiter of the Nissan GT-R sports car. In Japan, all domestic cars are programmed to be limited to a maximum of 112 or 118 mph top speed, but the Nissan GT-R has been designed to automatically authorize overriding of its own speed limiter when its GPS module determines that it has arrived at a sanctioned racetrack, where there is no speed limit.[35]

Firewall

Firewalls are filtering tools that act as barriers between the internal network and any other network, such as the Internet. They can be software based or hardware based and their job is to police the traffic coming in (ingress filtering) and going out (egress filtering) of the internal network according to predefined sets of criteria about what is and what is not authorized.[36] Upon receiving a network packet, the firewall analyzes its characteristics (source address, destination address, port number, network status, actual data delivered, etc.) and determines whether to let it go through, drop it, delay it, or redirect it for further inspection. In their simplest and most lightweight form, firewalls look at individual packets in isolation and take decisions based on static rules, but most firewalls are a bit more advanced than that (and less lightweight). Stateful firewalls keep a history of the packets inspected so as to track ongoing network sessions and anticipate what subsequent legitimate packets should look like; proxy firewalls protect users in the internal network by acting as intermediaries and establishing on their behalf any external connections that they require; deep packet inspection firewalls take the packets apart, analyze the data they carry, and look for particular content that would indicate a threat.[37]

---

[34]Ardagna, C. A., Cremonini, M., Damiani, E., di Vimercati, S. D. C., and Samarati, P. (2006). Supporting location-based conditions in access control policies. In *Proceedings of the 2006 ACM Symposium on Information, computer and communications security*, pp. 212–222, ACM, March 2006.

[35]Vijayenthiran, V. (2007) Nissan GT-R automatically unlocks speed limiter when you get to a circuit. Motor Authority, December 24, 2007.

[36]Bellovin, S. M. and Cheswick, W. R. (1994). Network firewalls. *Communications Magazine, IEEE*, Volume 32, No. 9, pp. 50–57.

[37]Beyond protection against cyber security threats, deep packet inspection can be equally useful to state censorship, surveillance, espionage, targeted advertising, copyright enforcement, and any other activity that benefits from the rapid and intelligent analysis of people's network traffic.

Its attractive proposition ("a system that prevents bad things from entering an organization's network") has made the firewall one of the most popular security products. However, its effectiveness is only as good as its configuration. In 2004, Wool's large-scale study[38] on real-world firewall configurations showed that the more complex the rulesets, the more errors, and consequently the less protection they offer. He reconfirmed this result with a separate study in 2010.[39]

Firewalls can prove useful in cyber-physical systems that involve communication over more than one network and where there is enough processing capacity to allow analyzing network traffic in real time. This can potentially include automobiles, for example to isolate the different in-vehicle networks, such as the high-speed and low-speed CAN buses, from each other and from external ones,[40] but more commonly firewalls are used in industrial control systems to isolate the SCADA control network from the corporate network and the Internet.[41] In the past, commercial firewalls would focus almost exclusively on communication protocols used in corporate networks and the Internet, but today DNP3, IEC, Modbus, and other industrial network protocols are well supported.

Intrusion Detection

Since it is very difficult to prevent all possible attacks against a system, it usually makes sense to put in place measures to detect intrusions when they occur.[42] Intrusion detection is the area of security where cyber-physical attacks may differ the most from conventional computer security attacks. The main differentiator is the very fact that they have an impact in physical space, and this impact can usually be observed. If an actuator behaves in a highly erratic manner or a group of sensors report data that appear to contradict the laws of physics, then

[38]Wool, A. (2004). A quantitative study of firewall configuration errors. *Computer*, Volume 37, No. 6, pp. 62–67.
[39]Wool, A. (2010). Trends in firewall configuration errors: Measuring the holes in swiss cheese. *Internet Computing, IEEE*, Volume 14, No. 4, pp. 58–65.
[40]Groll, A., Holle, J., Ruland, C., Wolf, M., Wollinger, T., and Zweers, F. (2009). OVERSEE: a secure and open communication and runtime platform for innovative automotive applications. In *7th ESCAR Embedded Security in Cars Conference*, Düsseldorf, Germany, November 2009.
[41]Byres, E., Karsch, J., and Carter, J. (2005). NISCC good practice guide on firewall deployment for SCADA and process control networks. *National Infrastructure Security Co-Ordination Centre.*
[42]Denning, D. E. (1987). An intrusion-detection model. *IEEE Transactions on Software Engineering*, Volume 13, No. 2, pp. 222–232.

these by themselves are good indications that there might be an attack going on. An intrusion detection system can make use of such information about the physical space in addition to information about the network and computational processes running on a system.

Intrusion detection mechanisms can be knowledge-based,[43] behavior-based,[44] or a combination of the two.[45] Knowledge-based approaches work by first compiling an attack dictionary. This is a database of known attacks, each exhibiting a particular pattern of network traffic rate, sequence of function calls, sensor measurements, and other characteristics that we refer to as the input features of the detection mechanism. (Some knowledge-based detection mechanisms make use of over 100 different input features.[46]) When deployed operationally, knowledge-based detection mechanisms monitor the current state of a system and look for these known attack patterns. If they do find one, they raise an alert and state which type of attack has been detected, usually accompanied by a level of confidence on this detection (e.g., low, moderate, high). Otherwise, they assume that there is no attack going on. A knowledge-based detection approach is meaningful to deploy if it is based on a large and well-defined attack dictionary. The attack patterns that are needed to populate the dictionary can be collected by launching simulated attacks against a system and recording the characteristic input features for each one. An attempt by Premaratne et al.[47] to develop an intrusion detection mechanism for electrical substation infrastructures involved simulating three types of attacks (denial of service, password cracking, and address resolution protocol spoofing[48]) against such an infrastructure, and measuring the number of failed

[43]Knowledge-based detection is also referred to as pattern-based, signature-based, or misuse detection.
[44]Behavior-based detection is also referred to as anomaly-based detection.
[45]Coppolino, L., D'Antonio, S., Romano, L., and Spagnuolo, G. (2010). An intrusion detection system for critical information infrastructures using wireless sensor network technologies. In *5th International Conference on Critical Infrastructure*, IEEE, September 2010.
[46]Tsang, C. H. and Kwong, S. (2005). Multi-agent intrusion detection system in industrial network using ant colony clustering approach and unsupervised feature extraction. In *IEEE International Conference on Industrial Technology*, pp. 51–56, IEEE, December 2005.
[47]Premaratne, U. K., Samarabandu, J., Sidhu, T. S., Beresh, R., and Tan, J. C. (2010). An intrusion detection system for IEC61850 automated substations. *IEEE Transactions on Power Delivery*, Volume 25, No. 4, pp. 2376–2383.
[48]In ARP spoofing, the attacker claims to have the address of another (legitimate) node in the same local area network, so as to intercept any traffic destined for that node.

login attempts, the rate of incoming traffic of a particular type, and other input features. However, developing an attack dictionary by simulating attacks one by one is inefficient. A more efficient approach is to use a honeypot, which is a computer system set up for the purpose of attracting attacks against it.[49] The honeypot approach can automate the process of collecting attack patterns and can be highly realistic, especially if it imitates a real cyber-physical system and its attackers are unaware that it is a honeypot. However, this is not an ideal solution either. It is most useful in helping build an attack dictionary for a particular cyber-physical system if it is sufficiently similar to it, but making a honeypot accessible to attackers reveals to them the configuration and potentially the vulnerabilities of the real system.

The majority of attacks that are commonly encountered are known and are already included in attack dictionaries. For these, knowledge-based approaches can be very accurate. They exhibit high likelihood of flagging a known malicious activity as an attack (true positive rate), low likelihood of flagging a normal activity as an attack (false positive rate), and low likelihood of failing to flag a known malicious activity as an attack (false negative rate). On the other hand, behavior-based approaches are much better at detecting attacks that have not been previously observed. They work by first defining what behavior should be considered as ordinary for a particular system and by then looking for evidence of behavior that is out of the ordinary. This makes them suitable for cyber-physical systems. As Mitchell and Chen have argued, attacks on cyber-physical systems can be highly sophisticated and may make use of several zero-day vulnerabilities due to the potentially very high payoff, as in the case of Stuxnet.[50] So, it is more important that their intrusion detection mechanisms can detect attacks that follow no known patterns than it is in conventional computer systems. Also, in the latter, where it is human users that trigger most activities, it is quite difficult to determine what ordinary is. As a result, behavior-based approaches have traditionally been less accurate for the majority of attack types on conventional computer systems and, consequently, less popular. However, in cyber-physical systems, most activities are triggered by automated

---

[49]Kreibich, C. and Crowcroft, J. (2004). Honeycomb: creating intrusion detection signatures using honeypots. *ACM SIGCOMM Computer Communication Review,* Volume 34, No. 1, pp. 51–56.

[50]Mitchell, R. and Chen, I. R. (2014). A survey of intrusion detection techniques for cyber-physical systems. *ACM Computing Surveys,* Volume 46, No. 4, 55:1–29.

processes and not by human users, and as such they are relatively predictable. For example, SCADA systems tend to involve routine and repetitive communication between known devices that may be operating in the same role and in the same predictable manner for years. In this context, determining what is ordinary is feasible and opting for a behavior-based approach usually makes sense.

If a particular SCADA communication protocol specifies that a server can receive but cannot initiate connection requests, then any attempt of a server to initiate requests should be seen as behavior that is out of the ordinary and hence suspicious. Cheung et al.[51] followed this approach for Modbus TCP to develop one of the first detection mechanisms for SCADA networks. Starting from the functions defined in the particular protocol's specification document,[52] they constructed a set of rules for the expected (and thus acceptable) behavior of the protocol for every possible function. Their detection mechanism would then consider a violation of any of these rules as evidence of an attack. The particular behavior-based approaches where there is a formal specification of the expected legitimate behavior are referred to as behavior-specification approaches. Thanks to their low false negative rates and ability to catch unknown attacks, behavior-specification approaches are among the most promising for the protection of highly critical cyber-physical systems, where a previously unknown type of attack can cause considerable physical damage if it evades detection. In fact, the specification does not have to be limited to the operation of the network, as in the example above, but the same logic can be used for a system's physical functions. Mitchell and Chen's intrusion detection mechanism for cyber-physical medical devices[53] specifies the expected behavior and interactions of their medical sensors and actuators rather than the network protocol that supports their communication. For instance, if a medical device is programmed to allow delivery of an analgesic only when the patient's pulse rate is above some threshold, then any user-generated or automated request to deliver

[51]Cheung, S., Dutertre, B., Fong, M., Lindqvist, U., Skinner, K., and Valdes, A. (2007). Using model-based intrusion detection for SCADA networks. In *Proceedings of the SCADA Security Scientific Symposium*, Volume 46, January 2007.

[52]Swales, A. (1999). Open Modbus/TCP Specification. *Schneider Electric*, March 29, 1999.

[53]Mitchell, R. and Chen, R. (2014). Behavior Rule Specification-based Intrusion Detection for Safety Critical Medical Cyber Physical Systems. In *IEEE Transactions on Dependable and Secure Computing*.

analgesic while the pulse rate is below that threshold should be flagged as indicative of a potential intrusion.

Behavior-specification approaches require a human expert to define what is ordinary. This can be a lengthy and complex process. The effectiveness of the intrusion detection ultimately depends on the quality of the rules set by the human expert (see Box 6.1 for an example exercise). Other behavior-based approaches aim to rely less on a human expert and more on automated processes that learn what ordinary is for a particular cyber-physical system by monitoring its behavior over time. Their aim is to determine ranges of usual values for relevant input features, such as the usual rate of network packets received at a particular industrial network[54] or the usual location of a particular medical sensor.[55]

As mentioned already, the fact that information from both cyber and physical elements can be used as input is a key characteristic of cyber-physical attack detection mechanisms. Cyberspace input features are largely the same as those used to detect attacks in conventional computer systems and networks (packet sources/destinations, timestamps, network traffic rates, types of messages, routing information, etc.). Physical space input features can be the measurements coming from sensors, the settings of actuators, the locations of devices, and so on (see Table 6.1). They too can be indicative of a potential intrusion and are frequently used together with cyberspace input features for electric grid,[56] automotive,[57] and other cyber-physical environments, but usually in a laboratory rather than real-world deployment. As an example, consider a SCADA system that is used to operate a water storage tank.[58] The rate at

[54]Shin, S., Kwon, T., Jo, G. Y., Park, Y., and Rhy, H. (2010). An experimental study of hierarchical intrusion detection for wireless industrial sensor networks. *Transactions on Industrial Informatics*, Volume 6, No. 4, IEEE.

[55]Park, K., Lin, Y., Metsis, V., Le, Z., and Makedon, F. (2010). Abnormal human behavioral pattern detection in assisted living environments. In *Proceedings of the 3rd International Conference on Pervasive Technologies Related to Assistive Environments*, ACM, June 2010.

[56]Koutsandria, G., Muthukumar, V., Parvania, M., Peisert, S., McParland, C., and Scaglione, A. (2014). A Hybrid Network IDS for Protective Digital Relays in the Power Transmission Grid. In *Proceedings of the 5th IEEE International Conference on Smart Grid Communication*, November 2014.

[57]Muter, M., Groll, A., and Freiling, F. C. (2010). A structured approach to anomaly detection for in-vehicle networks. In *Sixth International Conference on Information Assurance and Security*, pp. 92–98, IEEE, August 2010.

[58]Gao, W., Morris, T., Reaves, B., and Richey, D. (2010). On SCADA control system command and response injection and intrusion detection. In *eCrime Researchers Summit*, IEEE, October 2010.

Box 6.1 Exercise: Cyber-physical intrusion detection for a simple podcar

Also known as personal rapid transit systems, podcars are driverless vehicles that can carry individual passengers or small groups on networks of dedicated guideways. Let us consider such a podcar travelling on a 2,000 m straight line, as shown in Figure 6.1. It has roof-mounted GPS for estimating its approximate position (which can be off by up to 3 m), front-mounted ultrasonic sensors for detecting obstacles and avoiding collisions, and wireless connectivity for communicating with a control center.

In its normal operation, the podcar travels fully autonomously, monitoring its position, and starting, stopping, and controlling its speed without human interaction. However, an authorized operator at the control center can wirelessly send commands if there is an emergency. The communication protocol used is very simple. The operator sends one of three individual instructions (start, stop, travel at specified speed) in single network packets containing also an identifier for the particular operator (the packet source) and an identifier for the particular podcar (the packet destination). Each packet is 80 bits long. Upon receipt, the podcar sends an acknowledgment packet of 40 bits back to the operator. In addition, to ensure that emergency remote control is always possible, the podcar sends "ping" packets of 40 bits to the operator's room every 5 s, expecting an acknowledgement packet to each one (again 40 bits). If there is no acknowledgement, it has been programmed to stop immediately. It has also been programmed to stop immediately if it has reached its destination or the ultrasonic sensor has detected an obstacle within 10 m. The wireless communication channel can support only a very low transmission rate of 1 Kbit/s in either direction.

The particular podcar model can travel at up to 20 m/s, but its normal speed when travelling autonomously is limited to 10 m/s. That is both for comfort of the passengers and for safety, as the collision avoidance sensors cannot detect obstacles quickly enough for the podcar to brake in time. For the sake of simplicity, ignore the length of the podcar and any acceleration effects at the start of the journey, and consider the surface to be completely flat and the network delay to be negligible when the network operates normally.

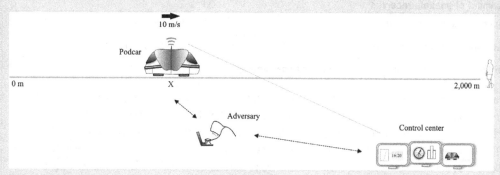

Figure 6.1 An adversary attempts to attack a podcar.

(Continued)

Box 6.1 (Continued)

Question 1: What rules would you consider including in a behavior-specification intrusion detection mechanism running as part of the embedded software of this podcar? Since processing power is limited, your detection mechanism cannot check all rules continuously, but only once every 10 s. The only data available are the following: Total number of packets sent P_s, total number of bits sent B_s, total number of packets received P_r, total number of bits received B_r, GPS-location X. The difference between the current value and the value 10 s ago for each one of these is denoted with the Greek letter Δ. For example, ΔPr is the total number of packets received in the last 10 s and ΔX is the total distance covered in the last 10 s according to the GPS module.

Answer: Since it is a behavior-specification intrusion detection mechanism that is required, we start by specifying what behavior is ordinary. From the cyber perspective, the exercise provides information only for the communication protocol. Since we are limited to one check every 10 s, the rules should reflect this. Network delay is negligible in normal operation. So, the podcar will send at least two ping packets (rule A) and will receive at least two ping acknowledgments (rule B) in any 10 s time window.

Since the sizes of legitimate packets are known, we can use these as the next rules. We notice that both types of legitimate packets sent from the podcar are always 40 bits long. Since we do not check each packet individually, only total numbers over 10 s, we can check that the average size of the packets sent in 10 s stays at exactly 40 bits (rule C). For received packets, the legitimate packet size is 40 or 80 bits. Using the same logic, in normal operation, the average received packet's size should be between 40 and 80 bits (rule D). In fact, since there will be at least two 40-bit inbound (ping) packets in the 10 s, the average over this duration can never be equal to 80 bits (there will never be only 80-bit packets received in these 10 s), but it can be equal to 40 bits (if all inbound packets are ping acknowledgments and no 80-bit packet is received). The protocol also specifies that there is an acknowledgement packet for every packet sent. So, the difference between the number of packets sent and received should be zero.

Cyber Input Feature	Rule
A. Number of packets sent	$\Delta P_s \geq 2$
B. Number of packets received	$\Delta P_r \geq 2$
C. Average packet size sent	$\frac{\Delta B_s}{\Delta P_s} = 40$ bits
D. Average packet size received	$80 \text{bits} > \frac{\Delta B_r}{\Delta P_r} \geq 40$ bits
E. Difference between number of packets sent and received	$\Delta P_s - \Delta P_r = 0$

In terms of the physical behavior specification, we can start with the podcar's normal speed, which is 10 m/s. Travelling at up to that speed, the podcar cannot cover more than 100 m in 10 s. However, the exercise specifies that each GPS measurement can be off by up to 3 m. Since the location is estimated via GPS and it takes two location measurements to calculate a distance ΔX, the latter can be off by up to 6 m. Any value greater than 106 m would be false or indicative of an attack that increased the podcar's speed beyond the safe maximum. Also, the location X can only be between 0 m (the starting point) and 2,000 m (the end of the guideway). Any value reported outside this range (after adjusting with the maximum GPS error of ± 3 m) would be false.

(Continued)

Box 6.1 (Continued)

Physical Input Feature	Rule
F. Distance travelled	$\triangle X \leq 106$
G. Location	$2{,}003 \geq X \geq -3$

Question 2: Which of the rules that you defined in Question 1 would be violated during (1) a denial of service attack based on a flood of illegitimate instruction packets of 80 bits each, (2) a jamming attack on the wireless channel, (3) a GPS spoofing attack, (4) a command injection attack aiming to increase the speed of the podcar to an unsafe 20 m/s, (5) a malware attack against the control center, or (6) a code injection attack?

Answer:

1. A typical denial of service attack involves receiving a large number of illegitimate packets. The very low transmission rate supported by the wireless channel will not be sufficient to accommodate all packets transmitted during the attack, thus causing some to be dropped or delayed. As a result, it would be likely that not all packets would be followed by acknowledgements, hence rule E would be violated. If the rate of illegitimate 80-bit packets received was sufficiently high to prevent any legitimate 40-bit ping acknowledgement to arrive within a time window of 10 s, then rule D would also be violated, since the average rate of received packets within this time window would be equal to 80 bits.

2. A jamming attack would disrupt the transmission of network packets. This could lead to violation of rules A, B, D, and E.

3. Violation of rules F and G would point toward an error in the podcar's geopositioning mechanism, which may be internal (e.g., faulty GPS receiver), but could also be the result of an erroneous GPS signal due to GPS spoofing or meaconing. Of course, a carefully crafted GPS signal could provide a location X that is erroneous but still within the rules' specified ranges, and thus avoid violating either.

4. The podcar would travel significantly more than 106 m and would violate rule F.

5. Different malware would have different impact. The worst-case scenario would be to hijack the operation of the control center. Rule F would be likely to be violated for the same reason as 4.

6. A code injection attack would alter the operation of the podcar's embedded software, possibly affecting the intrusion detection mechanism's data collection processes. Consequently, it could lead to erroneous data and a violation of any of the specified rules.

Note: It is rarely possible to detect an attack with confidence based on a single rule. Relying on more than one rule can be useful, but not a guarantee either. For example, if the GPS receiver experienced a natural failure, both rules F and G could be violated even if there were no attack in place. Several rules could also be violated due to a natural disruption of the wireless communication between the podcar and the control center (e.g., A, B, and E). For these reasons, behavior-specification approaches tend to have high false-positive rates. On the other hand, they are able to detect attacks that may be difficult to detect otherwise, such as the code injection attack.

Table 6.1 Examples of Physical Input Features That Can Be Used in Cyber-Physical Intrusion Detection

Physical Input Features	Example Attack	Example Areas of Application
GPS signal strength	GPS spoofing	Vehicles, smart grid
Rotational speed variations	Command injection attack	Centrifuges
Rate of change of water level	Command injection attack	Water treatment facility
Variation of received signal strength	Command injection attack, false data injection	Implants and on-body devices
Duration of message exchange	Relay	Medical devices, vehicles
Power consumption	Sleep deprivation	Medical devices, industrial control sensors
Voltage, current, phase	Aurora-like attack	Electric grid
Location & time/duration	Replay	Medical devices, vehicles

which the water level can change depends on the capacity of the tank and the diameters of the pipes. So, the SCADA system's intrusion detection system may monitor whether the water level data coming from the sensors appear to contradict the laws of physics (a water level that is beyond the physical capacity of the tank, or a change in the water level that is impossible given the diameters of the pipes). If they appear so, then either the sensors are faulty or an attack has altered the data coming from them. In mobile cyber-physical systems such as vehicles, the detection mechanism may also monitor the system's movement patterns.[59] If its location appears to jump from one place to another or if it appears to move at a speed that is greater than what is feasible for the particular type of vehicle, then its wheel speed sensor data or GPS signal may have been spoofed.

The latter brings us to the second type of physical space input data used in intrusion detection: data on the physical characteristics of the actual technology implementations used by the cyber-physical system. For instance, spoofed GPS signals coming from GPS satellite simulators are typically a lot stronger than legitimate GPS signals.[60] This is a physical characteristic of the technology involved. By monitoring the signal strength of a

[59]Mitchell, R. and Chen, R. (2013). On survivability of mobile cyber physical systems with intrusion detection. *Wireless personal communications*, Volume 68, No. 4, pp. 1377–1391.

[60]Warner, J. S. and Johnston, R. G. (2003). GPS spoofing countermeasures. *Homeland Security Journal*, LAUR-03-6163, pp. 22–30.

GPS receiver, it is possible to detect attacks that affect the integrity of GPS data. A similar observation has been made for the variation of the received signal strength of on-body versus off-body wireless communications. Based on this, one can detect whether a signal received by a medical implant comes from a (presumably legitimate) device that is placed very near the body or on the body, or from an external (and presumably malicious) source. The strength of the signal received from the latter is generally less stable.[61]

Apart from signal strength, time can also be useful. That is because cyber-physical systems are real-time systems, where the precise time that an instruction takes to execute is important. Zimmer et al. have shown that when an unexpected or unauthorized instruction is run on the system, the time that it takes the various code sections of its embedded software to run is affected noticeably.[62] So, by determining beforehand when or how long each section takes to run in normal circumstances, and then making very precise timing measurements, a behavior-specification intrusion detection system can help detect a code injection attack[63] that may otherwise be undetectable.

In large-scale cyber-physical systems such as traffic management systems and the smart grid, where the sensors and actuators are attached to several geographically dispersed nodes connected over large networks, intrusion detection can be performed in a distributed manner and can possibly benefit from cooperation between these nodes. For instance, naïve attacks may be detectable by an intrusion detection system sitting on an individual node (e.g., on a single smart meter), while more advanced attacks may be visible only to higher-level systems that aggregate raw data or intrusion detection reports from multiple nodes.[64] Cooperative intrusion detection in cyber-physical systems is expected to become more important with the advent of driverless vehicles. If a particular vehicle is observed to behave erratically on the road by other vehicles, the

---

[61]Shi, L., Li, M., Yu, S., and Yuan, J. (2013). BANA: body area network authentication exploiting channel characteristics. *IEEE Journal on Selected Areas in Communications*, Volume 31, No. 9, pp. 1803–1816.

[62]Zimmer, C., Bhat, B., Mueller, F., and Mohan, S. (2010). Time-based intrusion detection in cyber-physical systems. In *Proceedings of the 1st ACM/IEEE International Conference on Cyber-Physical Systems*, pp. 109–118, ACM, April 2010.

[63]Code injection is a type of malware attack, where malicious code is introduced in an existing computer program with the purpose of modifying its intended operation.

[64]Zhang, Y., Wang, L., Sun, W., Green, R. C., and Alam, M. (2011). Distributed intrusion detection system in a multi-layer network architecture of smart grids. *IEEE Transactions on Smart Grid*, Volume 2, No. 4, pp. 796–808.

latter can share their observations with each other to reach a consensus on whether there is a high probability that it has been compromised and it is unsafe to be near it.[65]

Antimalware

Antimalware countermeasures aim to prevent, detect, identify, and remove malware. As prevention we can consider any action taken to reduce the chances of malware finding its way into a system. Potentially the most effective of preventive measures is to have a program of awareness for malware and social engineering. The two have become closely interlinked in recent years. Social engineering has been made possible on a grand scale thanks to malware, and malware relies heavily on social engineering to propagate. For instance, a rented botnet may send spam e-mails to users worldwide, trying to manipulate them into clicking a link. By clicking it, the user is directed to a malicious web site, which infects the user's computer with a Trojan horse, possibly carrying a key logger and a rootkit. In fact, it can even convert it into a bot to be used in spam e-mail campaigns or other attacks.[66]

Awareness programs focus on informing users about the different social engineering techniques employed by hackers and simple cyber hygiene practices that are easy to follow and can dramatically reduce an organization's susceptibility to malware incidents. A good set of cyber hygiene practices has been proposed in a special publication of the National Institute of Standards and Technology.[67] A couple of examples are "Not opening suspicious e-mails or e-mail attachments, clicking on hyperlinks, etc. from unknown or known senders, or visiting web sites that are likely to contain malicious content," and "not

---

[65]Fagiolini, A., Pellinacci, M., Valenti, G., Dini, G., and Bicchi, A. (2008). Consensus-based distributed intrusion detection for multi-robot systems. In *International Conference on Robotics and Automation*, pp. 120–127, IEEE, May 2008.

[66]Note that during a botnet attack, the performance of the compromised computers (the bots) is also affected if they are ordered to send large amounts of network traffic to their target. As mentioned briefly in Chapter 2 (T2), the Port of Houston's computers may have been slowed down not because they were the target of the attack, but because they were used as bots. Whether this was true or not in that particular case is immaterial for our purposes. What matters is that it is possible that a computer critical for a physical operation can become a bot if it is connected to the Internet and becomes compromised.

[67]Souppaya, M. and Scarfone, K. (2013). Guide to malware incident prevention and handling for desktops and laptops. National Institute of Standards and Technology. Special Publication 800–83, Revision 1.

opening files with file extensions that are likely to be associated with malware (e.g., .bat, .com, .exe, .pif, .vbs)."

Antimalware applications[68] used to detect and identify (and usually remove too) malware most commonly scan the contents of a file and compare it against a blacklist of known malware. In this manner, they are very similar to knowledge-based intrusion detection systems. Note that for an antimalware application to be effective, it needs to always be up to date. However, this implies some form of Internet connectivity in order to always be able to download the latest malware signatures. In an industrial control system, where direct Internet connectivity on a server with access to the control network would be too risky, malware signatures may first be downloaded on an isolated computer and then be applied to the control network's computers manually.

An interesting alternative approach proposed by Gonzalez and Hinton[69] is to attempt to detect the execution of malware on an embedded system, such as a PLC, by monitoring the latter's power consumption. A PLC has rather predictable patterns of operation that result in known power consumption patterns. The rationale is that unusual power consumption may indicate the existence of malware altering the normal operation of the PLC.

In practice, advanced cyber-physical attacks such as Stuxnet are expected to utilize several attack approaches, elements used in different types of malware, and a variety of methods of propagation and infection, in what is known as a blended attack. This is where a defense-in-depth strategy (see later) can prove particularly beneficial.

Application Whitelisting

Rather predictably, whitelisting[70] is the opposite of blacklisting. Instead of blocking what is on a blacklist, it allows only what is on a whitelist. This means that it does not require millions of new entries of malware signatures every year to be up to date, and can still offer some protection against zero-day attacks and new variations of known malware before these are

[68]Antimalware applications are traditionally referred to as "antivirus" since they were first developed to address viruses.
[69]Gonzalez, C. A. and Hinton, A. (2014). Detecting Malicious Software Execution in Programmable Logic Controllers Using Power Fingerprinting. In *Critical Infrastructure Protection VIII*, pp. 15–27, Springer Berlin Heidelberg.
[70]Harrison, J. V. (2005). Enhancing network security by preventing user-initiated malware execution. In *International Conference on Information Technology: Coding and Computing*, Volume 2, pp. 597–602, IEEE, April 2005.

introduced to blacklists. Most commercial tools for application whitelisting allow a system's administrator to determine the list of executable files, directories, and software vendors that are trusted. An attempt to perform an action that is not explicitly included in a whitelist (e.g., to modify a trusted executable file or run an untrusted one) generates an automated alert to the administrator or is automatically blocked. This approach is commonly recommended for SCADA systems.

Flow Whitelisting

In computer networks, a network traffic flow is a stream of packets travelling from a source to a destination. Flow whitelisting can be seen as a special case of firewall configuration or behavior-specification intrusion detection, where a human expert determines all possible [source address, destination address] pairs[71] of legitimate network traffic. Any flow that is not found in the whitelist is considered malicious. Flow whitelisting has several advantages, since it is independent of the type of network protocol used and requires minimal resources to implement and run. It is not particularly practical in conventional computer networks, such as the Internet, where the potential legitimate flows are too many to include in a whitelist. This is not the case for cyber-physical systems' networks, where the number of flows is manageable and network traffic is generally repetitive and predictable.[72] As a result, most SCADA security guidelines published worldwide include recommendations similar to flow whitelisting, such as to "block all communications with the exception of specifically enabled communications."[73]

The flow whitelist does not need to be populated by a human expert. The alternative is to have a learning phase, where the whitelist is produced automatically by recording all flows that are present in that phase.[74] Any flow observed later is automatically considered legitimate if it had been recorded during the learning phase; otherwise it is considered malicious.

[71]A traffic flow can be more accurately defined by including, in addition to the source address and destination address, the source port, the destination port, and the protocol used.
[72]Yun, J. H., Jeon, S. H., Kim, K. H., and Kim, W. N. (2013). Burst-based Anomaly Detection on the DNP3 Protocol. *International Journal of Control & Automation*, Volume 6, No. 2.
[73]Stouffer, K., Falco, J., and Scarfone, K. (2011). Guide to industrial control systems (ICS) security. *NIST special publication*, pp. 800–882.
[74]Barbosa, R. R. R., Sadre, R., and Pras, A. (2013). Flow whitelisting in SCADA networks. *International journal of critical infrastructure protection*, Volume 6, No. 3, pp. 150–158.

Of course, this assumes that during the learning phase the network had not been under attack and all legitimate flows had been observed.

Cryptography

Central in the field of security, cryptography is the primary practice followed for the protection of confidentiality, integrity, and authenticity in modern computer and communication systems.[75] Let us start with a few definitions. **Encryption** is the process of transforming ordinary text (plaintext) into a coded form (ciphertext), and **decryption** is the reverse. **Cryptography** is the art and science of designing **ciphers**, which are the algorithms[76] used to encrypt and decrypt messages. Ciphers are also known as cryptographic systems. All modern ciphers use keys, which are sequences of bits that determine the output of a cipher.

In **symmetric** ciphers, there is one **secret key** for both encrypting and decrypting. The cipher takes as input the plaintext and the secret key and performs various substitutions and transformations over multiple steps. The end result is the ciphertext. To decrypt the latter and retrieve the plaintext, one needs to know the secret key. This introduces a significant challenge, as the intended recipient of a message needs to have somehow already received the secret key in a manner that cannot be intercepted by an adversary. Different environments require different approaches. What is interesting with symmetric cryptography in cyber-physical systems is that the exchange of the secret key can be achieved partly via physical means. This has led to novel techniques, albeit still tested only in a laboratory. For instance, a body's physiological state changes constantly and is quite unique at a given time. A device can generate a random secret key and hide it inside a message that contains these physiological measurements.[77] Another device receiving this message can tell what part is the secret key only if it has collected itself the same measurements and at roughly the same time.

[75]Also for nonrepudiation, which is about ensuring that the sender of a message cannot deny having sent it.
[76]In mathematics and computer science, an algorithm is a step-by-step procedure to solve a particular problem.
[77]Venkatasubramanian, K. K., Banerjee, A., and Gupta, S. K. S. (2010). PSKA: usable and secure key agreement scheme for body area networks. *IEEE Transactions on Information Technology in Biomedicine*, Volume 14, No. 1, pp. 60–68.

In **asymmetric** ciphers, there is a **private key** and a **public key**.[78] Anyone can encrypt a message using the public key (which is not secret), but only the owner of the private key (which is secret) can decrypt it. This means that the private key never needs to be shared, which addresses a significant weakness of symmetric cryptography. The downside is that asymmetric ciphers are generally much more complicated than symmetric ones, which makes them slower and less practical for large blocks of data. A common practice to get the best of both worlds is to use a symmetric cipher to encrypt the message and an asymmetric one to encrypt the secret key before sharing it with the intended recipient.

In addition to protecting confidentiality, the concept of asymmetric cryptography can also be used to create **digital signatures** that verify authenticity and integrity. The idea is that one can use a private (signature) key and apply a particular digital signing algorithm on a message to produce the digital signature, the authenticity of which anybody can check with the public key and a signature verification algorithm. The digital signature has also allowed the introduction of the **digital certificate**, which is an electronic document digitally signed by a trusted agency (the certificate authority) proving someone's ownership of their public key. Famously, the developers of Stuxnet used stolen certificates from well-known companies to make it look in the eyes of antimalware products as legitimate software developed by these companies.

While encryption is used pervasively in conventional computer systems, it is common to be absent, weak, or limited in scope when applied to cyber-physical systems. In a typical automobile, messages transmitted on the CAN buses are sent in plaintext because encryption would introduce a substantial processing power and time overhead, which cannot be afforded by resource-constrained ECUs with strict real-time requirements.[79] The use of cryptography is limited to authentication, for example, in unlocking the vehicle and disabling the immobilizer, using symmetric ciphers and short secret keys (see Box 3.5 in Chapter 3).

The same limitations are observed in the smart grid,[80] medical devices, and most other cyber-physical systems. The limited

[78]Diffie, W. and Hellman, M. E. (1976). New directions in cryptography. *IEEE Transactions on Information Theory*, Volume 22, No. 6, pp. 644–654.
[79]Wolf, M., Weimerskirch, A., and Paar, C. (2006). Secure in-vehicle communication. In *Embedded Security in Cars*, pp. 95–109, Springer Berlin Heidelberg.
[80]Wang, W. and Lu, Z. (2013). Cyber security in the smart grid: Survey and challenges. *Computer Networks*, Volume 57, No. 5, pp. 1344–1371, Elsevier.

processing power of embedded systems and the need to mini-mize latency dictate the use of relatively short secret keys and symmetric rather than asymmetric cryptography. To a large extent, these issues can be addressed by offloading to separate dedicated hardware the tasks of managing the keys and per-forming cryptographic operations. Two examples in the auto-motive sector are the German industry-led Secure Hardware Extension (SHE)[81] and the Hardware Security Module (HSM) designed in the EU-funded project EVITA.[82]

Integrity Verification

A way to affect the integrity of a cyber-physical system's oper-ation is to modify the firmware[83] and software applications run-ning on its embedded systems. The fact that most devices allow firmware updates so that manufacturers can address future issues or add features means that an adversary with physical access may attempt to upload onto it a counterfeit firmware update. Furthermore, the threat of counterfeit firmware is also one of the biggest concerns in supply chain security. For instance, a vehicle manufacturer relies on several different com-panies for the various software applications and sensing, actu-ation, and network subsystems, which in turn rely on their own suppliers for individual components within these subsystems, and so forth. A security breach in any of the companies across the supply chain is a potential reason behind integrity issues with the end product that is shipped to customers.

A standard approach for static analysis of the integrity of a file is to compare it against a baseline file that is trusted to be cor-rect, starting from their hashes and their sizes and continuing with more advanced tests on contents and operation. Various related approaches have been presented for the verification of firmware to be uploaded onto PLCs.[84]

The process of detecting unauthorized changes on a plat-form (a computer, embedded system, etc.) is called attestation.

---

[81]Escherich, R., Ledendecker, I., Schmal, C., Kuhls, B., Grothe, C., and Scharberth, F. (2009). SHE: Secure Hardware Extension—Functional Specification, Version 1.1. *Hersteller Initiative Software (HIS) AK Security, April.*

[82]Wolf, M. and Gendrullis, T. (2012). Design, implementation, and evaluation of a vehicular hardware security module. In *Information Security and Cryptology,* pp. 302–318, Springer Berlin Heidelberg.

[83]Firmware is the low-level permanent software that is programmed into an embedded system to allow it to function and support higher-level software applications.

[84]Garcia Jr, A. M. (2014). *Firmware Modification Analysis in Programmable Logic Controllers,* No. AFIT-ENG-14-M-32, Air Force Institute of Technology.

Remote attestation allows a platform to verify its state by sending measurements related to it to a remote server (the verifier), which compares them to the expected measurements for the correct state (assuming that the verifier already knows all legitimate configuration measurements), and by this determines whether the platform operates correctly. To carry out this process in a trustworthy manner, the usual approach is to employ a Trusted Platform Module (TPM).[85] TPM is a dedicated tamper-resistant microprocessor chip designed by a consortium of key industry players to carry out cryptographic operations securely. Unlike HSM, which is an external device, TPM needs to have already been included on the platform's motherboard and cannot be added externally. It is very common in conventional laptop and desktop PCs, but less so in PLCs and other resource-constrained embedded systems.

Where TPM is not available or impractical, attestation can be software-based.[86] It involves a challenge-response mechanism, where the verifier sends a random challenge to the platform, and then a verification mechanism running on the latter computes a response and presents it back to the verifier. The verifier then tries to determine whether the platform has been compromised based typically on the time taken to compute the response. An example of a challenge-response mechanism designed by Shah et al.[87] has been applied successfully on RTUs. However, it needs to be run when a RTU is taken offline so that the verification mechanism does not affect its real-time operation. Software-based attestation is not as reliable as hardware-based attestation, but has the advantage that it can be used in resource-constrained embedded systems such as smart meters.[88]

Survivability

Most protection mechanisms aim to detect and prevent cyber attacks. In ideal conditions, this makes perfect sense,

[85]Kinney, S. L. (2006). *Trusted platform module basics: using TPM in embedded systems*. Newnes.

[86]Armknecht, F., Sadeghi, A. R., Schulz, S., and Wachsmann, C. (2013). A security framework for the analysis and design of software attestation. In *Proceedings of the SIGSAC conference on Computer & communications security*, ACM, November 2013.

[87]Shah, A., Perrig, A., and Sinopoli, B. (2008). Mechanisms to provide integrity in SCADA and PCS devices. In *Proceedings of the International Workshop on Cyber-Physical Systems-Challenges and Applications*, June 2008.

[88]Song, K., Seo, D., Park, H., Lee, H., and Perrig, A. (2011). OMAP: One-way memory attestation protocol for smart meters. In *Ninth IEEE International Symposium on Parallel and Distributed Processing with Applications Workshops*, pp. 111–118, IEEE, May 2011.

since an attack that is detected early enough and is thwarted will have little impact on its target. In practice though, attacks do often go through, especially if they are based on zero-day exploits or they are the work of an insider. For this reason, there are classes of protection approaches that assume that attacks do succeed and, instead of (or in addition to) preventing them, aim to minimize their impact. Depending on one's background and particular focus in this area, the goals of these approaches are resilience, dependability, fault tolerance, intrusion tolerance, survivability, and so on. Here, we choose to use the term survivability, which is the ability of a system to operate correctly and with minimal performance degradation even if malicious actors have compromised parts of it.[89]

Survivability mechanisms are geared primarily toward maintaining availability and integrity. The most obvious approach is redundancy (Table 6.2). If there are 10 different network channels from one device to another, even if nine are disrupted there will still be one left to maintain communication between them. Whether such level of redundancy is wasteful or not depends on its cost and on how damaging and how likely a disruption of communication would be. The latter is not straightforward. The probability of random failure of a communication device can be measured by testing several copies of that device for a sufficiently long period of time, but the probability of intentional failure caused by a cyber attacker is much more difficult to estimate.[90]

In cyber-physical systems, redundancy with diversity can be used to protect the availability not only of communication but also of actuation, processing, sensing, and so forth. For example, a vehicle's cruise control system that measures velocity based only on the wheel speed sensors will be disrupted if they are physically damaged or the communication link with them is severed. However, if it can infer velocity also through GPS, then the cruise control system will continue functioning during an attack against the wheel speed sensors.[91]

---

[89]Kirsch, J., Goose, S., Amir, Y., and Skare, P. (2011). Toward survivable SCADA. In *Proceedings of the Seventh Annual Workshop on Cyber Security and Information Intelligence Research*. ACM, October 2011.

[90]Littlewood, B. and Strigini, L. (2004). Redundancy and diversity in security. In *Computer Security–ESORICS 2004*, pp. 423–438, Springer Berlin Heidelberg.

[91]Pajic, M., Bezzo, N., Weimer, J., Alur, R., Mangharam, R., Michael, N., Papas, G. J., Sokolsky, O., Tabuada, P., Weirich, S., and Lee, I. (2013). Towards synthesis of platform-aware attack-resilient control systems. In *Proceedings of the 2nd ACM international conference on High confidence networked systems*, pp. 75–76, ACM, April 2013.

Table 6.2 Types of Redundancy Mechanisms

Type	Description	Protects	Applicability
Simple redundancy	Use of redundant critical components, so as to reduce the impact of a component's failure.	Integrity, Availability	Any cyber-physical system
Diversity	Use of redundant critical components with deliberate differences between them, e.g. different operating systems or networking technologies.	Integrity, Availability	Diversity of sensor technologies is used widely in safety critical systems, mainly to ensure accuracy of sensor data.
Hot Standby	Runs in parallel with the primary system. It takes over when it senses that the latter has malfunctioned.	Availability	Commonly used in industrial control systems
Replication	Use of multiple near-exact replicas of critical components. If some are compromised, the other replicas will maintain an acceptable performance and help flag the misbehaving ones.	Integrity, Availability	Proven experimentally for SCADA network firewalls and SCADA master applications. Also proposed for military vehicles.

A more granular version of redundancy is replication. The idea is to deploy multiple near-exact replicas of critical components of a system, so that if some are compromised, the other replicas will not only be sufficient to maintain an acceptable performance but will also help flag the misbehaving ones. For example, Bessani et al.[92] have suggested replicating the firewalls that protect the SCADA networks of critical infrastructures, with every replica having to receive all incoming network traffic and to apply on it the same set of filtering criteria. To let the incoming traffic through, a predetermined minimum number of replicas need to have approved it. To overcome this measure, an attacker would need to launch simultaneous successful attacks on a large number of the replicas, which can be difficult or take too long to be practical.[93] Of course, if the attacker is an insider, already in the network, firewalls do not offer much protection anyway. What can be helpful in this case

[92]Bessani, A. N., Sousa, P., Correia, M., Neves, N. F., and Verissimo, P. (2008). The CRUTIAL way of critical infrastructure protection. *Security & Privacy, IEEE*, Volume 6, No. 6, pp. 44–51.
[93]Veríssimo, P. E., Neves, N. F., and Correia, M. P. (2003). Intrusion-tolerant architectures: Concepts and design. In *Architecting Dependable Systems*, Springer Berlin Heidelberg, pp. 3–36.

is to have more than one SCADA master applications, for example a primary and a slightly different "Hot Standby" running in parallel, with the latter taking over when it senses that the primary has malfunctioned. Kirsch et al.[94] have taken the concept further with several replicas of the SCADA master application running in parallel. They should be equivalent in terms of functionality, but not identical, so as to reduce the chances of all having the same security vulnerabilities and being taken out by the same attack. A way to achieve this diversity is to run each replica on a different operating system.[95] As with the replicated firewalls, for an event to be approved for execution by the SCADA master application, a predetermined minimum number of replicas need to have agreed on it. Again, to overcome this and force execution of the wrong events or block legitimate ones, an attacker would need to hijack a large number of the replicas. The attacker's job becomes even more difficult if the system features some sort of rejuvenation scheme, whereby replicas are periodically reset to a clean state just in case they have been compromised.[96] Replication can also be used for the purpose of data integrity and data availability. If data storage is replicated and distributed across the network, the SCADA master can confirm the integrity of data it receives by checking whether they match the data received from other replicas.[97] The more the replicas the more difficult for an attacker to affect integrity and availability, but also the greater the overhead created in the network (as more messages are exchanged) and, crucially, the easier to breach data confidentiality, since there are many different places the adversary can target to acquire the same data.

As discussed in Chapter 4, one of the key requirements in industrial control systems is continuous availability. This makes the application of software updates particularly challenging, since one needs to minimize the downtime caused by it. In fact, most industrial control vendors recommend switching off the

[94]Kirsch, J., Goose, S., Amir, Y., Wei, D., and Skare, P. (2014). Survivable SCADA via intrusion-tolerant replication, *Transactions on Smart Grid, IEEE*, Volume 5, No. 1, pp. 60–70.
[95]Garcia, M., Bessani, A., Gashi, I., Neves, N., and Obelheiro, R. (2011). OS diversity for intrusion tolerance: Myth or reality? In *IEEE/IFIP 41st International Conference on Dependable Systems & Networks (DSN)*, IEEE, pp. 383–394, June 2011.
[96]Sousa, P., Bessani, A. N., Correia, M., Neves, N. F., and Verissimo, P. (2007). Resilient intrusion tolerance through proactive and reactive recovery. In *13th Pacific Rim International Symposium on Dependable Computing*, IEEE, pp. 373–380, December 2007.
[97]Germanus, D., Khelil, A., and Suri, N. (2010). Increasing the resilience of critical SCADA systems using peer-to-peer overlays. In *Architecting Critical Systems*, Springer Berlin Heidelberg, pp. 161–178.

automatic update feature of Microsoft Windows operating systems until their product is tested for each new update. Replication helps in that it allows applying an update first on an offline replica and testing it before applying it on the primary one.

A system that is based on multiple replicas can be highly survivable, but also quite challenging to run and to develop if they all need to run at the same time and use equally up-to-date data. As a result, it may be appropriate for industrial control systems and military vehicles,[98] where availability is paramount, but less so for cyber-physical systems of lower criticality or limited access to resources.

Of interest is the idea that the more confusing the design of a cyber-physical system, the more difficult for an adversary to know how to attack it to achieve a particular physical impact,[99] and hence the more naturally survivable it is. This idea has some merit, but precisely what is confusing for an attack in practice is not easy to define. A similar approach is to employ deception. An example that has been implemented successfully in a laboratory[100] is to incorporate a network of fake virtual hosts acting as honeypots in an industrial control network in order to attract attackers to them rather than to the real control system nodes.

If every survivability measure fails, then safety-critical cyber-physical systems usually are designed to resort to a fail-safe behavior that prevents them from causing unexpected or excessive physical damage. A malfunctioning UAV may be designed to autonomously land or return to base when communication to its operator is lost, while a robotic arm for remote surgical operations may be designed to automatically shut down and report the error when it senses that it has malfunctioned.[101] A similar but distinct concept is fail-secure, which means that in the event of a system's failure, nobody should have access to it

[98]Obi, O., Deshpande, A., Stipidis, E., and Charchalakis, P. (2013). Intrusion tolerant system for integrated vetronics survivability strategy. In *8th International System Safety Conference incorporating the Cyber Security Conference*, IET, October 16–17, 2013.

[99]Rieger, C. G., Gertman, D. I., and McQueen, M. A. (2009). Resilient control systems: next generation design research. In *2nd Conference on Human System Interactions*, pp. 632–636, IEEE, May 2009.

[100]Vollmer, D. and Manic, M. (2014). Cyber-Physical System Security with Deceptive Virtual Hosts for Industrial Control Networks, In *IEEE Transactions on Industrial Informatics*, Volume 10, No. 2, pp. 1337–1347.

[101]Butner, S. E. and Ghodoussi, M. (2003). Transforming a surgical robot for human telesurgery. In *IEEE Transactions on Robotics and Automation*, Volume 19, No. 5, pp. 818–824.

or to its data. Often fail-safe and fail-secure are at odds with each other. The classic example is the case of a building entry system. What should it do by default if it fails (through an elaborate cyber attack or just a power shutdown)? Lock all doors to ensure that no unauthorized person will enter the building (fail-secure) or open all doors to ensure that everyone can get out in case of a fire (fail-safe)?[102] In most cases, it is health and safety that wins the argument.[103]

Secure Design Principles

Most of the secure design principles that have stood the test of time in the field of information security are largely applicable for cyber-physical attacks too.[104] Examples that have been identified as particularly important are the principles of economy of mechanism, defense-in-depth, least-privilege, separation of privilege, the minimization of the attack surface (especially with regard to a system's network accessibility), isolation, open design, as well as the psychological acceptability of any security measure that is introduced.

Economy of Mechanism

The more the security technologies employed and the more complex, the higher the risk that a component will be misconfigured and the more difficult to verify its security. Since embedded systems, cyber-physical systems and Internet of Things devices are usually resource-constrained, economy of mechanism contributes also toward survivability. For instance, a robot's or implantable medical device's security mechanism that would consume a lot of battery when operating would be harmful by itself. In this case, an attack could achieve its target by merely triggering a security mechanism.

[102]Axelrod, C. W. (2013). Managing the risks of cyber-physical systems. In *Long Island Systems, Applications and Technology Conference (LISAT)*, IEEE, May 2013.
[103]The police are all too aware of this in situations where they try to contain the baddies in a large building, such as a hotel, because it is possible to automatically open all doors and make a swift getaway by causing the fire alarm to go off.
[104]Cardenas, A., Amin, S., Sinopoli, B., Giani, A., Perrig, A., and Sastry, S. (2009). Challenges for securing cyber physical systems. In *Workshop on future directions in cyber-physical systems security*, July 2009.

Defense-in-Depth

Inspired by the military tactic of employing multiple layers of defense to buy time for the defender, defense-in-depth is a common best practice recommendation in computer security. The rationale is that no single defense measure is able to thwart all attacks all the time; hence more than one defense measure is needed. In this sense, it shares the same logic with redundancy-based survivability approaches with a particular focus on redundancy with diversity for security measures.

The layered approach means that an attacker would need to penetrate multiple layers of protection before reaching a critical resource. Large-scale industrial control networks are typically divided into distinct zones (subnets) protected by firewalls.[105] Webservers and e-mail servers that need to be accessed from both the corporate subnet and the Internet are placed in a so-called demilitarized zone[106] (DMZ), while the data historian that needs to be accessed from both the control subnet and the corporate subnet is placed in a second DMZ, as shown in Figure 6.2. A DMZ is a subnet that exposes its resources and services to the subnets that it is immediately connected to, but restricts direct communication between the latter. For example, a user on the corporate subnet accesses the data collected on the control subnet through the data historian on the DMZ rather than directly. With this arrangement, an attacker originating from the Internet will find it easier to access the web and e-mail servers in the first DMZ than the corporate subnet that

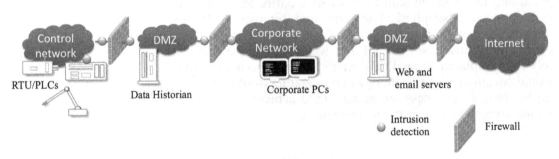

Figure 6.2 Intrusion detection and firewalls at multiple points of an industrial control network.

[105]Lippmann, R., Ingols, K., Scott, C., Piwowarski, K., Kratkiewicz, K., Artz, M., and Cunningham, R. (2006). Validating and restoring defense in depth using attack graphs. In *Military Communications Conference*, IEEE, October 2006.

[106]Stouffer, K., Falco, J., and Scarfone, K. (2011). Guide to industrial control systems (ICS) security. *NIST special publication*, pp. 800–882.

is hidden deeper inside the organization's network. Even if the corporate subnet is penetrated, the attacker will again not have direct connection to the control subnet, but to its neighboring DMZ.

Defense-in-depth is almost always a sound idea, but does not by itself guarantee protection. It has been characterized as "the cyber equivalent of physical walls and moats,"[107] but understanding cyber assets and their interdependencies is not as intuitive as understanding how physical defenses are arranged spatially in a medieval castle. For example, Stuxnet bypassed its target's layers of firewalls by propagating through removable USB media. This attack route would not have been apparent to the person who designed or implemented the particular nuclear facility's defense-in-depth strategy. Also, note that defense-in-depth naturally increases the complexity of the security design of a system, which can be at odds with the economy of mechanism principle.

Least-Privilege

Related to the "need to know" rule used in military and intelligence circles to restrict sensitive information, least-privilege was first articulated by Saltzer and Schroeder[108] in 1975 as the principle that "every program and every user should operate using the least set of privileges necessary to complete the job." Following this, if some particular functionality is not necessary, then it should not be implemented. If it is, then only users and programs that require it should be allowed access to it, and this access should be removed after it ceases to be necessary. Examples of violation of the principle are widespread in cyber-physical systems. For instance, the 2014 experimental attack against 100 traffic lights (Chapter 2, T7) was facilitated by the fact that a service designed for engineers to test a subsystem of the traffic lights prior to deployment was left enabled and accessible by external users after they were deployed.

In systems that involve multiple users, a common way to enforce the least-privilege principle is through role-based access control configured so that every role is assigned the least privileges necessary.

[107]Talbot, E. B., Frincke, D., and Bishop, M. (2010). Demythifying Cybersecurity. *Security & Privacy*, Volume 8, No. 3, pp. 56–59, IEEE.
[108]Saltzer, J. H. and Schroeder, M. D. (1975). The protection of information in computer systems. *Proceedings of the IEEE*, Volume 63, No. 9, pp. 1278–1308.

Separation of Privilege

Also known as "separation of duty," this is the principle that "a system should not grant permission based upon a single condition."[109] There should be more than one check before authorizing a critical action or access to sensitive information. Two-factor authentication is an example of this principle.

Minimization of Attack Surface

This principle requires that, as long as the functionalities required by the users are achieved, the number of entry points to a system (the attack surface) should be kept to a minimum. This can include the number of services running, the number of user accounts with administrative privileges, the number of networks with external access, and so on. Miller and Valasek[110] used the size of the attack surface as a metric for ranking automobiles on their susceptibility to cyber attacks.

Note that minimization of the attack surface is in direct contrast to the increasing functionality of modern cyber-physical systems. The average automobile's susceptibility to attacks has increased rapidly over the last decade as a result of new features requested by buyers, not only for entertainment and comfort, such as Bluetooth support, keyless entry, and telematics, but also for road safety. For instance, collision prevention and lane keep assist are some of the mechanisms that allow a vehicle to stop or change direction when particular messages are transmitted on the internal network.

Isolation

The sharing of hardware, software, and network resources between users and systems has always been a cause of security issues. To reduce these issues, it is common to isolate subsystems from each other, a user's processes, and data from other users', and critical resources from external or public access. At the network level, isolation can be performed to some degree by using firewalls and by encrypting any data travelling between two networks, such as a nuclear facility's corporate network and its industrial control network, so that security breaches in the former cannot easily affect the latter.

[109]Bishop, Matt (2003). *Computer Security: Art and Science*. Boston, MA: Addison-Wesley.
[110]Miller, C. and Valasek, C. (2014). A Survey of Remote Automotive Attack Surfaces, Black Hat 2014, Las Vegas, Nevada, USA.

An extreme case of network isolation is air gapping, which is about physically disconnecting a system from any external wired or wireless network. In the past, it has been used extensively and effectively to protect highly critical systems (e.g., avionics, medical, or military) from external threats. Today, complete physical isolation is usually impractical. For instance, for reasons of practicality, there needs to exist a continuous flow of real-time data from an industrial control network to the corporate network, or from a high-speed to a low-speed CAN bus in a modern automobile. Also, Stuxnet (Chapter 4) and Emsec attacks (Chapter 7) have proven false the assumption that air gapping renders a system completely secure from external attackers.

Open Design

The computer security community has long held the belief that a system whose design is publicly available (open design) can be trusted much more than one that is proprietary (closed design). The rationale is that the more independent experts have scrutinized a system's security and have helped fix its vulnerabilities, the more one can depend on it.[111] The universality of this principle is debatable.[112] Nevertheless, it is certainly wise to reject the opposite concept, which is that a closed design is more secure than an open one because it is not readily available to adversaries (security through obscurity). For instance, no matter how obscure a proprietary industrial control network is, a determined adversary, such as an enemy state, would have both the motivation and the resources to analyze it and identify exploitable weaknesses. Also, of particular relevance are medical devices, whose security vulnerabilities are usually caused by errors in the design or implementation of their proprietary software, communication protocols, or cryptographic systems.

Psychological Acceptability

Psychological acceptability is where many security mechanisms fail. If a particular security mechanism hinders a system's usability or accessibility, the users may reject it or look for a way to circumvent it. For instance, biometric authentication

[111]Hoepman, J. H. and Jacobs, B. (2007). Increased security through open source. *Communications of the ACM*, Volume 50, No. 1, pp. 79–83.
[112]Anderson, Ross (2002). Security in open versus closed systems – the dance of Boltzmann, Coase and Moore. In *Conference on open source software: economics, law and policy*, June 2002.

and identification technologies that are based on retinal scanning are consistently ranked among the most effective. They are also among the least popular in terms of their acceptance by the users[113] because they require conscious effort (to peep into an eye-piece and focus on a specific spot) and in some cases can reveal medical conditions like hypertension.[114]

Summary

Most families of security mechanisms developed for cyber attacks are applicable whether there is adverse impact in physical space or not. Nevertheless, there are meaningful differences between conventional computer systems and cyber-physical systems in terms of the deployment and effectiveness of each security mechanism (see Table 6.3). Unlike conventional computer systems, where confidentiality is the primary concern, the emphasis of cyber-physical system security is on availability and integrity. Resource-restricted devices are challenging when it comes to the implementation of cryptographic protections, firewalls, and blacklist-based antimalware applications. On the other hand, network traffic patterns and applications required are predictable and can be specified in whitelists, which are considerably less demanding in terms of resources. Also, biometric features, proximity, location, and other measurable characteristics that originate in physical space are highly relevant for use by authentication and access control mechanisms. Similarly, intrusion detection can benefit from taking into account not only cyber input features but also physical input features, such as suspicious changes in power consumption, water level, mobility, and so on.

Cyber-physical systems are attractive targets for highly capable adversaries, and security mechanisms designed specifically for them are still relatively immature. This combination means that it is not difficult for a particular mechanism to fail to protect against a cyber-physical attack. This places increased importance in survivability mechanisms, such as redundancy with diversity and replication, and to the age-old principles for secure design in cyberspace that have stood the test of time, and especially defense-in-depth and isolation.

---

[113]McMillan, T. and Abernathy, R. (2013). *CISSP Cert Guide*. Pearson Education.
[114]Jain, A. K., Ross, A., and Prabhakar, S. (2004). An introduction to biometric recognition. *IEEE Transactions on Circuits and Systems for Video Technology*, Volume 14, No. 1, pp. 4–20.

Table 6.3 Differences between Cyber-Physical and Conventional Computer Security Measures

Defense Measures	Conventional Computer Security	Cyber-Physical Security
Authentication	In most situations, password/passphrase or token-based authentication is the most practical.	Biometrics, proximity, and location-based authentication can be particularly suitable.
Access control	Most approaches focus primarily on confidentiality and integrity.	Focus can be extended to real-time availability of cyber-physical systems by using attribute-based access control with attributes whose values may depend on time.
Intrusion Detection	Makes use of only cyber input features. Knowledge-based approaches are usually preferable. Primary performance metrics are the false-positive, false-negative, and true-positive rates.	Makes use of both cyber and physical input features. Behavior-based and especially behavior-specification approaches are very promising. The true-positive rate and detection latency[115] (how long it takes to detect a threat) are particularly important.
Firewall	Used in the majority of computer networks.	Vital for protecting industrial control networks that are connected to corporate networks or the Internet, but less common in other cyber-physical systems.
Antimalware	Used in the vast majority of personal computing and enterprise environments. Updates are usually performed automatically over the Internet.	May be too demanding for resource-restricted systems. Updates on real-time systems are applied only when they are offline and the updates have already been tried on a backup system.
Application whitelisting	Increasingly popular, but somewhat impractical if flexibility is important.	Naturally suitable for cyber-physical systems because of low resource requirements and a short list of needed applications.
Flow whitelisting	Impractical in most Internet-based and user-driven environments because of the vast range of possible legitimate traffic flows.	Naturally suitable because the network traffic flows are generally repetitive and predictable and their number is manageable.
Cryptography	A primary mechanism for protecting confidentiality, integrity, and authenticity.	Due to processing power and time restrictions in cyber-physical systems, cryptography is often

(*Continued*)

[115]Striki, M., Manousakis, K., Kindred, D., Sterne, D., Lawler, G., Ivanic, N., and Tran, G. (2009). Quantifying resiliency and detection latency of intrusion detection structures. In *Military Communications Conference*, IEEE, October 2009.

Table 6.3 (Continued)

Defense Measures	Conventional Computer Security	Cyber-Physical Security
	By securing communications and online transactions, cryptography is an enabling technology for the Internet.	absent, weak, or limited to token-based authentication and secure streaming of real-time data. Integration of dedicated cryptographic hardware modules can address real-time and processing restrictions.
Integrity verification	Hardware-based attestation employing TPM is used widely in PCs for several years	TPM is not as widely used as in PCs. Software-based mechanisms may be better suited for resource-constrained embedded systems.
Survivability	Emphasis is more commonly on redundant data storage and prevention of data corruption and data loss.	Due to strict real-time requirements, emphasis is on the continuous availability of critical components, including the network infrastructure.

Follow-Up Questions and Exercises

1. Which of the following statements are correct?
   a. Behavior-based intrusion detection methods are generally better than knowledge-based ones at detecting zero-day cyber-physical attacks.
   b. The effectiveness of a knowledge-based intrusion detection method is partly based on how up to date its attack dictionary is.
   c. Behavior-specification approaches typically exhibit high false negative detection rates.
   d. Behavior-specification intrusion detection approaches are particularly useful in securing cyber-physical systems mainly because they can take into account physical input features.
2. Provide two examples of physical input features that could be incorporated in an intrusion detection system designed to detect Stuxnet-like attacks on a nuclear facility's centrifuges.
3. Which of the following statements are correct?
   a. In cyber-physical systems, whitelist-based protection mechanisms are generally more appropriate than blacklist-based ones.
   b. Most antimalware applications are blacklist-based.

    c. Blended attacks are unsuitable for targeting cyber-physical systems.

    d. Updating the operating system and any antimalware applications applied to a cyber-physical system is best to be done automatically, so as to protect from the latest threats.

4. For which of the following reasons is the application of cryptography in cyber-physical systems relatively limited?

    a. Strong encryption is demanding in terms of processing resources. These are often limited in cyber-physical systems.

    b. Some applications of cryptography, such as digital signatures and digital certificates, are not relevant to cyber-physical systems.

    c. Cryptography addresses security attributes that are of low importance to cyber-physical systems.

    d. Strong encryption can introduce time delays, which may be unacceptable for cyber-physical systems with strict real-time requirements.

5. After a series of reports of security breaches on older models that have hurt sales, an automobile manufacturer has decided to ramp up the cyber security of its latest model. They have installed a cyber-physical intrusion detection system running on the engine control module, several firewalls across its internal network infrastructure, and a two-factor authentication system for the driver based on a retinal scanner and a smart key. Which of the following secure design principles have been satisfied?

    a. Minimization of attack surface

    b. Separation of privilege

    c. Psychological acceptability

    d. Defense-in-depth

PHYSICAL-CYBER ATTACKS

7

Chapter Summary

Cyber-physical attacks are not the only attacks that exploit interactions between cyberspace and physical space. The reverse, where an attack in physical space aims to affect the availability, integrity, or confidentiality of information in cyberspace, is by no means new or uncommon. During war, telecommunication cables have always been a prime target for physical attacks, and the intelligence community has long known of advanced techniques for eavesdropping on information leaked in physical space. We describe three representative categories of such physical-cyber attacks, including physical and electromagnetic attacks affecting availability, intentional manipulation of physical input to sensors affecting integrity, and exploitation of compromising emanations affecting confidentiality.

Key Terms: Physical-cyber attack; Tempest; Emsec; side channel attack; sensor input manipulation; physical damage; cyber-physical-cyber attack; physical-cyber-physical attack

Computers and network devices have allowed the birth and the growth of what we call cyberspace, but they themselves are physical objects that obviously exist in physical space. Up to now, our focus has been on cyber-physical attacks, where a compromise in cyberspace affects physical space, but physical-cyber attacks, where the reverse is the case, are equally intriguing. Some of these are obvious. Physically cutting the only network cable will, of course, disrupt the network. Others are less so. They may exploit the manner in which cryptographic techniques are implemented in practice, the way we interact with computers and smart devices, or the physical input to the sensors on which a cyber-physical system depends. We propose the following general definition:

A physical-cyber attack is an attack performed in physical space that adversely affects cyberspace.

In this chapter, we start with old-fashioned physical damage for affecting data availability, and physical manipulation of sensor input for breaching data integrity, before moving on to the technically more complex attacks that breach data confidentiality by exploiting compromising emanations in physical space.

Breaching Availability through Damage in Physical Space

It is self-evident that the availability of data in cyberspace relies on the well-being of the underlying physical infrastructure: the hard disks where they are stored, the network devices and cables through which they are received, the processors, the power supplies, and so on. All these can be damaged, potentially at a grand scale, as a result of natural disasters, accidents, or intentional human action.

Direct Physical Damage

Often, cyber attacks are seen as more capable than physical attacks of causing disproportionate damage. Incidents such as a high school student singlehandedly taking down the web sites of Amazon, eBay, CNN, and several other major organizations, causing financial damage of millions of dollars,[1] have always gained wide publicity. Large-scale cyber damage caused by relatively small-scale physical damage rarely gains the same publicity, although there have been several such incidents.

In 2011, an elderly woman scavenging for copper near Tbilisi, Georgia, accidentally damaged a fiber-optic cable, rather spectacularly causing most of neighboring Armenia to lose Internet connectivity for 5 hours. It emerged that Georgia provides 90% of Armenia's Internet and the cable had been exposed due to landslides and heavy rain.[2] More commonly, physical damage of network infrastructure is the result of fire, flood, or other disasters experienced in physical space. For example, when a freight train carrying chemicals derailed and caught fire in a downtown Baltimore tunnel in 2001,[3] it led to the destruction of key fiber-optic cables and widespread loss of network connectivity for 2 days. Geographically, the tunnel was a very convenient location for placing underground cables and other equipment to connect the various networks in the city. In fact, there also were several redundant cables in case the main ones were somehow unavailable. However, being located in the same place meant that a single disaster in physical space could destroy them all at the same time (including the redundant ones), which is precisely what happened.

Since the 1860s, when Brunel's SS *Great Eastern* laid the first lasting telegraph cables connecting Britain and North America, and later the Arabian Peninsula and India, long distance global telecommunications have depended on undersea cables. Today, most of the global Internet traffic travels through approximately 200 gigantic undersea fiber-optic cables,[4] which are not easy to protect against physical damage.[5] In 2006, an earthquake near Taiwan damaged undersea cables, leading to complete lack of

[1]Calce, M. and Silverman, C. (2008). *Mafiaboy: How I Cracked the Internet and why It' Still Broken*. Penguin Group Canada.
[2]Parfitt, T. (2011). Georgian woman cuts off web access to whole of Armenia, The Guardian, April 6, 2011.
[3]Carter, M. R., Howard, M. P., Owens, N., Register, D., Kennedy, J., Pecheux, K., and Newton, A. (2002). Effects of catastrophic events on transportation system management and operations, Howard Street Tunnel Fire, Baltimore City, Maryland, July 18, 2001: Findings.
[4]TeleGeography maintains a wonderful map of the undersea telecommunication cables at www.submarinecablemap.com.
[5]Anyanova, E. (2011). Oceans apart: overview of the international law regime for submarine cables. *International Journal of Private Law*, Volume 4, No. 1, pp. 100–110.

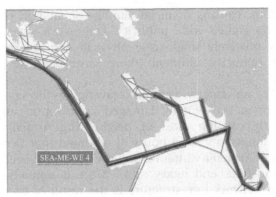

Figure 7.1 Several incidents of large-scale disruption of Internet services in the Middle East have been caused by physical damage to the South East Asia–Middle East–Western Europe 4 (SEA-ME-WE 4) submarine cable.

Internet access in Hong Kong and a 74% reduction in China.[6] In 2008, two more cables were cut off the coast of Alexandria, causing Internet connectivity to be lost in Egypt, India, Pakistan, and Kuwait (see Figure 7.1). A few months later, another three cables were cut south of Sicily, disrupting the connectivity of Egypt, Sudan, Zambia, India, Pakistan, and other countries.[7] Such events are not uncommon; there are dozens every year, usually attributed to accidental damage caused by ship anchors or just friction against rock. Sabotage is not unheard of either. In fact, undersea cable-cutting used to be a common military tactic. Britain's first offensive act of World War I was carried out by a small civilian ship ordered to locate and cut German telecommunication cables in the Atlantic Ocean.[8] This hindered severely the Germans' communications with their embassies in the Americas. Today, such sabotage is rather less likely. In the long run, one can gain a lot more from an undersea cable by attaching to it eavesdropping devices or by compromising its landing station than by damaging it.[9] Nevertheless, in March 2013, Egyptian authorities arrested three divers alleged to have been trying to cut an undersea cable of Egypt's main

[6]Kitamura, Y., Youngseok, L. E. E., Sakiyama, R., and Okamura, K. (2007). Experience with restoration of Asia Pacific network failures from Taiwan earthquake. *IEICE transactions on communications*, Volume 90, No. 11, pp. 3095–3103.
[7]Regan, J. (2008), Undersea cable breaks cut Internet in Mideast, Asia. Reuters, December 20, 2008.
[8]Downing, T. (2014). Secret Warriors: Key Scientists, Code Breakers and Propagandists of the Great War. Hachette UK.
[9]Sontag, S., Drew, C., and Drew, A. L. (2000). Blind Man' Bluff: The Untold Story of Cold War Submarine Espionage. Random House.

telecommunications provider, in the process causing a drop of 60% in Internet speeds.[10]

Electromagnetic Damage

Anyone who has lost precious files during a power surge knows that excess voltage can lead to dead hard disks and loss of any data that have not been backed up. Electronic components are designed to operate on standard currents and voltages, and when they exceed their limits, they overheat and can be permanently damaged. Lightning strikes are known to have such an effect to systems near their point of impact.

This brings us to the concept of the electromagnetic bomb,[11] a weapon that can disable the electronic components of the enemy's communication networks, vehicles, and buildings, in a manner not too dissimilar to a lightning strike. The principle behind it is the electromagnetic pulse (EMP) effect, which was first reported as one of the by-products of high altitude nuclear explosions.[12] The nuclear burst generates a fast pulse of gamma rays travelling away from the point of explosion and toward every direction, knocking electrons off the air molecules. Due to the earth's magnetic field, these electrons turn in a coordinated manner. This creates an electric current and a powerful electromagnetic field, producing, for a very brief period of time, thousands of volts on conductors of electricity, such as wires and antennas, as well as any device connected to them. People are not affected at all, since no radioactive particles reach the earth's surface, but exposed electronic devices are temporarily or permanently disabled.

EMP attacks are highly asymmetric, in the sense that the more advanced a nation the more it depends on electronic devices and the more vulnerable it is. The 2004 report of the commission to assess the EMP threat to the United States suggested that "terrorists or state actors that possess relatively unsophisticated missiles armed with nuclear weapons may well calculate that, instead of destroying a city or military base, they may obtain the greatest political-military utility from one or a few such weapons by using them — or threatening their use — in an EMP attack." In theory, a single 1.4 Megaton nuclear bomb detonating 250 miles (that is in the middle of the

[10]Chang, A. (2013), Undersea cables are actually more vulnerable than you might think, Wired, April 3, 2013.

[11]Kopp, C. (1996). The electromagnetic bomb – a weapon of electrical mass destruction. Monash University Clayton.

[12]Glasstone, S. (1964). The effects of nuclear weapons. US Department of Defense.

thermosphere) above Nebraska or Kansas can cause a blackout from coast to coast, disabling computers, vehicles, and mobile devices almost instantaneously.[13] Note that it will also damage communication and navigation satellites,[14] but in the circumstances this might be less important. In 1962, the United States performed such a high-altitude nuclear test (250 miles altitude; 1.4 Megatons) above Johnston Island in the Pacific Ocean. The resulting High-Altitude EMP (HEMP) caused electrical damage in civilian and military installations in Hawaii, 900 miles away from the detonation point. Similar tests over deserts in the Soviet Union resulted in damaged diesel generators and radar systems. Of course, at the time, there were no mobile phones or personal computers, and vehicles were not as dependent on electronics as today.

The potential of EMP to damage the electronic infrastructure of advanced nations has made it an attractive area of military research, especially on nonnuclear directed energy weapons. US research has focused on High Power Microwave (HPM) devices, which generate intense microwaves capable of disabling electronic equipment in their range.[15] Compared to HEMP, HPM attacks can be more destructive but over a much smaller area. It has been widely speculated that a US Air Force strike that disabled Iraqi satellite TV in the early stages of the Iraq War used one such experimental nonnuclear weapon.[16]

EMP is particularly effective against modern commercial off-the-shelf electronic devices. By being increasingly miniaturized, these devices have to depend on tiny components and circuits, which are very vulnerable to excess currents and voltages. Military-grade devices are usually hardened against electromagnetic interference to protect from jamming and eavesdropping (more on this later), and this protection would be largely effective against EMP too. The idea is to enclose a device in a conductive material, in order to distribute any charge created by the EMP effect around the exterior and protect the interior. Also, note that optical fibers are naturally resilient to EMP

---

[13]Raloff, J. (1981). EMP – a Sleeping Electronic Dragon. Science News, Volume 119, pp. 300–302.

[14]Conrad, E. E., Gurtman, G. A., Kweder, G., Mandell, M. J., and White, W. W. (2010). Collateral Damage to Satellites from an EMP Attack (No. DTRA-IR-10-22). Defense Threat Reduction Agency, Fort Belvoir, VA, USA.

[15]Wilson, C. (2008). High altitude electromagnetic pulse (HEMP) and high power microwave (HPM) devices: Threat assessments. Library of Congress, Washington DC Congressional Research Service, July 2008.

[16]Roberts, J. U.S. drops 'e-bomb' on Iraqi TV, CBS, March 25, 2003.

attacks. So, another protection technique is to replace copper cables with fiber optic ones.[17]

Note that an effect similar to EMP can be caused naturally as a result of a severe solar flare, which is an event of intense variation of the sun's brightness caused by the sudden and rapid release of magnetic energy in its atmosphere. In 1989, a solar flare caused a 12-hour electrical power blackout across the entire province of Quebec, Canada, widespread incidents of power loss across the United States, a loss of control of some satellites, as well as the jamming of some radio signals.[18]

Cyber-Physical Resilience of Computer Networks

Sterbenz et al.[19] have defined network resilience as "the ability of the network to provide and maintain an acceptable level of service in the face of various faults and challenges to normal operation." Until a few years ago, whenever anyone mentioned resilience at a scientific conference, it was almost always assumed that the discussion would be about either random physical faults[20] or Internet worms, excessive network traffic, and other cyberspace concerns. This is not surprising. The first decade of the twenty-first century saw high-profile denial of service attacks and computer worm epidemics on a global scale. Intentional physical damage of equipment has always been a concern, but not necessarily a scientific one. IT equipment is expected to fail at some point anyway, and when it does it needs to be replaced. Physical security personnel, redundant network devices and cables, and a backup site are enough to alleviate most IT directors' concerns of intentional physical damage. Cyber concerns are seen as the most complex and most deserving of the attention of technical innovators.

This perception is largely justified, but scientists have started seeing the resilience of networks in relation to their geographical distribution too. For instance, Gorman et al. were the first to

---

[17]McCormack, R. G. and Sieber, D. C. (1976). *Fiber Optic Communications Link Performance in EMP and Intense Light Transient Environments* (No. CERL-IR-E-94). Construction Engineering Research Lab (Army) Champaign Ill.

[18]Allen, J., Sauer, H., Frank, L., and Reiff, P. (1989). Effects of the March 1989 solar activity. *Eos, Transactions American Geophysical Union*, Volume 70, No. 46, pp. 1479–1488.

[19]Sterbenz, J. P., Hutchison, D., Çetinkaya, E. K., Jabbar, A., Rohrer, J. P., Schöller, M., and Smith, P. (2010). Resilience and survivability in communication networks: Strategies, principles, and survey of disciplines. *Computer Networks*, Volume 54, No. 8, pp. 1245–1265.

[20]Cohen, R., Erez, K., Ben-Avraham, D., and Havlin, S. (2000). Resilience of the Internet to random breakdowns. *Physical review letters*, Volume 85, No. 21, p. 4626.

try to map the fiber-optic network of the United States geographically and try to estimate the impact of hypothetical network failures on specific cities.[21] Since then, Neumayer et al. have developed mathematical models that help predict the extent of disruption in cyberspace due to an EMP attack, natural disaster, or other event in physical space.[22] As part of their work, they also developed a methodology for identifying the point on the map where a physical disaster would cause the worst network disruption. Agarwal et al. have since extended the scope of this area of research with models that take into account multiple concurrent (and presumably man-made) disasters occurring in different geographical locations. Using these they can estimate the probability of a physical disaster affecting a particular section of the network infrastructure.[23] This can be used by an EMP attacker to pick the optimal target(s), or by network designers to choose a geographical distribution that would maximize the network's resilience to such threats.

Breaching Integrity through Physical Manipulation of Sensor Input

By definition (Chapter 1), cyber-physical attacks that involve sensors are carried out by breaching the security of information that the sensors have already collected. Of course, an attacker would not be limited by such academic definitions and subtle distinctions. In some cases, it may be more effective to physically alter the environment that a cyber-physical system's sensors monitor around it. The approach used in each case depends on the type of sensor.

Examples of Sensor Failures

Let us start with lidar. Developed in the 1960s, it is a technology that uses laser to measure distance to a target by analyzing the reflected light. Its accuracy has made it very

[21]Gorman, S. P., Schintler, L., Kulkarni, R., and Stough, R. (2004). The revenge of distance: Vulnerability analysis of critical information infrastructure. *Journal of Contingencies and Crisis Management*, Volume 12, No. 2, pp. 48–63.

[22]Neumayer, S., Zussman, G., Cohen, R., and Modiano, E. (2011). Assessing the vulnerability of the fiber infrastructure to disasters. *IEEE/ACM Transactions on Networking*, Volume 19, No. 6, pp. 1610–1623.

[23]Agarwal, P. K., Efrat, A., Ganjugunte, S., Hay, D., Sankararaman, S., and Zussman, G. (2011). The resilience of WDM networks to probabilistic geographical failures. In *Proceeding of INFOCOM*, IEEE, pp. 1521–1529, April 2011.

popular for map-making and related applications but it is also used to aid the navigation of autonomous vehicles by mapping the terrain around them. For example, Carnegie Mellon University's technology that allows a full-scale heli-copter[24] to land completely autonomously; BigDog,[25] the quadruped robot designed to accompany soldiers and carry their equipment on rough terrains; and Google's self-driving car, all rely heavily on lidar. (In fact, the latter carries $70,000 worth of lidar equipment,[26] which is what makes its mass production a little challenging.) However, naturally reflective items can confuse such laser-based technologies. A puddle on the road can make it think that an object's reflection on the puddle is the actual object, while absence of reflection from the puddle can make it think that the ground there drops to a cliff or a ditch.[27] So, anyone wishing to confuse a laser-based autonomous system may try to strategically place mirrors and other reflective objects in its field of view. A 2011 Al Qaida document containing 22 tips on avoiding UAV missile strikes[28] includes, in addition to advice on video feed inter-ception and jamming, a recommendation to add reflective pieces of glass on vehicles and building roofs, presumably to confuse the laser designators of air-to-ground weapons mounted on UAVs.

Glass can also affect the effectiveness of sensors that mea-sure the infrared radiation emitted by objects. This radiation is correlated to the temperature of the object, which is why infra-red sensors are used to detect objects that are warmer than their environment. A surveillance robot looking for human intruders would be equipped with such sensors,[29] since human bodies would have a different temperature than their immedi-ate environment. However, an adversary wishing to evade detection can try hiding behind ordinary window glass. Unlike

[24]Scherer, S., Chamberlain, L., and Singh, S. (2012). Autonomous landing at unprepared sites by a full-scale helicopter. *Robotics and Autonomous Systems*, Volume 60, No. 12, pp. 1545–1562.

[25]Raibert, M., Blankespoor, K., Nelson, G., and Playter, R. (2008). Bigdog, the rough-terrain quadruped robot. In *Proceedings of the 17th World Congress*, pp. 10823–10825, July 2008.

[26]Priddle A. and Woodyard, C. (2012). Google discloses costs of its driverless car tests, USA Today, June 14, 2012.

[27]Zoz (2013). Hacking Driverless Vehicles. DEFCON 21.

[28]Associated Press. The Al-Qaida Papers – Drones, February 2013.

[29]Fernández-Caballero, A., Castillo, J. C., Martínez-Cantos, J., and Martínez-Tomás, R. (2010). Optical flow or image subtraction in human detection from infrared camera on mobile robot. *Robotics and Autonomous Systems*, Volume 58, No. 12, pp. 1273–1281.

visible light, only a fraction of the human body's infrared radiation goes through the glass.[30] That is why infrared camera lenses are made of germanium, which is transparent to infrared radiation, rather than ordinary glass, which blocks it.

As a third example, we can mention the backscatter X-ray imaging technology used primarily in full-body security scanners at airports, prisons, courthouses, and the like. When an object such as a human body absorbs X-rays, low-energy photons are bounced back out and are picked up by a sensor to create an image of the object. The technology is not perfect though. Scanning metallic objects against a dark background, objects that are shaped to follow the contours of the human body, and materials that scatter X-rays at similar intensity as the human flesh can be missed by this technology. Initial analysis of a representative full-body scanner[31] has shown that it might fail to detect a pancake-shaped plastic device with beveled edges if it were taped to the abdomen,[32] a fire-arm affixed to the outside of the leg and scanned against a dark background, and so on.

In general, there are several techniques for confusing different sensing technologies by exploiting their limitations in terms of physics. An ultrasonic motion sensor can be bypassed if the adversary moves very slowly in front of it or wears a costume made of foam or other material with anechoic properties (i.e., material that absorbs sound waves); a microphone can be defeated with a white noise generator, and so on. The precise mechanisms are not within the scope of this book, but what is important to note is that a technically sophisticated and adaptive adversary would invest time in finding out how to manipulate the physical input to any kind of sensor. Because the operation of cyber-physical systems usually depends on real-time sensor measurements, their designers take precautions to ensure their integrity.

---

[30]This is not always the case. It depends on the characteristics of the glass and the sensor. Also, an infrared sensor used as a security system would typically trigger an alarm when the glass would pass in front of another object in the background. It would not see the glass, but it would notice the sudden reduction of infrared radiation emitted by any objects behind the glass.

[31]Mowery, K., Wustrow, E., Wypych, T., Singleton, C., Comfort, C., Rescorla, E., Checkoway, S., Halderman, J. A., and Shacham, H. (2014). Security analysis of a full-body scanner. In *23rd USENIX Security Symposium*, August 20–22, 2014, San Diego, CA.

[32]Kaufman, L. and Carlson, J. W. (2011). An evaluation of airport x-ray backscatter units based on image characteristics. *Journal of Transportation Security*, Volume 4, No. 1, pp. 73–94.

Detection of Sensor Failures

In order to detect whether a sensor has provided abnormal measurements, one needs to be able to estimate what a normal measurement is in the first place. Here, we will borrow the classification of Sharma et al.,[33] who have divided detection methods into rule-based, learning-based, time series-based, and estimation-based.

In rule-based approaches, one uses prior knowledge of the environment that is monitored to set lower and upper limits of what is deemed to be realistic. Any measurement outside this range is an indication that the sensor may have been tampered with. The limits may relate to the actual value measured, its rate of change or its standard deviation,[34] and are chosen by human experts with knowledge of the particular domain of application. For example, if a robot uses an ultrasonic sensor to estimate distance from a particular stationary obstacle, the distance measurements should not have an unrealistically low or high value and should not increase at a rate that is greater than the robot's actual speed. Rule-based methods can be highly effective, but their accuracy depends almost entirely on the choice of limits. This can be somewhat overcome with the use of artificial intelligence, whereby normal values are not dictated from the beginning but are learned through actual use. In this context, the most common learning approach is of the supervised variety, which includes a training phase. The sensor is first used in various known normal and abnormal conditions, so that a cyber-physical system using it would learn the difference and would be able to recognize failures in the future.

In particular for sensors measuring natural phenomena that exhibit patterns, for example based on the time of day, it is common to employ time series forecasting. This involves the design of a mathematical model that estimates future measurements based on previous ones. A significant difference between actual sensor measurements and forecasted ones would be an indication of a failure.[35] These methods are particularly

---

[33]Sharma, A. B., Golubchik, L., and Govindan, R. (2010). Sensor faults: Detection methods and prevalence in real-world datasets. *ACM Transactions on Sensor Networks (TOSN)*, Volume 6, No. 3.

[34]Standard deviation is a statistical measure of the variation or dispersion from the average value.

[35]Osborne, M. A., Roberts, S. J., Rogers, A., Ramchurn, S. D., and Jennings, N. R. (2008). Towards real-time information processing of sensor network data using computationally efficient multi-output Gaussian processes. In *Proceedings of the 7th international conference on Information processing in sensor networks*, pp. 109–120, IEEE Computer Society.

effective at detecting failures of short duration, but have a tendency to produce false positives (erroneously detecting failures that have not occurred).

Failure detection can also benefit from redundant sensors gathering the same measurements, since inconsistencies between them would point toward a fault or intentional manipulation of at least one of them. This is a practical solution in many cases, especially as sensors are becoming less expensive, but if the failure is the result of a physical attack, all may have been affected. This can be addressed to an extent by using sensors of a different type for the same purpose. For example, an autonomous robot may employ both ultrasonic and infrared sensors to avoid obstacles. A physical attack that would deceive one would not necessarily deceive the other. In a similar manner, using a full-body scanner's X-ray backscatter technology both from the front and the sides would thwart most attempts to conceal an object via physical means.

In recent years, the focus of researchers has shifted to networks of large numbers of inexpensive sensors with wireless communication capability. In the context of security, they have the advantage of being able to interact with each other and collaboratively detect the ones that produce untrustworthy measurements. For this, they often use estimation-based methods. If a wireless sensor network monitors natural phenomena, such as light or ambient temperature in a room, one can estimate the normal value expected from a particular sensor based on the values reported by other sensors around it. In this manner, sensors detect inconsistencies in the measurements gathered by their neighbors[36] and can also score them in terms of their trustworthiness. This creates a reputation system,[37] whereby more weight is placed on the measurements of sensors with higher reputation scores. This is an elegant approach for detecting sensors that are naturally unreliable, for instance due to faulty electronics. However, the implicit assumption of any reputation system, which is that past behavior can predict future behavior, may not hold if there is a sophisticated adversary involved. In fact, somewhat ironically, it is the sensors with the highest reputation that would be targeted by an attacker. Deceiving a few

[36]Koushanfar, F., Potkonjak, M., and Sangiovanni-Vincentelli, A. (2003). On-line fault detection of sensor measurements. In *Proceedings of IEEE Sensors*, IEEE, Volume 2, pp. 974–979, October 2003.
[37]Ganeriwal, S., Balzano, L. K., and Srivastava, M. B. (2008). Reputation-based framework for high integrity sensor networks. *ACM Transactions on Sensor Networks (TOSN)*, Volume 4, No. 3.

reputable sensors would cause far more damage than deceiving those that are already perceived as unreliable.

Breaching Confidentiality through Emsec Attacks

Computers consist of a multitude of mechanical and electronic components. As a result, when they are in operation and especially when they process information, they produce heat, sounds, stray electrical signals through power cables, as well as electromagnetic radiation. For most people, these emanations are nothing but noise and possibly interference (especially for the pilot on your flight), but for crafty attackers they are sources of valuable information. Attacks based on the exploitation of compromising emanations are referred to as Emsec (emission security or emanation security), Tempest[38] (named after the code name of the corresponding NSA program), or side channel attacks (because information is accessed through a channel other than the intended one). The differences of these terms are rather blurry. Emsec is general enough to encompass most such attacks, whereas Tempest is used primarily for electromagnetic emanation leaks and especially for the corresponding government-certified countermeasures. Side channel attacks are predominantly employed in the analysis of cryptographic systems (known as side channel cryptanalysis), but the term is also used in relation to acoustic emanations, optical emanations, eavesdropping based on motion sensors, and so on. Emsec has been a primary concern for military organizations and a significant area of classified research for several decades, but it is only in the last three decades that the scientific community has published related work.

Electromagnetic Emsec Attacks

During World War II, one of the main devices used by the US army and navy to encrypt text was the Bell 131-B2. According to a declassified NSA report,[39] the device was already deployed and in wide use when a researcher at Bell Labs observed a very worrying phenomenon while testing it. Every time it was used,

---

[38]Although various sources have suggested that Tempest is an acronym for Telecommunications Electronics Material Protected from Emanating Spurious Transmissions, or for Transient Electromagnetic Pulse Emanation Standard, it is probably nothing more than a nice codename.

[39]Friedman, J. (1972). TEMPEST: A signal Problem, NSA Cryptologic Spectrum.

spikes would appear on an oscilloscope[40] located in a distant part of the laboratory. Carefully looking at the patterns of these spikes, he was even able to guess the text that was being encrypted. Because the Bell 131-B2 was already in use in the war, the Signal Corps was reluctant to take any action before more convincing evidence was presented. So, Bell engineers conducted an experiment. Placed 80 feet away from a Signal Corps building, they recorded for 1 hour the unintended electromagnetic signals that were emitted when the device was in use. It took them only 3 to 4 hours to produce 75% of the text that was processed. The Signal Corps was impressed with the experiment, but not with the extent of modifications that were proposed by Bell Labs to protect against this new threat. So, the solution actually followed was to advise commanders to use the device only if they had control of an area of 100 feet in diameter around them. The whole issue was forgotten until 1951 when the CIA, unaware of the Bell Labs experiments, made exactly the same observations and informed the NSA. NSA tested the Bell 131-B2 and every other encryption machine and confirmed that all of them emitted unintended electromagnetic signals that could be used to guess the text that was being processed. Interestingly, in 1954, the Soviets published a set of standards for suppressing interference caused by devices emitting electromagnetic radiation, but these standards were much more stringent for their communication devices than for equipment that causes considerably more interference, such as industrial motors. Presumably, it was not interference that they were worried about, but data leakage through Emsec attacks.

Almost all electronic devices that have not been shielded to a military grade of protection emit nonnegligible stray electromagnetic radiation. Naturally, this includes common television sets and computer monitors. Emsec attacks exploiting their electromagnetic emanations are often called Van Eck attacks (or Van Eck phreaking), named after the Dutch computer scientist who was the first to demonstrate their feasibility to the wider public.[41] Van Eck observed that the stray signals emanating from a television set in operation correlate remarkably to the video signals that provide the image displayed on it. Based on this observation, he demonstrated that an adversary can use a directional antenna and an

[40]Oscilloscopes are among the most common devices found in an electronics laboratory. They measure the voltage, time, and frequency characteristics of electrical signals and display them on a screen.
[41]Van Eck, W. (1985). Electromagnetic radiation from video display units: an eavesdropping risk? *Computers & Security*, Volume 4, No. 4, pp. 269–286.

antenna amplifier to pick them up and use these to replicate the image (albeit in much lower quality) on another black-and-white television. Since they were conducted in the early 1980s, Van Eck's experiments were on old cathode ray tube (CRT) monitors, but Markus Kuhn has shown that Emsec attacks may also be applicable on a modern flat-panel liquid-crystal display (LCD) by picking up emanations not from the display itself but from the cable that connects it to the computer.[42] The importance of Van Eck and similar attacks lies in the fact that computer screens are involved in almost every interaction between a user and a computer. So, any text typed by the user, e-mails received, images or other information displayed on a screen may be eavesdropped on. After a demonstration of such an attack prior to the 2006 Dutch national elections,[43] the Dutch government issued a requirement that voting equipment should be protected from leaking information up to a distance of 5 meters.[44]

After the first public demonstrations of Emsec attacks on computer monitors, researchers expanded to other computer components and peripheral devices, such as the common RS-232 serial cables used to connect printers and mice in the 1990s,[45] the PS/2[46] and USB cables used to connect keyboards, as well as the actual wireless and laptop keyboards.[47] All of these produce compromising emanations at considerable distance, usually in the order of tens of meters if not more.

Today, demonstrations of new attacks, where information is leaked through stray signals radiated or conducted through cables, have become regular occurrence. Take, for example, X-10, a communication technology, which has been popular for home automation networks because it is inexpensive and can use the existing

---

[42]Kuhn, M. G. (2005). Electromagnetic eavesdropping risks of flat-panel displays. In *Privacy Enhancing Technologies*, Springer Berlin Heidelberg, pp. 88–107, January 2005.

[43]There is only a small number of candidates that one can pick from on the voting machine, and each choice generates a slightly different pattern of electromagnetic emanations. A small group of eavesdroppers can quickly learn which pattern corresponds to which vote by voting themselves and recording the emanations. Alternatively, they can try to match the pattern that appeared more often with the candidate who has actually won the election.

[44]Anderson, R. (2008). *Security engineering*. John Wiley & Sons, p. 536.

[45]Smulders, P. (1990). The threat of information theft by reception of electromagnetic radiation from RS-232 cables. *Computers & Security*, Volume 9, No. 1, pp. 53–58.

[46]Wang, L. and Yu, B. (2013). Research on the compromising electromagnetic emanations of PS/2 keyboard. In Proceedings of the International Conference on Communication, Electronics and Automation Engineering, pp. 23–29. Springer Berlin Heidelberg, January 2013.

[47]Vuagnoux, M. and Pasini, S. (2009). Compromising Electromagnetic Emanations of Wired and Wireless Keyboards. In *USENIX Security Symposium*, pp. 1–16, August 2009.

power lines of the building to control lights, door locks, air conditioning, and so on. By using these lines, X-10 signals leak through the power grid and can be picked up by an adversary in the same neighborhood. Add to this its lack of encryption or any other mechanism to protect information, and it is not difficult to see a potential burglar eavesdropping on the messages sent from X-10 occupancy sensors to find out whether the owners are inside.[48]

Other times, it is not stray signals that provide compromising information, but measurements on the operation of a device. Since the late 1990s, the cryptographic systems of smartcards have been consistently targeted by a variety of such side channel attacks. Among the first and certainly the most influential was the work of Paul Kocher, who demonstrated that cryptographic systems can be defeated by statistically analyzing the power drawn[49] (see Box 7.1) or the time taken to process different inputs.[50] These techniques have proven to be so effective in practice that they have made side channel cryptanalysis an area of intense research in industry, academia, and intelligence communities. They have shown beyond doubt that it does not matter how secure a system is in theory if the physical components it is built on leak information, whether naturally or when actively stimulated by an attacker (see later for active attacks). They may have generated interest mostly in relation to cryptanalysis, but systematic measurements of the power drawn can reveal information in other settings too. One of these relates to the experiments conducted by Clark et al., who successfully identified web pages visited by a user based only on the power that the computer draws while displaying them.[51] This might have been too difficult in the past, but today's web pages feature such a variety of graphics technologies, streaming videos, and other rich content that the power drawn fluctuates considerably based on their content. So, by tapping the power outlet, it is possible to compare with patterns of power corresponding to web pages that the user has previously visited. It obviously cannot identify the precise web page if it has not been visited

[48]Kennedy, D., and Simon, R. (2011). Pentesting over power lines. In *DEFCON conference*, Las Vegas, Nevada, USA, August 5, 2011.
[49]Kocher, P., Jaffe, J., and Jun, B. (1999). Differential power analysis. In *Advances in Cryptology – CRYPTO'99*, Springer Berlin Heidelberg. pp. 388–397, January 1999.
[50]Kocher, P. C. (1996). Timing attacks on implementations of Diffie-Hellman, RSA, DSS, and other systems. In *Advances in Cryptology—CRYPTO'96*, Springer Berlin Heidelberg, pp. 104–113, January 1996.
[51]Clark, S. S., Mustafa, H., Ransford, B., Sorber, J., Fu, K., and Xu, W. (2013). Current events: Identifying webpages by tapping the electrical outlet. In *Computer Security–ESORICS 2013*, Springer Berlin Heidelberg, pp. 700–717.

Box 7.1 Power Analysis

Consider a smartcard, RFID, or other device, which performs a cryptographic operation to authenticate some process (e.g., to ensure that the car key inserted in the ignition lock cylinder is the correct one for this car). Two of the best-known approaches for power analysis of such devices, where the attacker aims to uncover the secrets of the cryptographic system based on the power it consumes, are Simple Power Analysis (SPA) and Differential Power Analysis (DPA), both developed by Kocher et al. and formalized by Messerges et al.:[52]

SPA. The attacker connects the device to an oscilloscope and visually observes its power consumption while it is performing cryptographic operations. Each operation consists of a number of instructions to the device's microprocessor (e.g., multiplication, squaring, inversion, etc.), and different instructions result in noticeably different patterns of current drawn, to the extent that one can potentially tell which instruction or group of instructions is running (see Figure 7.2, left). For example, the Data Encryption Standard (DES) involves 16 repetitions of the same group of instructions. These DES rounds can be clearly seen as a particular pattern of current drawn that is repeated 16 times (see Figure 7.2, right).

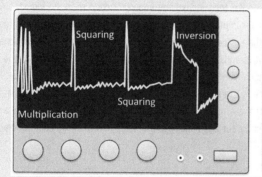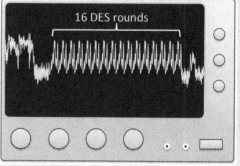

Figure 7.2 The current fluctuates based on the instruction performed by the device's microprocessor.

In addition, if the sequence of instructions defined by a specific cryptographic system depends on the data processed, then one can even guess part of the secret data. For the sake of explanation, consider a cipher (one which, we hasten to emphasize, does not exist; a hypothetical one), which always starts with a multiplication, and then continues with one more multiplication if the secret key's first bit is 0 or with a squaring if it is 1. An attacker would know whether the first bit is 0 or 1 by looking at the current drawn. If there is a pattern that is repeated at the beginning, then it must correspond to the two consecutive multiplications, and the first bit must be 0; otherwise, it must be 1.

(*Continued*)

[52]Messerges, T. S., Dabbish, E. A., and Sloan, R. H. (2002). Examining smart-card security under the threat of power analysis attacks. *IEEE Transactions on Computers*, Volume 51, No. 5, pp. 541–552.

Box 7.1 (Continued)

Preventing SPA attacks is relatively straightforward. If the designer of a cryptographic system ensures that the sequence of instructions performed is always the same and does not depend on the data processed, then there is little that SPA can achieve.

DPA. In practice, SPA is rarely sufficient to break a modern device's cryptographic protection. A much more powerful approach is DPA. It works based on the observation that the actual values of the data manipulated in a cryptographic operation cause variations in the power drawn. These variations are not as pronounced as those seen in Figure 7.2, which relate to the particular instruction running; they are minute in comparison but they are there nonetheless. Also, a lot of the variations of the current drawn are just noise due to imperfections of the device and have nothing to do with its cryptographic inner workings. In DPA, the attacker measures the current drawn over hundreds of experiments using the same secret key, and then employs advanced statistical and signal processing techniques to remove noise from the measurements and to uncover correlations between the data processed and the current measured. These correlations would not have been obvious to the human eye. In practice, one uses DPA to guess a few of the bits of a secret key and then applies a brute force attack on the rest. Protecting cryptographic devices from DPA and similar techniques is an important concern in the industry. A common approach is to try to make the power consumption of the device constant regardless of the instructions performed. This can be achieved by adding on the device some dummy components that consume additional power so that the total power consumption always adds up to a specific constant value. Alternatively, one may add randomness in the cryptographic process, such as a random number or sequence of instructions,[53] or generate a new secret key every time the device is used, so as to render previously captured keys practically meaningless. Such techniques make the work of the attacker a bit more difficult, but they also introduce a performance overhead, as the device needs to carry out additional operations as part of these countermeasures.

before, but the concept of measuring power to detect web pages is intriguing nonetheless.

Optical Emsec Attacks

Another important medium for the transmission and representation of information is light.[54] Computer monitors display information to the user as light. Three short, three long, and again three short flashes of light with whatever lamp or mirror

[53]Ebeid, N. and Hasan, A. (2003). *Analysis of DPA countermeasures based on randomizing the binary algorithm*. Tech. Report CORR 2003–4, Centre for Applied Cryptographic Research (CACR), University of Waterloo.
[54]Light is also a form of electromagnetic radiation, specifically in the frequency range from around 430 to 750 THz. Nevertheless, it makes sense to devote a separate section for optical emanations because they require very different skills and equipment to exploit them.

is at hand is the internationally recognized SOS distress signal, and fiber-optic, one of the highest-performing communication technologies, transmits information by sending pulses of light through thin glass tubes, the optical fibers. Whether low-tech or high-tech, light-based systems also produce compromising emanations. For example, consider a computer monitor and an adversary trying to eavesdrop on it from a distance. The obvious way is to point an amateur astronomy telescope toward it. If there is no direct line of sight, then perhaps the telescope can capture some compromising reflection of the monitor on the user's eyes or on a glass surface,[55] which can then be magnified and improved with the use of sophisticated image processing techniques.

In 2002, Markus Kuhn, rather impressively, showed that the image displayed on a CRT monitor can be reconstructed without any line of sight at all. A CRT monitor works by continuously updating its pixels[56] one after the other. It does so at a very high rate so that the human eye sees the image without any flickering. If the next pixel that is to be updated is a bright white, then the total light emitted by the monitor is very slightly increased. If it is black, then it is very slightly reduced. So, if one has a capable photodetector[57] and can measure these slight variations, then it is possible to tell the luminosity of the latest pixel that was updated on the screen. Estimating the luminosity of each pixel is enough to approximately reconstruct the entire image, even from the diffuse reflections[58] on the wall or the user's face,[59] especially if the room is relatively dark. This technique would not work for liquid-crystal display (LCD) monitors though, as they update all pixels in a line at the same time rather than one after the other.

---

[55]Backes, M., Durmuth, M., and Unruh, D. (2008). Compromising reflections-or-how to read LCD monitors around the corner. In *Symposium on Security and Privacy*, IEEE, pp. 158–169, May 2008.

[56]Pixel is short for "picture element." Pixels are the tiny dots that collectively form what is displayed on the computer monitor. If the resolution of the monitor is set to 2560×1600, then this means that the image displayed has 1,600 lines of 2,560 pixels each. A CRT monitor updates its pixels one by one, while a LCD monitor updates all pixels of the same line at the same time.

[57]A photodetector (or photosensor) is an electronic component that measures the amount of light that hits it.

[58]When a ray of light hits a surface and is then reflected at many angles rather than just one, this is a diffuse reflection. Matte paint, clothing, and skin usually create diffuse reflection.

[59]Kuhn, M. G. (2002). Optical time-domain eavesdropping risks of CRT displays. In *Proceedings of IEEE Symposium on Security and Privacy*, pp. 3–18.

At around the same time, Joe Loughry and David Umphress showed that some of the light-emitting diode (LED) status indicators on common communication equipment, such as the "Transmitted data" and "Received data" indicators on modems and the "Fast Serial" indicator on routers, blink in a manner that strongly correlates with the series of zeros and ones that they transmit.[60] This is because, for cost reasons, the LEDs may be powered through electronic components that are also used in the data transmission circuits of this equipment. So, if one places a sufficiently fast photodetector near the LEDs and observes how their brightness continuously oscillates between low and high, it is possible to read exactly what is transmitted through the device.

Directly observing information input through a computer system does not necessarily need any deep technical knowledge. For example, keys pressed on a smartphone's virtual keypad can be relatively easily inferred by visually observing the smudges (oily residues) that are left on the touchscreen surface by the user's finger.[61] Practices of installing cameras pointing toward ATM keypads (or keyboards of computer systems) or looking over a potential victim's shoulders to steal a numeric code (or password, identifying gesture, etc.) are even more obvious and well known. It is also widely known that occlusion (using one's body or hands to block view to the keypad, and manufacturers designing keypad shrouds that occlude some angles) can protect effectively against most of such "shoulder surfing" techniques. What is less well known is that an attacker can capture what has been typed even after the victim has left. When pressing a key, we transfer heat from our body to the particular key, especially if it is plastic. As a result, for a few seconds after the legitimate user has left, an attacker can point a thermal camera to the keypad and, as long as the keypad is not metallic, observe thermal residue on the keys that were pressed.[62] In fact, one can even tell their sequence, as the key whose thermal residue disappeared first is probably the one that was pressed first. Such attacks are not particularly new, but

[60]Loughry, J. and Umphress, D. A. (2002). Information leakage from optical emanations. *ACM Transactions on Information and System Security (TISSEC)*, Volume 5, No. 3, pp. 262–289.
[61]Aviv, A. J., Gibson, K., Mossop, E., Blaze, M., and Smith, J. M. (2010). Smudge Attacks on Smartphone Touch Screens. In *Proceedings of the 4th USENIX conference on Offensive technologies*, August 2010.
[62]Mowery, K., Meiklejohn, S., and Savage, S. (2011). Heat of the moment: characterizing the efficacy of thermal camera-based attacks. In *Proceedings of the 5th USENIX conference on Offensive technologies*, August 2011.

are becoming quite practical as thermal cameras are getting less and less expensive, and can even be attached as smart-phone extensions.[63] Of course, if there is any suspicion of a thermal camera-based attack, prevention is rather straightforward: rest the whole hand on the keypad, press more keys after entering the correct code, and so on. Also, the lighter the touch and the colder the user's hands the more difficult for the attacker to capture the code.

Acoustic Emsec Attacks

The possibility of attacks exploiting sound emanations has been known in intelligence circles since at least the 1950s. For example, in his autobiography, *Spycatcher*,[64] former MI5 scientist Peter Wright described how in 1956 the British were spying on the Egyptian embassy by listening to the sounds produced by its encryption devices. A partially declassified report on NSA's TEMPEST program mentions that "keyboards, printers, relays—these produce sound and consequently can be sources of compromise."[65]

Take, for example, a conventional computer keyboard. Because different keys on a keyboard are not completely identical, they produce slightly different sounds when pressed.[66] Based on this observation, researchers from IBM developed software that can learn the sound of each key and then try to infer which one is pressed based solely on the sound recorded on a microphone. Although not perfect (as the differences are minute), this approach allowed them to detect the correct keystroke most of the times, using only their software and an inexpensive off-the-shelf parabolic microphone at a distance from the keyboard (Figure 7.3). The approach was shown to work on other types of push button devices, such as the keypads of telephones and ATM machines, and to be independent of the user's typing style. Although the possibility of exploiting the acoustic emanations of devices was known, this was the first nonclassified experiment of this type and naturally generated considerable interest when it was published in 2004. A year later,

[63]Kreft, E. The simple way to thwart an alarming new tool to steal ATM code. The Blaze, August 29, 2014.

[64]Wright, P. and Greengrass, P. (1987). Spycatcher: The candid autobiography of a senior intelligence officer (pp. 111–112). New York: Viking, p. 82.

[65]NSA (1982) NACSIM 5000 Tempest Fundamentals, letter of promulgation, February 1982. Partially declassified transcript.

[66]Asonov, D. and Agrawal, R. (2004). Keyboard acoustic emanations. In IEEE Symposium on Security and Privacy, pp. 3–11, May 2004.

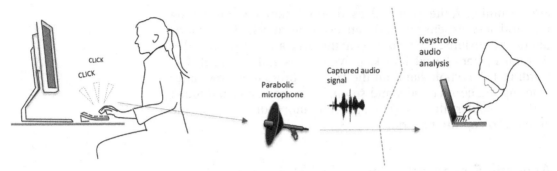

Figure 7.3 An adversary records and analyzes a keyboard's acoustic emanations.

another team following a similar principle managed to improve its accuracy to the point of recovering up to 96% of characters from the recorded sound of a user typing English text.[67] It was also discovered that the sound of each key correlates to its physical location on the keyboard.[68] So, Q, W, and E sound similar, and differ noticeably to P. If the sequence of keystrokes that is analyzed is a word in the dictionary (normal text or a poorly chosen password), even approximately guessing what part of the keyboard each keystroke sound comes from is enough to guess the whole of the word. With the concept now proven, the research community expanded to other devices too. For example, Backes et al. were able to recover 72% of the words typed on an old dot-matrix printer by placing a microphone next to it.[69] As one would expect, the sound emitted by the printer becomes slightly louder if more needles strike the paper,[70] and this can help distinguish different characters.

In the past, acoustic side channel attacks such as these were seen as scientifically interesting but too impractical. They require physical access to place a wireless microphone near the target computer so as to transmit the recorded sound to a

---

[67]Zhuang, L., Zhou, F., and Tygar, J. D. (2005). Keyboard acoustic emanations revisited. In Proceedings of the 12th ACM conference on Computer and communications security, ACM, pp. 373–382, November 2005.

[68]Berger, Y., Wool, A., and Yeredor, A. (2006). Dictionary attacks using keyboard acoustic emanations. In *Proceedings of the 13th ACM conference on Computer and communications security*, pp. 245–254, ACM, October 2006.

[69]Backes, M., Dürmuth, M., Gerling, S., Pinkal, M., and Sporleder, C. (2010). Acoustic Side-Channel Attacks on Printers. In *USENIX Security Symposium*, pp. 307–322, August 2010.

[70]Although an old technology, dot matrix printers are still in wide use in hospitals, banks, and other organizations. They activate a particular subset of their needles to produce the dots of ink that comprise each character.

nearby computer, where one can then try to isolate the sound of the keystrokes, analyze it, and capture passwords. With the same physical access, it would be far easier to just attach a hardware keylogger device or install a software keylogger application.[71] For an acoustic attack to be even remotely practical, it needs a target that carries its own equipment for recording sounds, can preferably process these by itself, and can be compromised remotely and in an automated manner. This is precisely what smartphones are for an attacker. They carry a high-quality microphone, have powerful processing capacity, and are increasingly targeted by malware with access to its microphone, the camera, and other sensors. An example is Soundcomber, an experimental Trojan horse application designed by Schlegel et al., which records the tones produced when digits are pressed and uses the processing power of the smartphone to analyze the sounds and identify them.[72] After the information has been captured, it is then transmitted to a remote computer controlled by the attacker. This technique works on conversations where the user of the smartphone needs to type PINs or credit card numbers, for example when calling menu-driven customer service systems.

All the acoustic Emsec approaches mentioned in this section are applicable only for cases where the target is manually typing words. They are accurate enough for short sequences of characters and preferably for known words that can be found in a dictionary, but cannot be used for secret keys that are processed by a computer. These are rather long and are not manually typed by the user. Nevertheless, Shamir and Tromer[73] noticed that even if there is no keyboard involved, computers produce sounds that can leak information. In particular, the electronic components on the computer motherboard that regulate the power to the processor produce slightly different sounds depending on the operations performed. They also showed that when the processor is performing a cryptographic operation,

[71]A hardware key logger is a device that the attacker needs to physically attach somewhere between the keyboard and the computer, for example as an innocent-looking extension of the keyboard cable. It captures the keystrokes as they are sent from the keyboard to the computer and stores them in an internal memory until the attacker comes back to retrieve it. A software key logger is an application that runs on the background and stores keystrokes in a file or sends them to the attacker over the Internet.
[72]Schlegel, R., Zhang, K., Zhou, X. Y., Intwala, M., Kapadia, A., and Wang, X. (2011). Soundcomber: A Stealthy and Context-Aware Sound Trojan for Smartphones. In *NDSS*, Volume 11, pp. 17–33, February 2011.
[73]Shamir, A. and Tromer, E. (2004). Acoustic cryptanalysis: on nosy people and noisy machines. *Eurocrypt2004 Rump Session*, May 2004.

the sound differs depending on the secret key that is used, to the point that one can potentially recognize a secret key if it has been used before and its sound has been recorded.

Motion Sensor-Based Side Channel Attacks on Smartphones and Tablets

Consider the usual scenario of a smartphone placed next to a computer keyboard while the user is typing. Based on the previous discussion, if the microphone is enabled, the smartphone can record the sound of the keystrokes and use one of several techniques proposed by scientists to process it and guess the words being typed. Even if the microphone is disabled, the smartphone also carries gyroscopes and accelerometers, which are sensors that can detect movement of the device. They are typically used to determine whether the display on the smartphone should turn from portrait to landscape and vice versa, but are so accurate that they can rather impressively also detect the minute vibrations of the smartphone caused by keys being pressed on a nearby keyboard. Marquardt et al.[74] have used this to identify the words that are typed based on the relative position and distance between each vibration that is sensed by the smartphone's accelerometers. This approach is not as accurate as acoustic ones, especially if the smartphone is placed farther than a few inches from the keyboard or at an angle. Nevertheless, it is a technically impressive achievement and has the advantage that motion sensors are seen as less susceptible to eavesdropping, hence less likely to be blocked.

Touch-based interactions between physical space and cyberspace have become particularly important thanks to the intuitive control that they allow, especially in smartphones.[75] However, touching a device also causes movement of the device. So, in addition to collecting information about other devices in the vicinity of a smartphone, motion-based sensors can also be used to infer what is typed on its own touchscreen. There are several examples in the academic literature of

[74]Marquardt, P., Verma, A., Carter, H., and Traynor, P. (2011). (sp)iPhone: decoding vibrations from nearby keyboards using mobile phone accelerometers. In Proceedings of the 18th ACM conference on Computer and communications security, ACM, pp. 551–562, October 2011.
[75]Chen, L., Pan, G., and Li, S. (2011). Touch-driven Interaction Between Physical Space and Cyberspace with NFC. In International Conference on Internet of Things (iThings/CPSCom) and 4th International Conference on Cyber, Physical and Social Computing, pp. 258–265, IEEE, October 2011.

experimental apps designed to demonstrate motion sensor-based side channel threats. Some of the first and most prominent ones are TouchLogger,[76] ACCessory,[77] and TapLogger.[78] Their underlying techniques may vary, but they are all broadly based on the same phenomenon: whenever a user taps anything on a touchscreen, the force of the finger causes a small but not insignificant movement of the device, which is measured by the motion sensors and can be used to infer what area of the touchscreen was tapped. This is equivalent to knowing what was typed on a virtual keypad. What makes this attack significant is that it is not seen as unusual for an app running in the background; for example, a pedometer app used by runners, to continue collecting motion sensor data even while the user is typing a PIN or a password. So, an adversary can produce perhaps a pedometer app, which does function as one, to avoid raising suspicions, but at the same time also captures text typed by the user. In fact, Michalevsky et al.[79] have demonstrated that modern smartphones' gyroscopes are so sensitive that they can pick up vibrations caused by nearby sounds. Employing advanced signal processing techniques on vibration data collected, they had some success in identifying speakers and words (from a small group of speakers and a small vocabulary). Such research, as well as MIT's "visual microphone"[80] (an impressive set of techniques that allow recovering audio from the minute vibrations visually observed on nearby objects), has uncovered new physical side channels that can leak information in a most unexpected manner.

[76]Cai, L. and Chen, H. (2011). Touchlogger: inferring keystrokes on touch screen from smartphone motion. In Proceedings of the 6th USENIX conference on Hot topics in security, August 2011.

[77]Owusu, E., Han, J., Das, S., Perrig, A., and Zhang, J. (2012). Accessory: password inference using accelerometers on smartphones. In Proceedings of the Twelfth Workshop on Mobile Computing Systems & Applications. ACM, February 2012.

[78]Xu, Z., Bai, K., and Zhu, S. (2012). Taplogger: Inferring user inputs on smartphone touchscreens using on-board motion sensors. In Proceedings of the fifth ACM conference on Security and Privacy in Wireless and Mobile Networks, ACM, pp. 113–124, April 2012.

[79]Michalevsky, Y., Boneh, D., and Nakibly, G. (2014). Gyrophone: Recognizing Speech From Gyroscope Signals. In *Proceedings of the 23rd USENIX Security Symposium*, August 20–22, 2014.

[80]Davis, A., Rubinstein, M., Wadhwa, N., Mysore, G. J., Durand, F., and Freeman, W. T. (2014). The visual microphone: passive recovery of sound from video. *ACM Transactions on Graphics (TOG)*, Volume 33, No. 4, p. 79.

Active Emsec Attacks: Artificially Stimulating Emanations

All Emsec attacks discussed up to now are passive attacks, since the user observes the emanations that a system produces naturally. Most of the attacks reported in the open literature fall into this category. However, a system's emanations can also be artificially stimulated, so as to make it easier for the attacker to exploit them. In military circles, these are known as Teapot[81] attacks. They usually involve the transmission of carefully crafted signals, which cause the target device to generate electromagnetic emanations.[82] Markus Kuhn and Ross Anderson have remarked that even beams of microwave radiation have been used for this purpose, which "may explain the old Soviet practice of flooding U.S. and allied diplomatic premises in the USSR with microwave radiation."[83]

Active attacks are not limited to electromagnetic emanations. For example, consider the optical attacks discussed earlier. If the blinking of a LED indicator is imperceptible to the human eye but sufficient for a photodetector to discern, then it becomes a covert channel for communication. In the appendix of their paper on information leakage from optical emanations,[84] Joe Loughry and David Umphress provided the code for a computer virus that can make the keyboard's LEDs reveal what the user is typing. Its considerable advantage is that it does not need an active network connection between the target and the attacker to leak information. All it needs is a telescope powerful enough to record the blinking. A similar logic can be used for covert acoustical communication. For example, Hanspach and Goetz[85] attracted public attention when they demonstrated that laptops infected with malware can be programmed to form covert acoustical networks, transmitting and

---

[81]Like Tempest, Teapot is just a codename, and a well chosen one at that, considering that the American English idiom "Tempest in a teapot" means to exaggerate a small event.

[82]Markettos, A. T. (2011). *Active electromagnetic attacks on secure hardware*, Doctoral Dissertation, University of Cambridge.

[83]Kuhn, M. G. and Anderson, R. J. (1998). Soft tempest: Hidden data transmission using electromagnetic emanations. In *Information Hiding*, Springer Berlin Heidelberg, pp. 124–142, January 1998.

[84]Loughry, J. and Umphress, D. A. (2002). Information leakage from optical emanations. *ACM Transactions on Information and System Security (TISSEC)*, Volume 5, No. 3, pp. 262–289.

[85]Michael Hanspach and Michael Goetz. (2013). On Covert Acoustical Mesh Networks in Air. *Journal of Communications*, Volume 8, No. 11, pp. 758–767, Engineering and Technology Publishing, November 2013.

sharing information between each other using their built-in speakers and microphones.

Active attacks are also particularly powerful in side channel cryptanalysis. They usually involve inducing some sort of fault and causing the targeted device to operate in an unpredicted manner, which in some cases reveals information about the secret key or the operation of the device's cryptographic system. Manipulation of the voltage to the device[86] or application of different kinds of radiation, even illumination of electronic components with a laser pointer,[87] can lead to such faults.

Emsec Countermeasures

The lower-tech approach for protecting against Emsec attacks is to ensure control of the geographical area around systems that process highly confidential material. This was the approach taken by the US Signal Corps for the Bell 131-B2 in World War II, and is also the basis of NATO's zoning policy. This policy defines different Tempest protection standards for different environments. Equipment operating in NATO Zone 0 should produce no exploitable emanations at a distance of roughly one meter. Zone 1 extends this to 20 meters and Zone 2 to 100 meters or so. Commercial off-the-shelf personal computers are usually classified as Zone 2, which means that military personnel can use them if there is no risk of a potential eavesdropper next door and the information processed is unclassified. Equipment certified for Zone 0 can be used in environments with more stringent requirements, such as embassies, but due to shielding is orders of magnitude more expensive.

Shielding is the practice of reducing electromagnetic emanations by protecting equipment with a material that blocks them. Depending on the requirements, a shielded device may be made of special components that produce reduced emanations or may be a normal off-the-shelf device that is enclosed in a metallic casing. Occasionally, whole chambers in a building may need to be shielded,[88] but this solution is by far the most expensive and is adopted less and less since the end of the Cold War.

---

[86]Anderson, R. and Kuhn, M. (1996). Tamper resistance-a cautionary note. In *Proceedings of the second Usenix workshop on electronic commerce*, Volume 2, pp. 1–11, November 1996.
[87]Skorobogatov, S. P. and Anderson, R. J. (2003). Optical fault induction attacks. In *Cryptographic Hardware and Embedded Systems-CHES 2002*, Springer Berlin Heidelberg, pp. 2–12.
[88]Hemming, L. H. (2000). Architectural Electromagnetic Shielding Handbook: a design and specification guide. John Wiley & Sons.

Another approach is jamming.[89] In the context of Tempest protection, it is the practice of artificially generating additional emanations that carry no useful information and overwhelm any potentially compromising ones. Considering that analyzing emanations to extract confidential information from them is already a technically challenging process, jamming aims to make it even more challenging for the adversary.

Possibly the most elegant of countermeasures proposed to date is the "Tempest font"[90] introduced by Markus Kuhn and Ross Anderson. They found that by slightly blurring[91] the font used on a computer, the quality of the font is only slightly reduced, but the information leaked through electromagnetic emanations is reduced dramatically. Significantly, this was a convincing demonstration that Emsec countermeasures should not be limited to physical space, as more cost-effective software-based solutions[92] can be found in cyberspace.

Cyber-Physical-Cyber and Physical-Cyber-Physical Attacks

As discussed throughout this chapter, there are multiple ways in which physical space can be exploited so as to affect cyberspace. Since exploiting the latter can again affect physical space, with some of the techniques presented in Chapters 3, 4, and 5, it is possible to lead to a cyber-physical attack starting from physical space. This would make it a rather comically named physical-cyber-physical attack. For instance, considering that network disruption can directly affect physical space, especially if it supports SCADA systems, an EMP attack targeting the network infrastructure would belong to this category. Another example, briefly mentioned in Chapter 3, would be to place a magnet near the particular implantable defibrillator analyzed by

[89]Suzuki, Y. and Akiyama, Y. (2010). Jamming technique to prevent information leakage caused by unintentional emissions of PC video signals. In International Symposium on Electromagnetic Compatibility (EMC), IEEE, pp. 132–137, July 2010.
[90]Kuhn, M. G. and Anderson, R. J. (1998). Soft tempest: Hidden data transmission using electromagnetic emanations. In *Information Hiding*, Springer Berlin Heidelberg, pp. 124–142, January 1998.
[91]To be more accurate, by slightly blurring we refer to the application of a low-pass filter that removes the top 30% of the Fourier transform of the font's image. Most of the information contained in its compromising emanations belongs to the high frequency part of the video signal. If this is removed with a low-pass filter, the eavesdropper has a lot less information to work with.
[92]Anderson, R. J., and Kuhn, M. G. (1999). Soft tempest – An opportunity for NATO. *Protecting NATO Information Systems in the 21st Century.*

Halperin et al.[93] (physical space), to keep triggering the transmission of data (cyberspace), not specifically for the data but to exhaust the device's battery (physical space).

An equally comically named cyber-physical-cyber attack is also possible and rather more interesting. A cyber-physical attack against the smart grid that would cut the power in an area would also affect its network availability.[94] Other examples are the software-based active attacks that stimulate emanations (see earlier). An adversary infects a computer with a virus (cyberspace), which causes one of the computer's components to produce or amplify light, sound, heat, electromagnetic radiation, or any other emanation (physical space), which in turn is analyzed to reveal confidential information from the computer (cyberspace).

A cyber-physical-cyber attack that has attracted attention is the work of Diao et al.,[95] who reported in 2014 that a way to bypass the permission settings of a smartphone is to use its speaker-microphone pair as a communication channel. Unlike most malware that require sensitive privileges to function, their experimental application needed not much more than access to the speaker. A command such as "call x number" would be whispered through the speaker, picked up by the microphone, and recognized by the phone's built-in voice activation service (e.g., Google Voice Services), which would then initiate the call. This could be considered as an attack by itself, especially if the number called were a premium rate one, but the interesting part is that these commands could also request sensitive information, such as the owner's calendar, IP address, location, and so on. The application could then use a built-in text-to-audio service (e.g., Google Text-to-Speech) to convert the sensitive text data into audio and play it back to a telephone number controlled by the attacker. Obviously, relying on audible sounds whispered through the speaker means that the owner would notice the attack sooner or later, unless perhaps launched late at night.

---

[93]Halperin, D., Heydt-Benjamin, T. S., Ransford, B., Clark, S. S., Defend, B., Morgan, W., Fu, K., Kohno, T., and Maisel, W. H. (2008). Pacemakers and implantable cardiac defibrillators: Software radio attacks and zero-power defenses. In *IEEE Symposium on Security and Privacy (SP 2008)*, IEEE, pp. 129–142.

[94]Neuman, C. and Tan, K. (2011). Mediating cyber and physical threat propagation in secure smart grid architectures. In *IEEE International Conference on Smart Grid Communications*, pp. 238–243, IEEE, October 2011.

[95]Diao, W., Liu, X., Zhou, Z., and Zhang, K. (2014). Your Voice Assistant is Mine: How to Abuse Speakers to Steal Information and Control Your Phone. *arXiv preprint arXiv:1407.4923*.

An even more exotic attack would be the so-called "subliminal attack" proposed by Martinovic et al. for brain-computer interfaces (BCI).[96] These are headset-like devices with electrodes that measure activity in the brain (electroencephalography) originally for applications in healthcare but increasingly in the entertainment and gaming industry. They work like a mind-controlled joystick that interprets thoughts into commands. For instance, a game character will move to the left if the player thinks of moving to the left. There are even app markets, similar to the ones for smartphones, where one can download third-party BCI applications. The researchers showed that a BCI game or any other seemingly benign application could momentarily display on the screen stimuli that generate subconscious thoughts on private information, such as whether the user knows a person displayed on the screen, a geographical location, or parts of a PIN number. These thoughts are picked up by the BCI device and are then forwarded to an adversary who can try to analyze them and infer the private information.

Cyber-physical-cyber attacks are, by nature, very complex. To be worth the effort, they need to be ambitious in terms of their targets. An ambitious such example is Ben-Gurion University's AirHopper,[97] which is an experimental attack for exfiltrating sensitive data from air-gapped computers. It involves physically accessing the target computers to infect them with malware, which causes the computers to start leaking data through frequency modulation (FM) radio emanations. The researchers showed how to generate these emanations and how to pick them up on the FM receiver of a nearby mobile phone, assuming that the latter has also been infected with malware designed by the attacker. The concept of exfiltrating information through FM emanations is fascinating academically, but the whole attack is prohibitively complex for most attackers and most situations, with the possible exception of advanced persistent threats. In this context, a complex cyber-physical-cyber attack with the potential to overcome air gaps and other barriers to conventional cyber attacks should not be outright dismissed as unrealistic.

[96]Martinovic, I., Davies, D., Frank, M., Perito, D., Ros, T., and Song, D. (2012). On the feasibility of side-channel attacks with brain-computer interfaces. In *Proceedings of the 21st USENIX Security Symposium*, pp. 143–158, August 2012.
[97]Guri, M., Kedma, G., Kachlon, A., and Elovici, Y. (2014). AirHopper: Bridging the Air-Gap between Isolated Networks and Mobile Phones using Radio Frequencies. 9th IEEE International Conference on Malicious and Unwanted Software, October 28–30, 2014.

Summary

Physical-cyber attacks exploit the physical aspects of computers and network equipment to affect the availability, integrity, and confidentiality of information in cyberspace. Whether due to physical disasters, metal scavengers, ship anchors, or sabotage, it is not unheard of that a whole country loses Internet connection because of a single severed cable. The less advanced nations are particularly vulnerable in this respect, since most of their long-distance network traffic goes through a very small number of cables, the maintenance of which is rather expensive. More advanced nations are vulnerable to a different kind of threat. The greater their dependence on computers, networks, and electronics in general, the more vulnerable they are to EMP. A nuclear explosion in the upper layers of the atmosphere would generate this effect and would probably disable most civilian and some military electronic equipment over a geographical area the size of the United States or Europe. Since this is within the capabilities of any nuclear state with a ballistic missile program, and dependence on electronic systems that are vulnerable to EMP will undoubtedly continue, scientists have started developing mathematical models to predict the impact that EMP and other disasters in physical space would have on a particular area's telecommunications.

Since it is sensors that gather information from physical space to present it in cyberspace, any physical attack against them would also affect the quality of the information they collect. Of particular interest are attacks that aim to deceive a sensor by exploiting its natural weaknesses; lidar is confused by reflective surfaces, infrared by common window glass, ultrasonic by rough surfaces, and so on. Approaches used to detect faulty sensors are largely applicable also in detecting sensors that report unusual measurements due to a physical attack.

Possibly the most interesting physical-cyber attacks are the ones that exploit compromising emanations in physical space to eavesdrop on confidential information in cyberspace. For example, it does not matter how mathematically secure a cryptographic system is if the power it consumes or the time it takes to process information is enough to infer parts of the secret key. The image displayed on a computer monitor can be revealed through the electromagnetic emanations produced by the monitor itself, the cable that connects it to the computer, and even the variations in light emitted in the room. A keyboard produces sounds and vibrations that can reveal what is typed, especially if there is a compromised smartphone next to it. In fact, such side channel communication can be a mechanism for an adversary to extract confidential information from facilities that have no network connection: A computer virus grabs the information and then transmits it in the form of light, sound, electromagnetic radiation, or any other compromising emanation in a manner that the adversary can interpret.

This chapter serves as a reminder that the security of cyberspace depends on the manner it has been implemented in physical space. While cyber-physical attacks are a relatively new threat, the reverse has always been the case. Telecommunication cables have always been prime targets during war, and the intelligence community has long known of techniques for deceiving sensors or eavesdropping on TEMPEST information.

Follow-Up Questions and Exercises

1. Use one of the undersea cable maps available online to identify the Internet traffic of the countries that would be affected by a natural disaster affecting cables in the Gulf of Suez.
2. Fill in the missing words:
   a. An adversary wearing a suit of anechoic material would potentially deceive a(n) _____ sensor.
   b. An object sitting behind a common glass window may go undetected by a(n) _____ sensor.
   c. Reflective surfaces and even paddles on the road can confuse _____.
3. Which of the following statements are true?
   a. Acoustic Emsec attacks are limited to eavesdropping on users typing on keyboards.
   b. Acoustic Emsec channel attacks exploit sound emanations produced by devices that are processing information.
   c. While electromagnetic Emsec attacks were known at least since the wartime experiments on the Bell 131-B2 device, it was IBM researchers that first discussed the possibility of exploiting sound emanations in 2004.
   d. Different keys on a keyboard may produce slightly different sound when pressed. It is possible to identify what someone has typed based on the recorded sound.
4. Smartphones, tablets, and other intelligent portable devices carry multiple sensors. Provide three ways in which a technically capable adversary can exploit these sensors to steal the PIN for a user's online banking account.

5. Describe an example of a cyber-physical attack that would involve the exploitation of compromising emanations.

6. Consider a smartcard using a hypothetical cipher, which starts with a squaring, an inversion, and again a squaring if the secret key is even, or with a squaring, an inversion, and a multiplication if it is odd. How can you determine whether the secret key is even or odd with the help of an oscilloscope?

INDEX

Note: Page numbers followed by "*f*," "*t*," and "*b*" refer to figures, tables, and boxes, respectively.

Printed in the United States
By Bookmasters